# PAINKILLER ADDICT

## FROM WRECKAGE TO REDEMPTION
## MY TRUE STORY

CATHRYN KEMP

PIATKUS

First published in Great Britain in 2012 by Piatkus





ISBN 978-0-7499-5806-0

Text on pp. 303–4 reprinted by permission of
NA World Services, Inc. All rights reserved,

Typeset in Swift by M Rules
Printed and bound in Great Britain by
Clays Ltd, St Ives plc

Papers used by Piatkus are from well-managed forests
and other responsible sources.

MIX
Paper from
responsible sources
FSC® C104740

Piatkus
An imprint of
Little, Brown Book Group
100 Victoria Embankment
London EC4Y 0DY

An Hachette UK Company
www.hachette.co.uk

www.piatkus.co.uk

# Contents

'Nothing has more power over us than the truth . . .'

*The Palace of Illusions*,
Chitra Banerjee Divakaruni

# Acknowledgements

This book is dedicated to all those who showed me there is another way.

To the staff and patients at my rehab – I was honoured to witness their journeys and privileged that they became part of mine. To my GP who had the courage to trust in my process. To the recovery people in my life who support me daily. To Caroline, my sponsor and dear loving friend, who held my hand and carried me gently through the first two years of recovery – and who is still my guiding light.

To my agents Jen and Jane of Graham Maw Christie who saw the seeds of my story and nurtured its path into becoming. To my editor Anne Lawrance at Piatkus for the sensitivity and gentleness to witness my confessions without judgement or blame, and who prodded me into crafting my story into something I shall always be proud of. To all the staff at Little, Brown for their unremitting encouragement and interest in the greater picture beyond this narrative.

To my parents, my sister and her family and my friends who stuck by me through terrifying illness and the degradation of rampant addiction, I say thank you and acknowledge it can never be enough. To my husband and step-son I have no words, except to say thank you for wishing this story into being.

Mostly, this story of mine is gifted to those addicts out there who have not yet found recovery – this work is yours, this story is yours, and this path out of the suffering of addiction may be yours, God willing.

# Introduction

I used to think a drug addict was someone who lived on the far edges of society. Wild-eyed, shaven-headed and living in a filthy squat. That was until I became one.

How does it feel? That is what people ask me. Was the feeling I got from the drugs worth the deceit, the destruction, the carnage of my broken life? Was it worth the lies and manipulation, the bullying, the demanding and the shame you will read about in these pages?

Maybe you already know the answer, or, if by the grace of fate and fortune you have not yet taken a strong painkiller, you are only ever one car accident, one operation, one case of back pain away from finding out.

The good feeling, the hazy, numbing, everything-is-all-right sensation is just a prescription away – and that's what makes it so easy, so dangerous, and ultimately, so exquisitely destructive.

If, like me, you are someone who has crossed the thin line between pain and addiction, between sticking to your prescription and taking an extra painkiller, or even if you live in the underworld taking anonymous narcotics, then you already know.

And yes, it's good. It's so good, so rare, so special. It is the ultimate feeling of blissed-out, blessed-up connection with the world, the universe and possibly even with God. It's a supreme narcotic heaven; it's a place where everything makes sense, where peace and friendship, love and trust gently, softly collide into pleasure, a deep sense of relaxed pleasure which goes far beyond the realm of everyday life. It is serene and beautiful – and it is a lie.

When I was chasing the peace, nothing and no one else mattered. I say this knowing the pain it will cause my family and my husband and friends who witnessed me fall into a pit of my own making. I was detached in my own world of suffering and redemption, too ill and tired to make sense of their shattered feelings. Addicts in the tight clutches of their addiction wreck others' lives, not just their own. They trail a slime of lies, of cheating, of deception, manipulation and more lies. And it is only by hitting the bottom of the pit (if they are lucky enough to get that far) that sanity and tentative healing can slowly emerge.

I am a recovering addict. I will never relinquish that tag, nor the taboo, the societal condemnation, the judgments and blame attached to it. But today I am clean and sober, and I pray I stay this way.

This account is based on the twenty diaries in which I recorded my seven-year journey and I meet each with a cringing and wary disbelief. Did all that really happen?

I am startled at how little I recognise of the person who wrote them. Littered through the paper sheets are quotes, poems, images from postcards or photographs – all talismans, all a desperate search for guidance and strength.

Strong painkillers saved my life, but then they almost killed me. And the way it happened to me, it could happen to anyone. My story of addiction is a tale of our times, as each year, more and more prescriptions are written for strong painkillers or tranquillisers. When powerful drugs are packaged as prescriptions, taking one more when the going gets tough can seem as harmless as having a drink to drown your sorrows. But I am hopeful that my story will be more than a cautionary tale. I hope it might reach out to someone who is struggling with addiction, or pain or illness – or struggling to support someone who is – and make them feel less alone in their fight. Mostly, I hope that anyone identifying with the utter hell of active addiction may seek help and recovery. If my story plants a seed for any of these things then my disclosure will be worthwhile.

CHAPTER 1

# Drug Addict

*February 2010*

'You're an addict,' announces my GP in his surgery on a sharply cold winter's day. 'I'm cutting you off.' I glance down at my expensive boots, as if to check that I'm still ok, still 'normal'. In the silence that follows, his words seem to float somewhere in the air between us, doctor and patient, dealer and junkie. I don't want them to find their way down, tangle themselves into my hair, ooze through my skin and sink like a lead bomb, waiting to go off in my mind.

Suddenly, I feel sick. I bend over and retch. Dr M. does nothing. Not a fucking thing. Doesn't rush to get me a sick bowl. Instead, he watches with something like professional curiosity as the horror, the mess, the shit hits my fan.

'I'm cutting you off,' he says again. Full stop.

My head is now spinning. I'm clutching my skull, rocking slightly. I run my hands through my hair, feeling the physicality of my skin, trying to grasp on to something. I feel like I'm drowning.

I'm numb with shock. I retch again and watch the bile gloop its slow path to the carpet. Stupidly, I notice the blue repeat pattern on the weave and think, It's the same as Mum's. I'm looking down at the carpet for minutes, or maybe seconds or maybe I just glance.

Time has left the room. It's just me, my drugs and a big, black nothing.

Part of my brain moves swiftly to calculate how many fentanyl lozenges I've got left. Thank God, I've got enough to last till I can figure this out. No matter what else is going on, regardless of how shocked, devastated, upset, hurt, traumatised I am, I always know how many lozenges I've got. That part of my head is always working. Always figuring out when and how to wheedle the next lot out of my doc.

Thinking about the lozenges makes me yearn for them. I shouldn't need one – I took six before I came out; I'm good for at least another half hour. Then the sweats and shakes will start, the uncontrollable urge swamping everything, the monster rearing inside me again, with acute regularity. The only constant in my life.

I agree with him. Of course I do. But inside I'm thinking, He can't make me stop. I need those drugs. I've been in terrible pain for five fucking years. He can't make me, because the drugs are the only thing giving me any relief from pain. They are giving me a life. Without them I can barely breathe.

I make it home to my little cottage in a small village. I can't recall how; did I stumble or run? Or crawl, on my hands and knees in the degradation of addiction. I probably walked slowly, head up, trying to look normal, like I usually do. Like I don't have this secret life, like I'm not higher than Concorde. Don't know. Don't care.

I have to block out the memories of who I was before this – before these drugs, before this village, before the horrors of my illness – because if I remember my life, the pure freedom of my old life, I feel I will simply dissolve away in the acid of regret and bitter recollection. I was once a travel writer and a moderately successful journalist. I lived in south London, ate in Nobu and The Ivy and wined and dined celebrities for the papers I wrote for, in between flying to exotic places. Now I am a drug addict. I simply don't recognise myself any more.

Once inside, I go straight to the drug cupboard where my hoard of prescription opiates is kept. My hands tremble as I rip open a strip of three lozenges. I cram two into my mouth (meant to be taken three-hourly – NHS warning) and wait. It only takes a couple of minutes before the warm, soothing hands of mother opiate bring me back to sanity. The fear dissolves gently. Time backs slowly into the room. I pick up a novel. I want to lose myself.

I don't know it, but I am already lost.

CHAPTER 2

# More Painful Than Childbirth

*8 October 2004*

I have had a nagging pain in my back for the past couple of days and I feel really sluggish and nauseous in the morning despite having had only a couple of glasses of wine the night before. My best friend jokes I might be pregnant, so I panic and book myself an appointment with my new local GP pronto.

I have just moved away from London after selling my flat and handing in my notice at the paper in Canary Wharf. My days as assistant features editor of a tabloid newspaper are over because I have decided to go freelance and move to the seaside. In the back of my mind, I am hoping I will finally meet someone special and start a family. It seems impossible to live a settled life in London; too many parties to attend, too many stories to chase and people to meet. I have lived south of the river for seven years and I am still looking for Mr Right, while experiencing a few Mr Wrongs on the way. The latest Mr Wrong has barely been in touch since I left the city a few weeks ago, and so I try not to think about him as I drive to the surgery.

I know I am a cliché. Single woman, fast approaching forty. Well, thirty-three to be precise, but time is ticking on and I am no nearer to meeting anyone who might remotely be the father of my future children. I drink a little too much – especially since I stopped smoking on my thirtieth birthday – I own far too many pairs of shoes and my fridge is constantly a bare, pitiful-looking place which usually contains something like a week-old pot of hummus, some celery sticks, a pot of chocolate mousse and two bottles of Petit Chablis. And now I might be pregnant to boot.

Once inside the doctor's surgery, I meet my new GP and tell him my symptoms. He does a quick pregnancy test after I've weed in the plastic cup provided and tells me it is negative. I am so relieved, I almost forget the ache in my back which is throbbing again. He feels my back and makes me bend down and touch my toes. Once I have done this, he tells me my problem is muscular and dispatches me with a leaflet on back pain.

Clutching the pale blue leaflet, I open the door to my new place: a penthouse apartment with a glass atrium revealing a sunlit balcony. I sigh with happiness when I look at the fruits of my labour. This flat is the hard-won result of the last seven years working seriously hard at seriously stressful jobs and I love it.

Later, I drive round to see Sid, my photographer friend who lives a few miles away, because we are working on a national newspaper feature together. As I am driving, the pain increases and starts pumping through my back. It begins to scare me; this doesn't seem right. By the time I pull up at Sid's I'm bent double and can barely make it up the stairs. His wife fetches me a glass of water while I wait for Sid to finish what he's doing and come down. When I heave up part of my lunch, I realise I can't drive myself home, so he drops me back, and I leave my car sitting outside his house.

At home, I get into bed and confront the fear that's hanging on this pain. I don't recognise it. I feel like I'm going somewhere new and I really don't like it. I don't notice my gorgeous home any more; all I am aware of is the sensation that this niggling, fidgeting, burning pain is becoming more and more uncontrollable by the minute.

By 7.30 p.m., I can't cope. I call my friend Francesca who lives near by. She picks up the phone, thank God, and ten minutes later we're driving to A&E. We speed past the seafront and I see a man walking his dog. Somehow, I sense that I am about to lose what he has. That freedom. That simplicity. Ordinary life.

'What if I need a kidney transplant? It's definitely my kidneys. What if I need dialysis?' Fran snorts a reply. I've always been a drama queen. But this time it's real.

Someone is moaning and it takes me a moment to realise it's me. Pain is swallowing me whole. Like a pair of bellows pumping a squirming, terrifying, jarring feeling through my back to my stomach. I know it's wrong. There are good types of pain and bad ones. Good being the burning sensation of muscles during a workout, or scratching sore skin really hard or squeezing a nasty spot.

I've never felt bad pain before and I'm frightened, so scared I am beginning not to care what it is or what's causing it – I just want it to stop. By the time we pull up outside the hospital, I am desperate. We ditch the car on a double yellow. I am bellowing and panting like an animal.

'What's happening to me?' I ask. And there's no reply. I feel utterly alone, wading through a bad place.

Fifteen minutes later and I'm foetal on a trolley. Someone in the opposite cubicle – sounds like an old man – is screaming he wants to die. I know how he feels.

It's like Vegas here, but infinitely worse. There are no clocks. Time has stopped. I have no idea how long we've been here. There seems to be everything and nothing going on. Disconnected voices. Low murmuring. A sudden rush of people and trolleys. Nothing. A nurse eventually takes my details and gives me a round pink pill. Voltarol. It helps a little.

Several hours later and my blood tests come back normal. A female doctor tells me there seems to be nothing causing the pain. I feel relieved, but confused. At midnight, I'm discharged and Fran drives me home. I'm still in pain and, as the painkiller wears off, I feel distinctly rough again.

The next morning, I call my parents as they're eating breakfast. There's a surreal quality to the whole story, and even I think I sound like I'm exaggerating as I tell them I spent part of the night in a hospital bed. I begin to think I was imagining the pain. They decide I should come to their place for the next couple of days. I agree and an hour later, they appear at my new flat, pack my bag and bustle me into their car.

I haven't eaten anything for two days now. I'm starving, so Mum cooks chicken when we get in. Two hours later and I barely make it to the loo before I projectile vomit. The sick forms an arc. It's expelled from my body with such venom, I watch it with astonishment. Pain now comes in waves. Tsunamis. Welling up, forcing through me.

Again, that squirming feeling, like a deep itch inside me which gets stronger and stronger. This time I know it's real. This time the pain *is* me. It wraps itself around me and there's no escape.

I'm driven to my parents' local A&E at breakneck speed. I'm made to wait while some idiot receptionist writes down my address, slowly. I want to scream. Actually I want to punch her, but I am too busy trying to stay alive. I retch and vomit and shit into a wheelchair loo in my cubicle. Dignity is a luxury I've lost somewhere in this darkness. A young nurse comes in bearing two paracetamol tablets in a sick bowl. I scream at her to get me some proper fucking pain relief. I don't care what it is, but I want it now. She walks out, offended. I am crying and shaking, moaning in agony.

Eventually, the doctor decides I have kidney stones and I get a morphine shot. He says we should go back to the original hospital as the urinary department there is better. I'm bundled back in the car, still wearing my NHS gown, my knickers on show and clutching a thin blanket. The cannula (IV needle) is still in my right hand, the plastic tube sticking out grotesquely.

We drive for an hour. Nausea beats at my brain as the morphine does its work. I don't know which is worse – the pain or the sickness from the painkiller. I've got vomit down my pale yellow hospital gown. Flecks of spit and bile around my mouth. I'm cold.

Once there, I'm put on another trolley and taken to another cubicle with the thin polyester curtain drawn around me. I wait. We wait. Nurses and doctors come and go. We repeat the same information three times. Someone finally does a blood test.

Two hours later – two of the longest, hardest hours I have ever faced – and the results are in. It's pancreatitis. My amylase levels (digestive enzymes in the blood) are massively raised. They should be somewhere near twenty; mine are three thousand.

Normally, the pancreas produces then expels digestive enzymes (amylase, protease and lipase) when we eat and they break down the food after it passes through the stomach. For some reason nobody seems able to explain, mine are being produced, but not being expelled. I'm basically digesting myself.

Now the doctor really does have sympathy written into his face. He tells me it's the single most painful condition in existence. Several notches up from childbirth on the official NHS pain Richter scale. Unless it's caused by a blockage of gallstones, he tells me, there's no cure. He gives me a leaflet, printed on flimsy cheap pink paper and headed 'Living With Acute Pancreatitis'. I stare at it blankly in the seconds before the blackness of horror and despair descend.

It gets busy around me. I notice a change of pace. Nurses rig up a saline drip via the needle in my hand. I am given another morphine shot. An immediate feeling of warmth radiates through me as the drug enters my bloodstream. Bang, it's literally a hit. Time and space go into a different dimension; everything becomes woozy and creamy. I have seconds to enjoy it before the sickness jolts my stomach. My head feels like it weighs a million pounds. I lie back. This action makes me want to vomit though, so I prop my head back up with a pillow. I surrender to the narcotic parallel universe in the same room. My parents look miles away, in another galaxy of worry which I'm not part of any more. Here it's timeless, suspended reality.

Minutes or months later, a nurse opens the curtains. I notice she has rubber gloves on and implements in her hands. I feel utterly disconnected from her.

She's fitting me with a catheter. My legs are open and something feels strange and uncomfortable. Something's going up my wee-hole the wrong way. I'm wriggling to get free, but my mum holds me down.

Now I can't even piss for myself.

Hours later – I think. The machine next to my bed beeps every minute or so. A tinny, repetitive, mournful sound. Impersonal. My hand hurts where the needle sits, the saline moving into my hand in cold jerks. The morphine has worn off. Yet despite the insistent burning pain, I'm reluctant to ask for more as I can't bear being sick again.

My parents are long gone. I'm in a room filled with snoring, restless sick people. Hell's waiting room with harsh fluorescent lights and no dimmer switch for night-time. There's a constant patter of voices and footsteps somewhere in the warren of beds. There's no one here but me; there's every sick person on earth here with me. I'm confused still from the drugs.

Morning finally comes. I watch the black night turn purple, then grey. A sign above my bed says NBM – Nil By Mouth. No breakfast for me. I watch the other inmates spread cheap margarine on their white toast. I want to scream. Instead, I cry.

Tears roll down my face and I let them flow in an efflux of fear and despair. Somewhere out there women like me are living versions of my life. They're waking up in their one-bedroom flats in a leafy part of the city. They're drinking fruit smoothies and eating granola for breakfast. They're showering, deciding which clothes to wear, pulling on heels, a coat and walking to the station on their way to Canary Wharf. Or perhaps they are like the 'new' me – grabbing a black coffee on their way to the station before boarding the commuter train to Victoria, then the tube. I can picture them, heels clacking on the station concourse, laptops in their bags, each hoping to get a seat this morning. Then queuing afterwards at Pret for their first skinny latte of the day, clutching a breakfast muffin before buying all the red tops and maybe *The Times* and *Guardian* as well.

In my mind's eye I can see them, hordes of women like me, women who are me, who aren't me, walking into the office. The freedom, the luxury of walking and working and wearing expensive clothes makes me heave. How am I here? How am I not at my desk in the features department of a national newspaper? How am I not reading the papers, jotting down ideas for stories, girding my loins for conference at 10.45 a.m. with the editor? How am I not making plans to meet friends for dinner or working out where we will go for our next city break?

This is not my life. My life for the past seven years has been a whirlwind of deadlines and adrenaline rushes, travel to the far reaches of the planet or short trips with friends. It has been chaotic for sure. I haven't stayed in the UK for more than a few months at a time since leaving college and haven't had a regular boyfriend for most of that time, but it has been challenging, exciting, even dangerous sometimes. I have been held at gunpoint on a Russian train; almost drowned in the Mekong when the engine of the boat I was travelling in broke down and we headed for whirlpools in the swirling depths; and I was involved in a botched kidnap attempt by a cab driver in Riga for a brief, terrifying ten minutes, before managing to make a hasty escape.

So many bizarre and exhilarating moments and it has all come to this? This horrible place. This awful pain. It feels, to me, like a tragedy of Greek proportions.

At 8 a.m. a nurse comes round with a flannel and a plastic bowl filled with tepid water. This is for me to wash in. I'm hooked up to a drip, I have needles sticking out of my hands, I'm so weak from hunger and pain I can barely sit upright. And now I have to wash. By myself. I would laugh, if I wasn't so horrified by the thought of it.

I make a feeble attempt at washing. Drag the flannel under my armpits. The action releases a sour smell. I reek of animal sweat and fear. There's now a water stain blooming across my sheets and my gown is wet. I have roughed it before in Burma and Laos. I have slept on mats on earth floors in South America and washed in rivers which flow with the effluence of mountain villages in Peru, but nothing I have ever been through has prepared me for this total degradation, this place that is empty of dignity and this hurt which frames my world, frazzles my senses and leaves me in tatters, day and night.

I tell the nurse I am in pain. She raises her eyebrows and walks off. Twenty minutes later, she returns with a kidney bowl containing a needle. She opens up the cannula and injects the morphine into my open vein. Then again with an anti-emetic. Cold liquid meets warm blood. Cooling the fire inside my raging body. The hit.

My head rolls back, eyes closing. The sucking feeling drags me into the place where everything dissolves. I'm separate, hiding in the warm, dark womb of narco-dreaming. Sinking away from real things, real places. Disconnecting into relief.

The sound of wheels creaking in municipal transit wakes me. I've no idea what time it is, or even what day. The team of doctors came round earlier, but they practically ignored me, wrote up some more saline on my chart and left. No kind words.

No explanations either, come to think of it. Not that I care right now: let it flow past and maybe I'll slide out of here on a wave of disinterest. My head feels blurry, like I've got a hangover. A second or so later, I realise I've been groaning like a demented old lady. I feel something – sick maybe, desperate.

I stop moaning, in case people think I'm crazy. I'm embarrassed, which is pretty ridiculous considering I've got a plastic tube coming out of my wee-hole, another coming out of my arm and this vile flimsy gown which makes me look like something from bedlam. My hair is greasy, I've got no make-up on and no one has tried to clean my teeth, so my breath must be rank. My mouth feels dry, but I can't even sip water.

The tea trolley goes past and I realise it's afternoon. My mum and dad arrive some time later. I can see them try to hide the shock on their faces at the sight of me and the bag of yellow urine hanging like a bloated organ from one side of the bed. They stay till 5 p.m., munching on sandwiches and packets of crisps at my bedside. I know they're desperately worried and love me to bits, but the sight of them stuffing food in front of me taunts me, makes me angry. Even so, I feel like a small child, weak and pathetic when they go.

Alone, I watch the sun sink over the hospital car park. I'm spreadeagled in bed, shifting to get comfortable. I suddenly realise I need a shit. I reach my arm through the tangle of tubes to the buzzer and press. It flashes and I hear its nasal echo from the empty corridor. No one comes. I get a sudden sharp pain in my belly, which means I have to get to the loo fast. I'm not meant to get up because of all the opiates I've been given. But it's either that or shit the bed, and I'm still just about clinging to the last of my dignity.

The room shifts slightly as I stand up. Moves back into focus and I can walk. I grab the drip's metal pole as the supermarket trolley wheels on the end of it spin in three different directions. Compounding this, my gown flaps open and I have to hold my catheter bag and try to keep the back material flaps together with one hand while the other grasps the drip. I rattle down the ward like an old woman. I am an old woman, praying. Praying I'll get to the loo in time.

Opening the first cubicle door, I'm greeted by the sight – and stench – of a toilet seat covered in diarrhoea. There's an elderly man attempting to wash his hands at the sinks near by. I retch, shut the door and make it into the next loo. I glance at my feet, clad in thin hospital slippers. Have I stepped in the mess?

When I've finished, I spend five minutes pulling up my knickers with my one free hand. I get to the sinks and the man is still standing there. He looks confused and his gown is wide open at the back, revealing his arse. It's curiously pale and crinkled, like a delicate pink prune. As he moves off in front of me, back to our mixed ward, faeces are dripping down his legs and on to the floor. Like a grotesque parody of Hansel and Gretel, he is leaving a trail of diarrhoea down the length of the ward. I just want to get to my bed. Suddenly, it feels like the only safe place in the world.

My buzzer is still flashing and eventually someone comes. I'm angry. So angry I can hardly spit my words out. I tell her about the man, his river of shit, the dirty toilets and the sheer misery of being forced to be here in this dirty, shameful ward. She doesn't care and this makes me madder. She walks off, but I'm too uptight to shout after her. I don't want to cause a scene and the realisation defeats me.

I cry through the night. I don't stop, I don't sleep. I see the dawn again and I feel black inside.

I want to die.

Several days later, I am discharged with liquid morphine to keep taking at home as the acute phase of the pancreatitis has passed. My parents pick me up, like the weakling child I am, and I go back to theirs. I can't live alone in this pitiful state. I can barely stand, let alone feed and clothe myself. Almost overnight, I am a cripple. One life vanishes and is replaced by no life, no liveable life, anyway.

Two days later, I'm back in A&E. Rushed in by my parents; a puking, shivering, moaning mess as the pancreatitis strikes again.

Bloody faces flash past me and I hear the screaming voice of a girl who sounds drunk and shrill in her anger. Swear words litter the cramped air – it's Friday night in casualty and I'm doubled up, sobbing on a trolley, being pushed into the bowels of the yellow-painted waiting room.

'Not you again', says one of the male nurses. I smile weakly and puke strings of bile into a bed pan. The animal sound of teenage drunks boasting and arguing with the nurses fills me with fear. I feel so vulnerable in their anarchic vicinity. I'm frightened of them; I'm frightened of the pain which thunders through my shrinking body. There is no respite, no release as my lunchtime dose of liquid morphine has long-since worn off.

I want to use the wheelchair toilet, but I'm terrified one of the teenagers will come in and see me, shivering and retching in my debility. A male nurse helps me on to the chair, puts a box of tissues next to me. I'm pathetically grateful for any small kindness. I cry tears of shame and fright as I use it, afraid the smell of my shit will reach the drunks. Afraid someone will expose my frailty. My arms shake so violently I can't pull the tissues out to wipe myself and I have to call out for my mum. I'm thirty-three years old and I need my mum to wipe my bottom. Still, I'm so glad she's here. Yet so guilty she's here in this living hell with me, when she should be at home, asleep.

The doctors take forever to get to me. I cry out in pain, but no one seems to hear. An hour later, a stressed-looking female doctor opens the curtain. She's brusque, asks me if I drink. I say no. I haven't drunk any alcohol since the night before the first attack of pancreatitis. Why the hell would I willingly put myself in this position? Anyway, it's clear she doesn't believe me. Pancreatitis is known as the alcoholic's disease. She obviously thinks I've brought this on myself, that I've been sat at home drinking vodka. The sense of injustice overwhelms me. Now all the raised eyebrows make sense. They think I'm doing this to myself.

I need something for the pain. I can't go on. I'm pleading, begging for pain relief. I feel, rather than hear a guttural moan coming from inside me. More raised eyebrows and the doctor leaves. Mum and Dad look at me. We're alone. I'm alone, amid this unholy chaos.

Utter fear floods every cell in my terrorised body. Across from me a young man with a bloodied face looks up and catches my eye. There's a teenage girl with him. She's drunk, mouthing off at the passing nurses. She carries her stiletto heels, her tights ripped around the base of her feet. There's a man in the cubicle next to me. He has third-degree burns from a house fire. He's unconscious, his bedside crowded with the silent fear of his family and friends. I can hear a nurse making calls to burns units in other hospitals. She's saying they can't treat him here.

I would sympathise, but pain overwhelms me again. I grab the sick bowl and heave into my agony. I don't care about the others any more. I'm resentful they're taking medical help away from me. Pain is selfish. It claims me now, wraps round me and into me. Folded into myself, I pant and writhe. The world outside disappears. I see only the distress on my parents' faces, lit in garish pantomime by the stark greenish hue of the strip lights.

Hours and another shot of morphine later. Two men push and pull my trolley. They smell of cigarette smoke which makes my stomach heave. I catch glimpses of badly drawn tattoos scarring their arms. Their chat weaves in and out of my mind which hovers somewhere close to, but not inside, my body. Jan's husband left her, one says, trouble on Saturday night, the ambulance crew and shifts changing. Disconnected voices echoing in empty space. Empty, except for us.

I stare up at the lights in the deserted corridors of the hospital. They move past me like motorway headlights, blurred by the movement. It is black outside, harsh lighting making ghosts of our reflections. I am limp. Lying in supine surrender.

Then I am in a lift. I note the change with indifference. Juddering, changing space. Lift doors open. I feel woozy and sick now. The lift clanks, jolting me back to reality, briefly. Disgorged from the lift, we move down more corridors. Endless nowheres. The floors make a shushing sound underneath me. The footsteps of the men echo, swirl and vanish, disintegrating inside my ears.

I am pushed into a ward in semi-darkness. A curtain is pulled open and strangers' arms hold me under my arms and around my torso. I am lifted on to the bed, trailing wires and equipment in a cacophony of bleeping sounds. I'm surprised at how frail and small I am, as helpless as a baby.

My drip line pulls which jogs the needle in my hand. My catheter swings against the bed frame. A nurse writes something above my bed in silence, reaching over me like I'm not here, not existing. She places the buzzer from the side table into my hand. I'm to call if I need anything.

Where do I start?

Sometime around dawn, I wake up with a terrible burning pain from my back into my abdomen; my nerve endings are screaming at me. I press the buzzer, expecting a nurse to come. I wait. And wait. The buzzer echoes down the length of the ward. The initial anger I feel at being ignored turns to anxiety, then tears of fear as time passes. What if no one's there? What if I'm left in pain?

I don't know how long I wait, internally pleading with God knows what or whom for someone to come and take this burning away. I twist and turn in my sheets, which by now are stained with the sweat of my pain and fear.

A nurse comes, maybe an hour later. I chose the wrong time to be in pain, she says, as the shifts were changing over. I am incredulous, astonished into silence. I am convinced even an animal wouldn't have been left in agony for so long, but I'm frightened to complain in case she refuses me pain relief. I smile and say it's ok, as I writhe in obvious pain, pulling the bedclothes taut and digging my fingernails into my palms to deflect my attention from the fucking agony I've been left in.

I'm burning with rage and disbelief. Nurses are constantly hailed as angels for their care and sacrifice in helping patients and many, I'm sure, deserve the accolade. Not much is said though about the delicate balance of power between nurse and patient, of the subtle ways in which the sick are continually reminded of their place in the hospital hierarchy.

Twenty minutes later, she returns with a needle, lying inside a vomit bowl. She pulls the curtain and I struggle to sit up, obedient, helpful, desperate. She opens my cannula, leaking blood on to my soiled sheets. At this, she panics slightly, but keeps her steely expression. Finally, she gets the needle in, closes the cannula and leaves, telling me to press my buzzer if I need any help later.

'Ok, I will. And thank you,' I reply, smiling weakly.

Sadistic bitch, I think, as the drug seeps through my shattered body. I look down and see that my palms are bleeding.

Another day passes in the twilight of a hospital ward. People come and go. The sun rises and sets. My parents arrive and depart. My sister phones, but I'm too disconnected to take the call. Dinner is served. The last medicine round finishes and it's night-time again.

No one changes my bedding. I'm lying in my own sodden mess of blood and sweat until the next morning.

Today, I'm due for a gall bladder scan. All my hopes are pinned on this. If it's gallstones causing the pancreatitis, I'm home and dry. They'll be removed, the pancreatitis will stop and I'll be cured. I will get my life back.

Even as I wait to go down, I feel giddy with happiness. I could be about to find out what's causing all this. *Something* must be causing it. It's inexplicable and deeply frightening to think there may be no clear answer. I have to believe it's gallstones, for the sake of my sanity.

I wait all morning. I'm not allowed any fluids, so I'm thirsty, but nothing matters except getting this scan done. It's afternoon before two hospital orderlies arrive at my bedside. The morphine is wearing off. I'm starting to keen into the pain.

We won't be a jiffy, they say, then we wait for nearly an hour for my papers to be brought to my bedside. I'm refused pain relief by the nurse on duty because they're waiting for me down in the scan room. She says it like I've deliberately kept them all waiting.

I breathe into the pain now. My mental focus is on getting

through each minute, then, as time passes, each second. I'm taken down to the scanning department, slap bang next to A&E. I suffer the indignity of being on public display, my wee bag, saline drip, unkempt greasy hair, unmade-up face and all wheeled past the rows of 'normal' people. I try not to notice the curious looks I'm getting from some people. I expect they're thinking, Thank God it isn't me. I know I would be. Others look away like I'm too scary, too vulnerable to cope with.

I feel my mood slip into anger again, as my breathing becomes more shallow and urgent. I feel like a woman in labour, except there's no baby, no 'reward' at the end. If there is an end.

I'm scanned, told I have no gallstones and wheeled back to the ward. There must be thirty people in beds crammed into a space the size of two average front rooms. Suddenly, it feels hostile and hugely overcrowded.

It's visiting time. The noise of chairs scraping on the floor, people laughing and a loud TV somewhere playing the *Strictly Come Dancing* opening sequence greet me. Fractious sounds shattering my fragile peace.

I'm cowed, wanting to process the assault of feelings the scan result has hit me with. I can sense the yawning darkness hovering near by and I want to curl up in it, embrace it. But there's no room to feel anything. There are people everywhere. Chairs litter the room at awkward angles. Several times the orderlies ask people to move out the way as they wheel me through to my space. I thank the men as they leave.

It feels like nowhere is safe. Nowhere is quiet and private.

There's a male patient in the neighbouring bed, and his wife, their three children and his mother-in-law are all gathered around it. The mother-in-law is loudly asserting that Iceland's Black Forest Gateau is better than Tesco's. I didn't know gateaux still existed. I'm not sure I really want to know either. I lie in irritated silence, wanting to scream at them to shut up. I want to shout at them that my life is fucked, nobody knows what's wrong and I might die. Suddenly, I glimpse some understanding of why people flip and start shooting strangers. I'm becoming a monster.

An hour later, a bunch of flowers is delivered. The card says they're from the features desk at the *Mirror* newspaper. I look at the loops of handwriting scrawled in biro across the white card and see nothing. Feel nothing. I'm a blank. The card is for someone else. The old me.

The old me died the day I came into this shit-hole. Right now, I'd give anything to fall asleep and not wake up. If I could get to the window, I'd jump out. If I could get to the medications, I'd take the lot because I can't live like this. I turn away from the lilies, hating their sickly, sweet smell which curls through the room I lie in. I feel alone and apart, yet I'm surrounded by patients and their visitors.

I count each second, each painful minute while I wait. I wait for it to end. I wait to get better, to feel normal again, to walk again, or die. I wait for nothing and everything.

I bury myself in the sheets, lying in silence, squirming into my pain until a nurse arrives with a needle. She dabs my arm briskly with an alcohol wipe. I remind her it says on my chart I can't have alcohol. She tsks and grabs a towel which she then soaks in cold water from the tap and rubs on to my arm. Then I feel a sharp point penetrate my skin. It hurts, then it doesn't hurt. Then it's ok. I'm back in a safe place. Hiding from the agony of being.

Being here. With no foreseeable end.

CHAPTER 3

# Bad News

*October 2004*

Days later, as the winter sun begins to glow orange in preparation for setting, I have a visitor. A surgeon. He pulls the curtains round my bed. The movement holds me transfixed, suspended in time, and I suddenly realise my life is going to change and this is the moment before it does, my last moment of this part of me.

He sits down wearing sympathy on his face. This must be bad. From what I've seen, the doctors never come round to see patients out of hours. Strange how the ward seems to hush, even though everyone's talking. Or maybe it's the drugs again. My mind feels elastic – stretching out into the web of time and space and contracting without warning. Only me. Only this space.

Focus slides back, I'm nervously pulling at the frayed hem of my robe. I force myself to concentrate. He's drawing a diagram, as simple as a child's (they really do think we're idiots). I watch the pencil (HB) slide around the page. He's drawing a pancreas and some strange dots which are bile ducts, I think. Then there's the neck of the pancreas, and he's drawn it as a wobbly line. That can't be good.

Then he says something which penetrates my addled lethargy.

'You have acute-on-chronic pancreatitis.' Such a civilised name for such agony. 'We don't know what's causing the episodes,' he says. 'I think we have to accept that the cause for your pancreatitis is idiopathic. That means that we simply don't know the cause.' And with that, he waves his hand airily in my direction.

Who exactly has to accept? I think.

'So this acute-on-chronic pancreatitis can just keep happening and there's nothing you can do?' I ask. My tone is accusing.

'Yes,' he replies. And it's the worst 'yes' I've ever heard. 'There's something else,' he says.

This is it, I think.

'You're unlikely ever to be able to have children. We lose people with pancreatitis.'

It takes me a second or two to realise he means they die. I look into his eyes as he continues to speak.

'It's simply too dangerous for you to carry a child,' he says. 'I'm sorry.' His pity feels genuine.

Suddenly, I'm broken, shattered into tiny, scratchy fragments of sorrow and pain and disbelieving and many more emotions I can't name. They swell and break inside me, like waves against the shoreline. And I lie, prostrate, empty and dying.

He goes on, explaining that pregnancy can cause pancreatitis apparently, and that there's a high risk of diabetes. Anyway, I would have to be two years clear of an attack. Right now, I'm struggling to make it to two weeks without one. Two years seem vast, impossible. To him as well as me.

Just before he leaves, he turns and says he nearly forgot something. I look up, desolate – what else could there possibly be?

'We know you have been complaining of muscle aches and weakness,' he says. 'I've been speaking to the orthopods and they think you've probably got fibromyalgia as well.'

I look back at him, blankly.

'It's chronic fatigue syndrome or ME, but with muscle cramps over the entire body,' he adds.

I barely take this in. I am too hollowed out by his main mission – to tell me I won't ever be a mummy. Then he leaves, opening up the curtains again to the bedlam of the ward. As if my life hadn't been destroyed, shattered into fragments too small to mend.

I cry. And having started, I can't stop. I cry into nothing. I cry until my eyes are so sore I can barely open them. I keep crying as night falls.

As darkness takes the ward, I slide down into despair. This night, I say goodbye to my hopes and dreams of having a child. I was never greedy. I wanted just one girl. She would have worn stripy Pippi Longstocking tights and her brown hair would have been in two bunches sticking out at the sides of her sweet-smelling head. I can picture her as if I'd carried her and given birth to her. She was always as clear to me as the impression of a loved one just departed.

And that's what she is now.

Grief is a strange thing. I want to be in its bleak clutches. Held in memory of the little girl I will never have, it's as close as I will ever get to her. The sadness has a beauty, like a song which enchants and mesmerises and then vanishes without a trace. I feel mapped by this sadness. It traces lines through me, discovering me, reminding me I'm alive and I feel too much.

And I'm glad I'm awake. I need to be awake tonight because the worst has happened. For the first time in many days, I feel a kind of agonising peace. I can't struggle or fight against what I've been told. I guess this dense, deep feeling is that of surrender to something I cannot change. I am utterly powerless over all of this and it finally sinks in. It sinks right down, past my throat and sits, a warm, dark ache in the pit of my soul.

The night creeps onwards. When the pain rears again, I don't wait. I press the buzzer. I don't fight or complain or demand relief. I hit the buzzer and watch the orange light glow on and off. Someone eventually comes and I'm given the morphine and the anti-sickness. I feel like a sheep on its way to slaughter. I sit still while the nurse opens the cannula and I wait for the drug to rush into my blood, my bones, my skin. It doesn't take the real pain away, the great yawning black chasm where my heart used to be. But it makes this dreadful night more bearable, more liveable by taking away, albeit temporarily, the savage pounding of my damaged pancreas.

I watch as the first streaks of grey break up the darkness. Almost like clockwork, there are birds, then light – barely noticeable at first, then smearing itself across the blank sky.

Whatever happened last night, whatever it is I have fallen down deep into, I know one thing for sure: the next time I am carried or wheeled out of this hospital, I will leave my soul trampled into the stained floor of this Hades.

Slowly, slowly, the ward wakes up. The first of the legion of army sergeants in white pinafores and blue-striped uniforms bustles up the ward, pushing a trolley with locked sides. She looks at me. I'm almost shocked by the intimacy of her gaze.

I'm aware I must look even more of a state than ever. My eyes feel swollen and sore. I must look like where I've been – where I still am: locked away alone, inside my grief.

And here is a nurse – sweet-faced and blonde-haired – with the most agonising tenderness in her gaze. She's actually noticed me. She looks at me like she gives a shit.

When she finishes the morning medication round, she comes back and sits quietly at my bedside and rubs my back. I turn to her like she's an old friend and howl into her shoulder. She holds me like a mother and lets me cry. She tells me she is diabetic, so understands what I'm feeling. She has to inject insulin several times a day. She is dependent on her medication and she can't have more kids as it's too dangerous. She has two young boys though. So even as I lap up her sympathy, I'm measuring out my grief; knowing mine is bigger, wider, larger, heavier than hers. Like it's a twisted competition and I can shout that my pain is worse. And it comforts me at the same time as it sickens me.

Finally, when my crying subsides and I start to feel the awkwardness of being in a kind stranger's arms, I pull away. We look at each other and we know each other.

'There's a church service in the chapel this morning. Why don't you go?' she suggests, looking directly into my eyes in gentle command.

I find myself nodding, still too overcome to speak.

Squeezing my shoulder, she gets up to leave. Her white plastic clogs squeak as she walks down to the nurse's station. I will never see her again in all the times I will be flailing around in pain or debility in one of these stinking wards. But the image of her stays with me. And my faith in human nature, which is so broken and bruised, rises from the trampled ashes inside me – unbidden, unasked for, but there nonetheless. And I almost don't want it to, so scared am I of getting crushed again beneath the weight of this place.

Within half an hour, I'm being carried into a wheelchair, the weight of grief and mourning rendering me heavy and even slower than usual. I'm swathed in a blanket which looks like the ones I used to have in my pram, judging by old family photos. But I don't care. I can barely lift my head up to watch where I'm being taken. Instead my eyes trace the concrete floor as we move in quiet grace towards the chapel.

It's not a chapel, as it turns out. It's a room with an old green carpet and several bunches of plastic flowers sitting in incongruous proximity to the 'altar', which is a table covered with an embroidered cloth. Green linoleum-covered chairs line the small room. Most are filled with patients.

I'm parked at the side and the orderlies leave. Within minutes, the priest arrives, in ceremonial robes. It's a Catholic service. Barely aware of what's happening, I'm just grateful for being out of the ward. Staring at the same blank faces day in, day out is relentless and depressing. And as I think this, my mind transports me back there.

Most of the patients on my ward are elderly. Many clinging on for dear life, literally. Their families crowd their beds each weekend and I wonder what they are really getting out of life to fight death so long and hard. The woman opposite me has been fitted with a colostomy bag which she seems unable to use. She has no sense of smell which exacerbates the problem and I have lost count of the number of times I have had to call for a nurse because her bag is leaking and she is unaware of it. My stomach turns as I think of her. It might be cruel to say it, but isn't it more cruel to put your family through interminable visits to smelly hospital wards? And then expect them to monitor your bag? And worry about you, and keep you entertained? Yet every weekend her family come. And she considers herself blessed and is happy.

I turn away from the thoughts as I am feeling agitated and distressed. I feel hot shooting rage suddenly jolt me from my lethargy. Am I angry because I want to die and can't? And I'm being told every day I have to 'live' with this? Because I do actually really want to die. I want to leave this pain and this torment and this stinking hospital nightmare. I can't stand seeing people happy with their small lot. Happy with their smelly bag and their four hours of family time and their hospital food and their painkillers and medicines and nurses and tests. I can't stand people being happy in this place – for the simple reason that I cannot find my peace in here.

I cannot accustom myself to this small framework. It is not enough. It is not nearly enough for me.

I'm panting. I realise I've worked myself into a state. They'll think I'm mad. My breathing is coming fast and furious and I can't do anything about it, so I breathe. And I breathe some more. Then I hear the priest ask if anyone wants to take communion or receive a blessing.

As I'm NBM again, I guess communion is out of the question and I'm very sure that a sip of alcohol would probably kill me right this minute due to pancreatitis, so I settle for the blessing.

But I'm furious still; hiding behind a wall of anger as the priest walks towards me. I don't believe in this. I shouldn't have come.

He makes the sign of the cross over my head and touches the point of my forehead above and between my eyes. And I feel something. I feel something that isn't fear and isn't pain and isn't anger. It is something calm. It lasts for a split second and disappears and I feel confused. I don't believe in this God that needs formal ceremonies and interminable lectures and sermons. I don't agree with anything that tells me how to worship, how to behave. I don't believe in anything that treats me like a sinful child and tells me this man in the white frock knows more about the mysteries of the universe than I do.

And yet I feel something.

I'm wheeled back to the ward, frail and fragile, wrapped in the hospital blankets which are now keeping me warm. I am struggling to sit upright as the startling pain is now coming fast and steady, punching through my back to the top of my abdomen. Feeling peculiar, slightly embarrassed at having turned to a God I don't believe in, I arrive back at my bed. I feel strangely quiet. Empty inside. I spend the day watching the grey winter light spread thin shadows from nearby trees across the windows.

*

I'm expecting no visitors today.

My parents have been looking exhausted, and the more I see them, the guiltier I feel at having somehow orchestrated this drama, this medical stage play which never seems to end. So I've told them to stay home for tonight.

My sister rings again. I don't know what to say. I tell her I'm tired. More than that I can't say as I've barely acknowledged it all myself. I just want to hide away in a safe, dark place like an injured animal. I thank her for her texts – she has been sending short messages of love several times a day, for which I'm grateful. But even so, when I eventually turn my phone off, I'm glad of the silence.

It's gone 5 p.m. when I realise there's someone standing by my bed.

'You drifted off,' she says. It's a friend of mine, Ella. She's popped in. Being an hour's drive away, it's a long way to pop. I just want to shut my curtains and disappear behind the polyester patterns into the grief that's hovering close by, but I can't. She's come too far.

I pretend happiness at seeing her. She sits on the plastic brown armchair next to my bed. I think I've forgotten how to make polite conversation. Small talk seems so pointless and exhausting. I try my best, but I feel it's obvious my heart's not in it.

She doesn't seem to notice though. She wants to talk, so I let her, having no defence against unexpected kindnesses. She's giddy, excited, a whirl of emotions. Next thing, I hear her telling me about a sharp pain she felt in her groin that was so bad she was rushed to A&E. I get ready to sympathise. To be kind or reassuring or whatever she wants.

Then the world freezes. Time stops.

It's a baby. She's telling me she's having a baby.

My stomach lurches and tangles into a knot of shock and,

more than that, pure envy. This isn't about me, I tell myself. And I smile. I really do smile as God, the universe or whatever rips my life apart one more time.

She's so happy. She's crying with happiness. And there's part of me that wants to tear the smile off her face. I am a monster. I am evil and wretched and lost. So lost.

'I'm pregnant,' she says again. She tells me her partner is so excited he's been out buying vitamin pills for her. They've started looking for a bigger place to buy. He surprised her today by telling her that his parents have given them the down payment for a house. 'We can be a family,' she says.

Pure poisonous bile wells up inside me. I can taste the bitterness on my tongue.

I want to slap her. I want to kill her and destroy her luck and her happiness. All of it. I want to scream and cry and tear the throat out of God. I want to rip these fucking wires out of my arms and wee-hole and run away.

'That's wonderful,' I say. 'I'm so happy for you.'

But I don't look happy – although my friend hasn't noticed, and I'm grateful for it.

It's dark when she gets up to leave. Her face, animated and happy, looms in front of me. She kisses me, then turns and walks away. In the lull of the darkened ward, I feel the anguish grab me, overtake me. The ache becomes the pull, the slide down into a dark and empty place where I'll shrink and vanish. I am a willing prisoner in the bleak recesses of an emptied soul. I wish for oblivion. I wish for oblivion to take me away, to keep me far away.

There's pain in my back and my stomach and it grinds at me, wearing me down, eroding me into a shrunken ill person. And the pains all mix in, until eventually, only the orange buzzer at my bedside makes sense. I take it, hold the plastic control. The large circular button has the outline of a nurse on it, telling me to press for help. Press for help. So I press. And the faceless nurse comes.

And later she returns with a needle in a kidney bowl. She opens the cannula. She wipes away my leaking blood. And I watch, as the syringe compresses, pushing the clear liquid down, down, into my arm, into my open vein. And I'm overtaken. I don't see the nurse leave. I'm drowning, yet I'm safe.

I lie back and seconds later my head follows. I fix my sight on the small pattern of a flower on the curtains hanging round the bed. They're faded blue and the flower is a simple scribbled design. A few brushstrokes, repeated over and over. I try to count them, but my eyes hurt and I feel sick. I'm safer focusing on the whole flower, straight ahead of me, as if by doing so, I can keep the chaos at bay.

CHAPTER 4

# Sunrise

*July 2006*

At 10.11 a.m. the doctors enter the ward for their rounds. I watch them circle the room. As they move from patient to patient, they don't bother to keep their voices down. I can hear their Oxbridge accents as they ask whether the patient has had a bowel movement, whether they've passed gas, whether they've managed to eat. I shouldn't hunger for their – and my own – privacy; I shouldn't revolt against the gaping loss of personal dignity in a ward stuffed full of anxious faces, pale and helpless-looking in their confusion. It is pointless railing against this place, these people. But I do.

I have been in and out of this ward with regular attacks of pancreatitis for over a year and a half now. They always tell me there is nothing they can do to stop them. My beautiful flat has been left empty since the first time I fell ill, while I have bounced from my parents' home to hospital – back and forth in a never-ending dance.

Inside me, the anger builds. Always this anger. Is it because I feel so helpless and pathetic? I feel like a small child in here. Always having to ask for everything I need, being told what I'm doing and when. For someone who was used to packing a rucksack and taking off into the next job in the next place, the world being my office and my playground, this enforced dependence drives me to insanity, though I think anyone would feel the same, regardless of their life before this.

I feel like I'm going mad in here. I sit and watch as the doctors slowly get nearer and nearer and it's as if I'm staring at them through an invisible glass wall. As if they inhabit another realm in the real world, while I stare at them like a goldfish with the burden of the capacity for memory. A goldfish with a brain.

It is a cluttered fish tank, this glass-walled space at the end of Ward 11. It is the digestive ward, and nurses have to hold their breath as they walk through because of the stench of open wounds and digestive ailments. It is the ward that they have to acclimatise to. And I'm here in a bed at the far end of it, feeling suspended disbelief in the section of the ward which was built as a conservatory. It was meant to be a lounge area for the patients, but now it has fifteen beds crammed into it, all of us at strange angles to each other. The end of my bed almost touches my neighbour's. Two beds down from me there's a cubicle swathed in yellow plastic bin liners. They are tied to the bed frame and to a separate trolley which sits at the foot of the bed. Yellow is the sign of infection.

The patient has MRSA, but there isn't anywhere to isolate her from the rest of us.

My eyes keep being drawn to the yellow, the frightening yellow. I am fidgety.

It's hot under the glass, and as I shift in the cotton sheets, my legs stick to them and they wrinkle annoyingly under me.

And now it's my turn. I watch the doctors as they survey my chart, talking among themselves. I am told my pain relief is being reduced. They want to get me home. A thought that terrifies me, despite the third-world feel of this ward. I would fight for my corner in this hot, smelly place, but I cannot find the words.

A trickle of sweat is snaking slowly down my back, making me itch, stealing my concentration. Everything seems blurred and foggy in my mind.

They have moved on and I realise I'm going home. Well, going to my parents' home.

I have to eat the lunch and if I don't throw it up, I can go. I haven't been cured; I don't have a treatment plan, any help or contingency plan. Just that I have to not throw up my lunch and then I go.

I call my parents. They agree to pick me up at 4 p.m., thinking it will give me enough time to puke or not puke, and the chemist enough time to prepare my take-home meds. At 12 p.m. the lunch trolley is pushed into our section of the ward by a large red-faced nurse. She shouts something at one of the orderlies and they both laugh. She moves her hair back from her face, puts the wheel brake on the huge steel 1950s trolley, and opens the levered side door. It's like the worst ever in-flight meal service from a crappy airline. Like Aeroflot in the early days – the days when we used to clap every time it landed safely because the crash rate was so appalling. I smile even as I remember those days, until I realise my friends are still doing it. Still living 'my life', travelling the world and writing for a living. I push away the thought.

The nurse walks past my bed. I say I am to have lunch. She says I should've ordered my meal last night when the menus were brought round. I tell her I didn't know last night that I was going to be able to eat lunch today as the doctors have only just told me. She says there isn't much food left.

'What have you got?' I ask.

'What do you want?' she asks.

I say, 'I don't know, I haven't seen the menu. Can you tell me what there is, please?' Then I add, 'I am on a special medical low-fat diet.'

'We've got macaroni cheese, quiche or beef Wellington,' she replies.

'I need low-fat food. Surely you have something for low-fat diets?' I ask, with the now-familiar pleading nasal quality in my voice.

She says no, they don't.

I say: 'Can the kitchen make me something for a low-fat diet?'

She says, 'No. Everyone in the kitchens has now gone home. It's too late, and anyway they don't do personal requests.'

Personal requests?

With that, she pushes her head up and puts her hands on her hips.

I feel anger rising and surging inside me again. I want to throw the entire tray of macaroni cheese at her smug face.

Instead, I say: 'I'll have the quiche.' My words taste of defeat and resignation.

She plonks the tray on my lap, making it very clear she's annoyed at me. I would laugh, but it would be that awful hollow, choking laugh that comes from the realisation that you are utterly vanquished, completely defeated and destroyed. And that is how I feel as I watch her walk back down the ward, grabbing for her cigarettes at the nurses' station. I watch her leave, watch her all the way, mad as it sounds, as she walks down the corridor and finally turns the bend which leads to the lift, where she will press the ground-floor button, walk several steps ahead and through the sliding doors to the front of the hospital for her lunchtime fag. I imagine her drawing in the smoke with satisfaction and, honestly, I want to kill her. I want to hurt her for the months and months of petty humiliations, the tiny battles I have to lose each and every day in hospital. I want to blame her for all of them, and I want her to know this feeling; this red-hot rage which comes from deep within my bowels.

I eat as much of the quiche as I dare, given that it's made up of eggs and cheese which are in complete opposition to my doctor's instructions about food. I crunch on the lettuce, then suck the blackcurrant jelly off my spoon. Then I wait.

About thirty minutes after eating it starts. The pain. It builds up with a niggling, cringing sensation at the top of my abdomen as the food reaches where the pancreas ejects the digestive fluids. After forty-five minutes, I have to call for pain relief, but I haven't thrown my meal up, so I am still ahead. As the nurse goes to get the morphine, I get a sharp pain in my stomach which drives me to the bathroom. The meal has taken less than an hour to pass through me in a rush of light brown diarrhoea. I still haven't thrown up though, which I take to be a good sign.

By the time I get back to my bed, the nurse is waiting. I quietly ignore the fact that I can't eat without being propelled into agony. Because suddenly, I just want to get home. Not that I know where home is at the moment. But I want to get out of here with a ferocity that means I don't care any more about a cure or pain relief or tests. I want to go somewhere clean and safe, away from the beds crammed together, away from the clipboards and specialists. Away from the tiny shower room which has black mould around the edges of the tiles. Away from the toilets. Oh God, how I want to get away from the toilets.

It is amazing how the simple luxury of a clean loo can be so compelling, so desirable, the object of such fantasy. I dream of a white bowl with super-soft toilet roll in a clean, bright bathroom, with a window and a light, fresh scent of flowers or meadows or whatever those bleaches promise. I yearn for that loo, I really do.

Four p.m. and my parents are sitting at the end of the bed. Dad is impatient, restless, saying he has things to do and why aren't I ready yet. Mum opens her *Telegraph* and takes a small package of biscuits from her bag. She's carefully wrapped them in clingfilm and she nibbles on them slowly as she reads.

Dad marches off to find cups of tea. The hospital is not working to his schedule – I know how that feels. Fran has also arrived, and I note the quick register of shock when she sees me. I guess I have lost a lot of weight. Every time I eat, I end up either in acute pain or with full-blown pancreatitis, so I am in a continual battle to eat enough to live on. She bends over and kisses me. Her face is cool against my cheek. Mum and Dad are pleased to see her; they are grateful that my friends visit me, and I love them for that alone. Fran calmly twirls a lock of her long brown hair and curls it behind her ear before looking at me with serene scrutiny.

'Typical,' she says, finally.

'Go on,' I reply. 'What's typical?'

'You've lost at least a couple of stone, you're like a little dead bird, and your tits are still bigger than mine.'

I choke back my laugh, grabbing my stomach in pain as I try to stop the giggles. 'Ouch, that hurts. Don't bloody make me laugh again,' I say, in mock horror.

'I wouldn't dare,' she says and we smile at each other. Francesca has been the most regular visitor of all my friends. At least once a month, she drives over to spend a day with me, usually at my hospital bedside. She tells me the gossip, who has met whom, who has gone travelling, who wants to get pregnant. It is like a fresh breeze from the outside world coming into the stale air of my prison. I am elated in her company, but when she leaves I struggle not to sink lower still.

Half an hour later, a nurse comes up to us saying my meds are almost ready. By now, I am at the tail end of the last morphine dose and I am really feeling it. The burning feeling inside my stomach is back, and I am fidgeting into the sensation which feels like someone has placed a hot iron on to my stomach lining, leaving it scorched and raw and red, like slices of undercooked meat. This isn't an attack brewing. That pain is quite distinct, like losing control of sanity. This is what is left after each attack – one pain dissolving like molten lava into another. This pain is the 'safer' one, but it is pain and it is tiring and I am feeling so hot in the glasshouse inferno.

Eventually, another nurse appears with a large bag of medicines. She lays them all out on the bed, pausing only to open the discharge sheet. I see Fran's eyebrows raised in disbelief and I tell her this is normal for me now.

There's a confusing, long prescription: Buscopan for IBS cramps, paracetamol and ibuprofen for base-line pain relief, metoclopramide for nausea, tramadol for stronger pain relief and OxyContin (liquid morphine) for proper pain relief. She talks us through the drugs, but to be honest, I know them all so well now I hardly listen.

As I am wheeled by Dad through the hospital corridors in the blue standard-issue wheelchair, I allow myself the wild hope that this will be my last visit to this place or to any hospital. I let myself feel like it'll never happen again. I know it is foolish. I know I'm setting myself up for my hopes to be crushed again, but I cannot resist.

The sun is shining as we turn into the car park and I believe, I really believe, that this will be the last time. Maybe I'll never have an attack of pancreatitis again. Maybe I'll start getting better now and have my life back.

It takes less than twenty-four hours for me to be proved wrong.

Leaning my hot head against the coolness of the car window, I start to feel panic. This pain has become a thing of terror and the thought of being back out in the world as vulnerable as I am is horrifying. I know that within minutes Fran will be pulling crisp, cold sheets over me in a bedroom in my parents' home, and I feel anchorless, drifting, disconnected from the house, my friends and my life.

This home I'm going to is not mine. It's not my childhood home, this house in the countryside. I grew up in a semi in Redhill, an unremarkable part of Surrey. Then we moved up to Cheshire because my dad changed jobs and we lived in another square, 1960s semi in a cul-de-sac before moving again, back down south, to an equally faceless, but slightly bigger, detached house in another suburban cul-de-sac.

My dad worked hard and by the time I had left home and was working abroad, they'd bought themselves the shabby, unloved farmhouse in the countryside, with nice neighbours and nice surroundings. They then set about making it a home. They had made huge sacrifices for both my sister and me, sending us to college, etc. My mum's wages from her years doing the bookkeeping in a rural garage went straight into my bank account to supplement my paltry student grant.

But until all this started, I had spent little time here in their new home. It is another strange place to get used to. A nice place – but unfamiliar at a time when I crave something of my own to remind me I still exist and to comfort me.

I collapse back into the pillows, clutching the sick bowls we took from the hospital. Mum brings me vegetable soup. I barely manage a couple of mouthfuls. I know they're worried about my weight. I have lost almost a stone since all this began, and I wasn't exactly fat before. Now I'm barely nudging seven and a half stone.

Pain starts pounding my brain. No, my back. No, my stomach. I am a cripple in a bed that is not my own. I dribble soup down my new cotton M&S pyjamas. A thousand years seem to pass, then Mum opens the door with her foot, her hands occupied with a tray. On it is fruit, water and the bottle of liquid morphine I have been prescribed. I feel unbelievable relief. Tears prick my eyes and I blink them back.

Mum's hands are shaking; she can see I am suffering, so she is trying to open the bottle quickly. I am moaning and a trickle of spit settles on the side of my mouth. It tastes foul. I am foul. I swallow and it goes. All of it starts to go. And I am blacking out, thank God. Thank God.

I wake up. It is almost dark.

My dad is dozing on a wicker chair by the door. He has been sitting with me for maybe two hours by now. Something like my heart stirs with pity, but I don't know if it is for me or him. When he is sleeping he looks old. When he is awake he is a rocket, he is a god in a running vest and a marathon medal. He doesn't do illness. None of us did. Until now. Positive Mental Attitude, Dad says each time he sits with me, as I puke up the morphine into a vomit bowl. I don't blame him for not understanding. I can barely comprehend the severity of this illness myself, let alone expect anyone else to.

Even so, it grates after a while.

After an hour or so, he stirs, eyes unfocused. Rubbing his face, he gets up and immediately says we have to start moving my stuff from the other bedroom as this time I am staying in the larger back bedroom. I gaze at him from the bed, not sure what he means. How can I help when I am like this?

He says it again. By now, it is obvious he is not joking. He wants me to get out of bed and carry books into this bedroom. I wonder for a brief moment if all the stress of this illness has affected his brain. He is utterly serious.

'Dad, I can't help you. I can't walk and I keep being sick,' I reply, carefully phrasing my words. Even so, inside I feel a massive rush of anger and confusion.

There is silence, then Dad walks out of my room. He marches back in seconds later with a pile of books which he dumps in one of the corners. He walks out again. This time he's talking, wanting me to hear. He is saying that I am ungrateful, and why does he always have to do everything and this is typical of me. He is really angry now, working himself into a state, all the while carrying my possessions which amount to a few boxes stored in the spare room. He dumps them down as though my stuff isn't important, although actually parts of my life are stored in those meagre boxes.

I can't stop the anger exploding from me now. It is hot and powerful and it singes my tongue as I shout back: 'You fucking insensitive bastard. I can't believe you're doing this! How the fuck can I help you?'

'Don't you dare talk to me like that,' he replies. His voice is sharp, pointed. He is a different person.

'I dare, Dad. I bloody dare. Haven't you seen me lately? What the hell is going on with you? Can't you see how ill I am?' And with that, the anger slides into a hollow jolt in my stomach.

I feel sick. I am going to be sick. The soup is coming up and I can feel my abdomen tightening. There is a moaning sound and, this time, I know it is me. I know I am groaning into my sick bowl as my dad watches, tight-faced.

'You're so bloody ungrateful. Why should I have to do everything?' he shouts at me, oblivious to the effect he is having.

I tell him he is an unfeeling bastard as I spit small chunks of potato into the bowl.

At that, outraged by my frailty and probably desperate for my recovery, he loses it. He starts shouting until Mum appears in the doorway. She looks like we've stabbed her in the back.

'Not again,' she says with icy calm. 'Will you two please stop behaving like children.' She turns, leaving us in shamed silence.

Dad walks out, his footsteps stomping the length of the corridor. Seconds later, the door to the lounge downstairs shuts louder than it should. I barely reach the vomit bowl before my feelings flow out in a torrent of sick. So there is guilt and upset, hurt and anger and it is all in this room with this fucking illness which is tearing us all apart from each other.

We are sick of it. We are all sick of it. My dad, my mum, me – we are all at the end of our tethers. We are alone in this house, just us and a few vomit bowls, a pot of morphine and nothing else.

As silence settles back on to my room, I feel rejected, abandoned, scared and vulnerable. I can hear the TV downstairs and I feel so alone. I know that none of us is behaving rationally. But how can we? When every day we face something that refuses to leave, that refuses to be cured. I know my dad was shouting for his pain, for my pain, for the family's pain. But it still hurts.

The sun is fully set by now. My curtains are still open as I can't get up to draw them shut. Instead, I watch the blue become inky black with my overhead light projecting a ghostly orange orb on to the panes.

I am trying to ignore my body. I am trying to calm my mind and reassure myself that everything is ok. But I can sense my body will crumple into another attack. I can already feel the sick and squirmy feeling building in me again. The itch has started. The feeling that I am being devoured from the inside out is starting, and I know where it is leading and I am so scared. I will do anything not to go back to hospital.

Sounds from the TV break up the silence in my room. I can hear the tinny laughter of a game show. My parents are downstairs, light years away in 'normal' life and I am not there. I am here. I am here and it is starting and I don't want it to. And I am so scared. I cry like a small child.

Then nausea rises and I know I am lost. It is definitely coming now and I am lost, I have lost. I am beaten and desperate and defeated. I puke violently into my sick bowl. It splashes over the edge and on to the new clean sheets. Mum will kill me, I think before it happens again. And again.

I try to call out, but the sick keeps coming. They eventually hear. Mum's footsteps coming at a stately run up the stairs. 'Oh Christ,' she says. 'Albie, call the ambulance.'

Mum is always calm in a crisis. Dad panics. I can hear the fear in his voice. He is dialling and he is taking a long time. He hands the phone over to Mum and I hear her voice from far away asking for an ambulance. We wait. Well, they wait while I puke and moan.

Someone is panting and crying in the room. I don't like the noises, but I know they're coming from me. And they won't stop. It won't stop. I'm clutching my stomach, I am counting the seconds. I am shaking, I am moaning.

The ambulance will take too long. We have to go to A&E ourselves. Mum bundles me up in the blanket I bought on the Inca Trail in Peru, maybe to subconsciously remind me I have lived a life and this illness isn't the whole of me. She wraps me carefully in the scratchy folds of the llama wool blanket, and motions to Dad to lift me up. I don't want him to touch me; I still hate him from our fight. And now, even worse, I blame him for this latest episode. I hate him, and I am pretty sure he hates me right now. And yet he lifts me. And I let him.

Trailing the blanket, Dad carries me into the car. The pace of the pain quickens. I am now absorbed by the turmoil of the erupting agony inside me, its crescendo building as the seconds pass. Get me to hospital, I croak. The fight has left me. All I want now is to get to the relative safety of A&E. I am frightened. I need a doctor and I need morphine. I need IV fluids and an antiemetic.

I know my life could be in danger and the realisation hits my dad as well. Out of the bleary psychosis of the pain, I see my father's hands shaking as he turns the key in the ignition. Our argument is vanishing, slipping away, relegated and replaced by a fragile reconciliation in the car.

Dad drives fast, swearing at other drivers, hooting at pedestrians who are ambling drunkenly between the high-street pubs. He drives like a man possessed. He is a man possessed – of a sick daughter.

Twenty minutes later and the green hue of the A&E strip lights wink at us from the road. Dad turns the car into the hospital forecourt, parking haphazardly across a double yellow line. He leaps out, opens my door and lifts me out again. I can't be carried this time. I am being sick on to the road. I know I have an audience as we career through the doors, people watching me in morbid fascination.

The receptionist tells me to wait a minute and I tell her I can't. She looks up and sees me, dishevelled, white as a spectre with a sick bowl under my chin and says, 'I'll make you a priority.'

Thank fuck for that.

Within minutes, I am taken into a cubicle to wait for a doctor to assess me.

My dad, silent up to this point, his eyes wide with hurt and fear, takes my hand. 'It'll be ok,' he says. And in that moment, the shame and regret of our rows, our bickering and our fights fall away. In that one small sentence, I hear love and hope and care. He squeezes my hand gently – and all this is almost worth it. It's almost worth the shouting and the fighting because we are reconciled under the too-bright lights in the too-noisy room with the too-yellow walls and the too-loud drunks. We are father and daughter again, together against the world. Waiting and afraid – but together. And I am soothed like a small girl again, being tucked up in bed by my daddy to chase the monsters away.

*

Much later, and I am back in Ward 11. I think I am in the same bed as last time. Or was it the time before? I am hooked up again. The same old story. A saline drip, a cannula sticking out of my hand which irritates my vein. I am awake, but groggy. Dad left hours ago. He waited with me until I was admitted and then I told him to go home and get some sleep. Reluctantly, he left, leaving me back in the now horribly familiar ward.

It is early morning. Shapeless people move around. It is quiet; a rare moment of peace. I pull the white sheet up to my eyes and squint through the thin fabric. The world looks white and calm and safe. I am ok, I tell myself. It will all be ok.

I have put lavender oil on the sheets and I smell it. The scent of outside, of mellow sunshine and fields, sits incongruously on the cotton. A tear winds a slow path down my cheek. It is ok, I keep saying, as if I'll believe it.

This time, I am only in hospital for five days. Long enough for the pancreatitis to burn itself out and so I go home. Again. As I'm wheeled out, blinking into the sunshine, I know I will be back. I am stuck in a time machine which has stalled, propelling me back and forth within my own personal Groundhog Day.

As I sink under my acceptance that this is now my life, I feel a strange peace. There is literally nothing I can do, nothing I can change, nothing I can do differently. And so I wait now. I wait to see if I will survive, if this is all there will ever be.

Within an hour I am lifted carefully back into the cold bed in the end room of my parents' house, in the middle of the countryside. I feel as alone as I could ever be. The house is hushed, the only sound being a radio left to quietly fill the space between the walls of this home with the sound of Classic FM.

There is a bag of painkillers on the bedside cabinet. It is within reach, but I cannot move, I am so weak. Every four hours I hear the tread of my mother's footsteps as she comes up the stairs, along the corridor and into 'my' room. She asks me how I am. I say I am ok. We both know I am lying, but we both want to believe that it is true.

Mum marks the time in a notebook kept especially for the purpose of recording the doses of the various drugs I am taking. It is now 3 p.m. and I am due to take two paracetamol (500mg each), two tramadol (50mg each), 10ml of OxyContin and a metoclopramide. Mum holds my head up, cradling my neck in her arms which are soft and smell of roses. She lifts me just enough to swallow down the tablets, then the liquid morphine.

Once done, she settles me back down on to the pillow. She asks if I need the loo and I say I am ok for now. At the side of my bed is a bucket with a towel draped over it and a toilet roll beside it. This is my toilet as I cannot move myself out of bed. When I need to use it, my mum has to help me up out of the bed, pull up my nightie, half-carry and half-drag me to the bucket and hold me as I crouch and shiver over it. When I have finished, I hand the toilet roll to her and she has to struggle to rip off the required number of sheets while simultaneously holding me up, before wiping me clean. By this time, I am retching, as any movement makes me sick and shaking with cold and exhaustion. Each time we say we should have torn off the toilet roll beforehand.

Each time we forget. Each time.

My dignity is a far-off memory. My natural desire for a respectful distance between my private ablutions and my public presence has long since abandoned me. I used to cry every time I had to be heaved on to the bucket – weeping for my lost pride and self-respect. But now I give in to it. Whether I cry about it or accept it, there is little I can do about it anyway. I am sorely grateful. And that gratitude, that essential need to live off the kindness of those around me, has worn me into a shrivelled person, a smaller version of what I once was. It has done for me what the illness has not. It is the final angry nail in the coffin of my being. For me, it means that I always have to be nice. I can't be upset, annoyed or grumpy because I owe everyone around me so much. I owe them my life.

And so it rankles, slowly niggling away at me, until each smile feels like a betrayal, each thank you feels like another reason to give up, to feel shame, remorse and regret for everything that has happened to me.

I know I sound like a horrible person, and maybe I am. But I challenge anyone not to feel worn down after weeks and months of having to be grateful. When there is little enough left of your true self, somehow the gratitude feels like the last straw.

Or maybe I'm confusing the gratitude with the general tedium of being alive and yet not living. Each morning I wake up from what little sleep I've been allowed by the burning in my back and stomach to another day spent lying on my back, marooned in an empty landscape of discomfort. My eyes blink, my mouth talks, my ears listen, but I cannot sit up, I cannot brush my hair, clean my teeth or wash myself. I cannot read a book as I am too weak to hold one up. I cannot get out of bed to turn the light off or take myself to the bathroom. I exist. My mind is awake and churning, second by second in restless confusion, but I do not live.

I cannot fathom the change in my life and my health. Where did all this come from? My life has been ambushed, my body has been kidnapped and I am trapped.

Each morning at 7 a.m. Mum comes in to see if I'm ok. Crumpled in her nightie, her hair in post-sleeping disarray, she comes to check on me. If I need it, she lifts me up and on to my bucket. If not, she begins the morning medicine round, painkillers mostly, and the anti-sickness. Then she takes away my vomit bowl and brings another as I've almost always been sick overnight.

Depending on how I feel, some mornings if I am really bad,

she will wipe me down with some baby wipes. How apt they are. I am stranded like a helpless baby. On better days, she brings me a cup of tea before she and Dad hoist me out of bed and haul me along the corridor and into the bathroom for the shower routine.

There's a stool inside the shower and once my nightie is pulled over my small frame, I sit huddled and rocking, waiting for the first burst of water to hit my skin. I dread the shower. Mum reaches up for the shower head and runs the water, careful not to touch my raw skin until it is cool enough not to hurt, then she washes me. My head spins and the nausea builds as the sheer willpower involved in staying seated and not slumping on to the ceramic white floor of the shower defeats me.

My hair is washed, less gently as time passes. This is a hassle for Mum as well as me. She has a lot to do, and looking after an adult baby must be as unsettling and as emotionally draining as it is for me to be cared for. I keep my head down, so she won't see that often I'm crying in unrestrained grief not only for myself and my debility, but for her and the sense of duty and love which drives her to care for me endlessly like this. I cry for both of us because I know she won't. That at least I can do without help.

The shower, from start to finish, takes the best part of an hour, including dressing me in a clean nightie and holding me up for the short distance to the bed. I fall back on to the pillows, the sick bowl goes under my chin and I fight the urge to vomit.

Then Mum goes to shower and dress herself, arriving back again with a bowl of porridge and more tea. I try so hard to eat. I've seen myself as I'm shuffled past the bathroom mirror; I've glimpsed a skeletal body, one I don't even recognise. Where my bottom used to be, there's nothing; where my tummy – which I so hated – was, there is now flat, unnaturally flat nothing.

I am skin and bones, fading away before all of our eyes.

*

Incredibly though, through these dark days, I have managed to meet someone and we have very tentatively started a relationship. It is the strangest thing. We met three months ago when I contacted an alternative health clinic in desperation. Mum drove me to the practice, depositing me on a chair in the waiting area as the world spun round me and I fought the urge to vomit over the immaculate flooring.

The man I went to see – Adrian – listened to me and even made me laugh. He was the first to say I could get better. I saw him weekly after that and he started me on a course of herbal medicine. He came out to me after the first appointment as it was clear to both of us what it cost me to go to his practice.

Then we started speaking now and again on the phone – mostly frenetic, tearful calls from me during which he calmed and soothed me and got me laughing at his silly jokes. The calls became more frequent, the visits longer and longer.

Adrian doesn't seem to mind the illness and the deep depressions it sinks me into. He doesn't mind the lack of privacy, the bouts of sickness, the fact of being with someone who cannot walk or eat out or even watch TV for long. He talks to me, reads to me, even strokes my hair and chats with my mum. He is gentle and understanding and we find we share a love of travel and films which we talk incessantly about on days when I am well enough.

We all think Adrian is some kind of angel looking after me, because who meets someone when they are as ill as I am? We are convinced he is nothing short of a small miracle – sent to help all of us through the difficult days and darker endless nights with his infinite optimism and kindness.

He would hate us branding him as something divine though, so we just wonder, mystified, as he rings the doorbell, bounds up the stairs of my parents' farmhouse and taps his fingers along the corridor to announce he is coming, he is coming. Those moments are the highlight of my world – the sound of the doorbell, then the footsteps, then the joyous tapping and his face beaming as he looks round the door. As he looks with delight at me, propped up on pillows, face ashen and pale, without make-up or pretty clothes – just me in my pyjamas, waiting for the kindness of this virtual stranger to lift me out, however briefly, from this solitary hell.

I laugh now when I think of all the effort I used to make to attract a good man. I made sure I was always well dressed and had regular manicures, pedicures and massages so that I was always feeling my best. It used to take me an hour to do my hair and apply my war paint before work each day. And there were so many dates in trendy central London bars, dinners in nice restaurants, walks along the Greenwich docks. But I found no one special. No one who cared enough. And so I carried on living my high life, with the secret loneliness that only a single girl in her thirties understands. Outwardly, I was attractive and successful, but inside was that small ache that grows with time, mingling uncomfortably with the fear that time was passing too fast and I was going to be left on a glamorous shelf.

There is a sweetness to our growing affection for each other – an innocence I thought I had lost for ever. And the first time Adrian joins us on the mad dash to A&E, I know he is becoming more than just a friend. He holds my hand as I cry into the hospital pillow, as I pant in pain and fear yet again, and I am conscious that without him hovering in the foreground of my life, I would probably go insane.

I have time. So much time. The kind of time that turns an hour into a day, a day into a complete time zone. And it is in this time that I am forced to face the fact of my existence. And to wonder if I will still be here, like this, in bed, not moving, in a year's time, in five years' time. Or even if I will be here at all.

I am acutely aware that I cannot get enough calories down me to stop the slow descent into weightlessness. This frightens me more than I can say. As the numbers on the scales go inexorably downwards there is the growing knowledge that I can only go so low before I stop. Before my body collapses from within, for one last and final time.

We are so helpless in the face of this, we don't know what to do. Mum brings me porridge, she brings me toast and she makes me a fat-free cake which is full of sugar to give me the calories I need. But my treacherous body can barely take more than a couple of sips, a bite or two every hour or so. I am fighting a battle with my own body and I am losing. I am losing. And I am so afraid.

I tell Adrian this. I tell him everything. I feel he is my only point of safety in a frightening world.

More and more, I feel a sense of betrayal by my body, most strongly when the attacks come, as they do, every week or so for the next few months. Each time, I am shocked that part of me wants to hurt me so badly. It feels personal. It is personal. And I feel let down by the very skin that contains me. My Judas. My disloyal body.

Can it really be the same body that took me all over the globe in a reckless orgy of travel, passion and adventure? It is a continual revelation that it can't take me anywhere any more. Every day I feel like I am still catching up with myself, still coming to terms with having no mobility to speak of, in such sharp contrast to who I was before.

I am a burden now. I make no bones about it. And I am humbled by my parents' willingness to carry me through this. I haven't been the easiest daughter. I spent years worrying them by regularly disappearing on my travels. Then I worried them by working too hard, by burning the candle at both ends in London and in not finding someone to be with, to settle down with. And I worried them most of all, perhaps, by not being very much in touch with them, by moving away and living, thoughtlessly, for myself. Maybe this new dependency is my payback.

I burned myself out. That is the kindest way I can describe my descent into illness. Every second of every day, I took my life and my health for granted and I pushed myself harder and harder, working longer and longer hours. I see that now, lying in a state of mourning. I am like Lenin in his mausoleum. My skin has the same waxy sheen, my body the same locked-in rigidity. Except he is dead, and I am not. Yet.

I have never really thought about illness before now. I have sympathised with other people in the appropriate way, but I never made the effort to connect with anyone going through anything outside of my sphere. But maybe I am too harsh on myself? Maybe none of us really knows anything about suffering or incapacity until it happens to us?

I have a sense that I am meant to go deeper into this. To absorb some lesson, some spiritual journey of self-discovery. As time lengthens and as the days move with dinosaur grace into each other, I slowly start to unpick my thoughts, unravel my emotions until I can dissect each and every part of this slowly, with meaning and intent.

I see that there is still an essential part of me that remains unchanged – that is unconnected to the business of having to 'do' things in order to be human. A part that is curiously unaffected by this paralysis, in both my life and my body. A small, quiet space that is somehow impervious to the torments inside me. I don't know what this place or this space is. But as time moves on, I find it stays, immortal and unmoving.

I look back at my life and scrub away the perceived glamour and high living and I see instead what I refused to see for so long. That the woman doing all those things, flying to all those places, working so hard, living so hard, was, in fact, so lonely. So lonely and so very scared. There is a soreness to these new findings – they expose more of me than my public ablutions ever could. Parts of my past behaviour sit with me now in prickly silence, just out of reach, but hovering, in continual reproach. The newness of my culpability is creating a rawness that chafes almost as much as the enforced stillness.

I see someone who chased hard after money and success, who ran full tilt at adventure and experience as a way of avoiding the relationships in her life. I see a woman whose personal life was littered with failed relationships, who reached out for love in cold, dark places, and who was abandoned, rejected and sometimes abused.

And I notice how the relationships I did manage to cling to are starting to fade away. My friends have lives of their own and they move onwards, like a film reel before me. In the time that I've been ill, I have watched them buy bigger houses, get better jobs, meet future spouses, plan their children, invest in pensions. All the time I watch, I listen, I accept their excuses for coming less frequently, I understand. I would be living like that too if I could. I would be too busy to meet up, catch up.

The torment grinds on, relentless, dogged and unyielding. I wake up to the darkness of the early morning, finding myself yet again in a hospital bed, yet again with a drip attached to a needle in my arm, yet again surrounded by the rheumy wheezing of the infirm and it feels like I never left. So frequently am I here now. In and out, like a yo-yo.

I lie for a while, digesting my thoughts, watching the light turn gradually grey to the beginnings of blue until I realise I need to pee. I don't bother with the buzzer. Can't face the fuss. I don't want yet another stranger to hoist me up and out into the loo. So I ease myself up, gripping the cool metal rod of the drip pole, leaning my weight into it like a peculiar walking stick. My gown is crumpled and my hair is itching my scalp where it needs washing and brushing.

The other patients are breathing heavily in collective harmony, like a slumbering beast. I carefully slip a foot into each of the white flat slippers provided by the ward. My bed is at the end of the ward, so I only have to take a few more faltering steps to get to the corridor. I shuffle slowly, clinging on to the walls and my pole, not really sure I'll make it on my own.

As I turn the corner from the ward and into the corridor I am struck by light which is streaming with decadent relish into the corridor. I stop, startled into silent wonder as the dazzling radiance of the sunlight fills me up, fills up my vision and saturates a place somewhere deep inside of me.

I open my eyes, having shut them in reaction to all that brilliance, and I see the view properly for the first time. The hospital slouches at the edge of the town, and just past its straggling borders is lush countryside that pulls me into the depths of its scope. The scene, reminiscent of a Gainsborough, melts into the lazy, hazy beauty of pinks and oranges and fresh early-morning blues. So pure. So strong. So astonishingly enchantingly beautiful, it literally takes my breath away.

Blinking back watering eyes which are so unused to daylight, I stand in wonder.

My crumpled gown, my crumpled body and soul swoon into the sunshine, glorifying in the feel of it on my skin and, without realising, I start to laugh. I laugh into the sunrise like it is the first I have ever seen. I laugh and laugh and I don't stop, even though the nurses will think I'm mad. I laugh, I chuckle, then I am silent.

The sun has done for me what a million therapists couldn't. It has planted a seed of hope. An irrational, illogical, unsearched-for seed of hope.

CHAPTER 5

# The Sit-In

*October 2006*

The surgeon is portly, with a waistcoat tightly buttoned around his wide girth and sandy-coloured hair which is thinning quite spectacularly on top. He walks over to my bed. I'm back in Ward 11. I'm lying on my bed, clasping my sick bowl, having just thrown up my lunch. I've been in and out of this ward countless times in the past months and I'm worn out.

He shakes my feeble hand and then asks me to lie back. I try to lie so I am comfortable, but the action makes me feel sicker, my head spins and I have to count down the seconds to stop myself puking on his lily-white hands which are now feeling my abdomen. He says nothing after the examination, so I say I need help eating as I've lost so much weight. My wasted body has shrunk to six and a half stone, which is dangerously thin for my height and this is really worrying me. Eating is painful and, after a few days, it always seems to cause another attack of pancreatitis. I have told the doctors and nurses repeatedly, yet nothing has been done or even suggested.

So I try again.

'I really need to get some calories inside me; I'm frightened I'll waste away ...' My voice trails off as the surgeon turns round. He was already halfway through departing my bedside. He swings round and, as he does, he tells me he thinks I look like a supermodel and pats my arm, smiling vacantly in my direction. With that he leaves.

If this was a pantomime, there would be a puff of green smoke and the crowd would boo. But this is an NHS hospital, and instead I am hit by a moment of truth: no one is listening to me. If I carry on losing weight like this, then I don't know what will happen to me. I am scared and I can't see any end to my plight.

I am wasting away in front of the eyes of all these medics and none of them seems concerned about it. This revelation punches me in the gut. I need to take action and regain control over what happens to me. If I don't stand up for myself in this place, I will just continue to deteriorate and actually, I am not ready to fade out in this way.

I fight the sudden urge to vomit again, pick up my mobile phone, my hand trembling with a mixture of nerves and determination, and dial the number of my local doctor's surgery. The ring tone repeats and repeats. Eventually, a receptionist picks up and I say I urgently need to speak to my GP. She takes my number and says he will ring me after his clinic. I wait frantically, checking my phone every minute to make sure I haven't missed his call.

Less than an hour later, my phone rings and I snatch it up and answer. I tell my GP I need a referral to a specialist and I need it now. He pauses. I hear him tapping on his computer keys. I tell him that an ex-boyfriend of mine has a cousin who works in the pancreatic department of a London hospital and I want to go there.

I tell him I have asked my surgeons here several times for a referral to a specialist, but they've said there is nothing anyone can do for me. There is no surgery that will deal with acute-on-chronic pancreatitis, they tell me over and over again. Well there must be something someone can do for me, and it is time to find out, I say.

My GP listens in silence as I read the riot act. He says he will send the letter tomorrow. I hang up, my heart beating out of my body. If I could pace around the ward I would. Instead, I pick up my latest book and try to read the first few pages, but this fails to distract me and so I put it down and just lie there, my thoughts churning in restless internal monologues.

Three days later, I am discharged. There is no word from my GP, yet I go with a lighter heart. This hospital may have washed its hands of me, but I have started to fight for myself, and I feel a small glimmer of unfounded hope.

Several weeks later, I am lying in bed at my parents' and realise I have still heard nothing from the GP about my appointment with the pancreatic specialist. I have only been home from my latest admission for a day and I feel weak and nauseous from the combined effects of the pancreatitis and the morphine injections. I call my GP again.

'Was the letter sent?' I ask, trying hard to concentrate through the sick feeling.

He tells me it wasn't.

'Why wasn't it sent?' I say incredulously, as a surge of anger brings a hot, bitter taste to my mouth. In the silence that follows I get a rush of sound in my ears like the visual noise of a damaged TV. 'I want to see you today,' I tell him. 'I want that letter done and sent and I want to see you writing it,' I add, as firmly as I can manage.

Twenty minutes later, I'm bundled into Mum's car and we drive to the surgery. I can hardly walk, but my anger propels me into the waiting room where I sit slumped until I can go in.

Once I have struggled the ten-metre walk into the consulting room, I sit down with difficulty. My body hurts in every conceivable place, it aches and burns and I fight with it endlessly, trying to reassert some control over it. I don't have the energy to argue with my GP. Instead, I tell him again simply that I want to see him write to the London specialist while I am here, in this surgery. I say that I'm feeling exhausted and wretched and betrayed by my doctor. I am scared I will give up, give in, lose the fight and wither away like a Victorian consumptive – frightened I will lose any hope and, in doing so, lose myself along the way.

So I am here, I explain, to make my GP accountable, to make him take responsibility for some part of this, my illness, my affliction.

Dr M. dictates my letter into his dictaphone. When he is done I ask if I can take the dictaphone to the receptionist. He agrees.

I get up slowly. I thank him for his time and for seeing me at such short notice. I take the small black object in my hand and make my slow way back to reception. I swing open the door with some difficulty. There is a child screaming and the smell of detergent. The place seems overpowering, rendering me smaller, giddy, less of a person. I keep to my course, aware I will need to be very sick some time soon with the effort this has cost me. I wait my turn at the desk, barely able to stand, gripping the side of the counter, and I hand the machine to the receptionist. I tell her it is urgent and I thank her too.

Back in the car, my anger dissolves into tears. I submit to being taken home, gently escorted up the stairs and back into bed where, before long, my stomach muscles cramp into themselves and the soup I had for lunch pours back up, hardly touching the inside of my mouth, as it exits in a hot, foamy mess. Once it is up and out of me, I feel better. I feel emptied and peaceful. I feel back in some kind of control. It cost me almost everything I had in energy to go there today, but I did it.

*

Three weeks later, and I am slumped against the passenger window of Adrian's car. I have been almost looking forward to today's appointment at the London hospital as it means we will spend a whole day together. I haven't seen him as much lately. He has been busier in his practice. I know he is occupied at work with new patients, so I don't ask him to come more often, but I miss him and his visits, although I don't have the courage to tell him so.

I have taken double my anti-sickness dose, but it is not long before nausea beats at my brain, overwhelming me as we drive. As my stomach starts to empty periodically on to several roadside verges, I realise I need a shit. I squirm into the feeling for a few miles more, but I know that I will need to stop and go somewhere. We have come by the back roads as there has been a pile-up on the M25, so there are no service stations or restaurants to rescue me.

Tears smart in my eyes. I feel ashamed and embarrassed before I've done anything because I know it is coming. I know the smelly rivulets of brown shit are coming and there is nothing I can do to stop them. I admit to Adrian that I have to go. I can hear myself saying this in sobs, rather than words. Mortified, humiliated and exposed beyond measure, I ask him to pull over. He screeches the car to a halt at a grassy verge which has some cover from prying roadside eyes, and he runs round to my door. I almost spill out in my haste to get cover before my insides explode. I am crying, I am moaning and I am furious, hating every inch of my body. Hating my bowels, hating my sickening tyrannical pancreas, loathing my fucked-up stomach and intestines. I hate all of it. This is my final indignity – shitting at the roadside with my boyfriend holding me up as I do it.

I manage to pull my tracksuit bottoms down. My legs are shaking furiously with the stress of crouching (my muscles are long-since wasted due to lack of use), while my body jerks and spasms with the effort and the deep, deep shame. I am crying, grieving my dignity, howling out my pain, shivering and shaking in remorse and suffering. When I'm done, I crouch as I wipe myself with the loo roll Adrian has brought from the car, kept in case of emergencies like this. I stand, then pull up my knickers and my trousers. Whimpering, I make my way back to the car where he's waiting for me. He is gentle and kind. He says he's seen worse and it's nothing to be ashamed of as we all do it. We all do it. But I am sunken in ignominy, smeared for ever with the stigma of today.

At the hospital he finds me a wheelchair and I am wheeled into the outpatients department. There are rows and rows of people waiting in several different sections; a bewildering display of NHS bureaucracy. We finally find where we have to sit. We are forty minutes early for my appointment, so we settle down to wait. He goes to buy a cup of tea and I sit, not taking my eyes off the consulting rooms in my desperation to see someone who may help me. The time passes slowly. I slump deeper into the wheelchair. He reads a paper from cover to cover. Then when he's finished, he reads it again.

Our 1.40 p.m. slot slides past. It's 2.40 p.m., 3.40 p.m., 4.40 p.m. before we pluck up the courage to leave our spot at the front of the rows of chairs, but as we turn round, we see the crowd of waiting patients has thinned dramatically. There are now just a couple of other people and us. We ask at the desk. The receptionist looks through the patients' notes which form a small pile now in her inbox.

'Sorry, but your notes aren't here. Are you sure you're here on the right day?' She's brusque, efficient-sounding.

I scrabble for my NHS appointment card, hands shaking as the start of fear creeps cold tremors into my mind. 'Yes, it's definitely today,' I say, brandishing the card in relief as proof of what I was already sure of.

'Your notes aren't here,' she says simply. 'I'll find out what's happened to them.'

We move back to the front of the rows of mostly empty chairs. Five o'clock comes and we see the receptionist putting on her coat, getting ready to leave.

Adrian goes over to her. I can hear the low murmur of his voice.

The notes have gone missing, he reports back to me. They were apparently collected from the hospital archive earlier, but at some point in the frenzied machinations of a day in this London hospital, they disappeared. When he finishes telling me, we stare at each other. We know what this has cost us, what it has cost me to come here. And I don't mean in money – any activity, any event is paid for by me in kind these days. In sickness and nausea. In dignity and self-respect. In exhaustion and fear.

Not knowing what to do or where to go, we wheel back to the receptionist.

'We're not moving from this spot,' I tell her. 'I don't care who lost my notes or why they were lost, I'm staying here until I see the consultant,' I say, my teeth bared in unmasked hostility.

'The consultant left half an hour ago. I'm sorry, but you can't see him today. You'll have to make another appointment,' the receptionist squares up to me. If it's a battle of wills she wants, I think, it's a battle she'll get.

'I'm not leaving until I see the consultant. If I have to wait all night, I am not leaving,' I say with finality, looking her hard in the eyes.

She stares back at me.

She is a slim, elegant African woman with a navy blue dress and a hairclip which glints back at me under the fierce hospital strip lights.

With a sigh, and an exaggerated shrug of her shoulders, she replies, 'I'll try him on his mobile, but I warn you now, he won't come back.'

'I'm not leaving until I see him,' I say again. This time louder.

This time angry. This time confronting her and meaning it, meaning the threat, meaning I will stay here, sitting in. I will sit here through the night ahead, if I have to.

I am not leaving and I dare her to leave me here, a slumped cripple in a wheelchair with a sick bowl hovering permanently below my chin. I dare her to leave me here all night.

Whether this woman, who was clearly on her way out and probably wants to get home, relax and eat dinner with her family, takes pity on me, or sees my determination, I don't know. I feel dreadful and know I must look ghostly white and drawn by now. I haven't sat up for this long for months and am at the point of crying from desperation and the physical pain of being semi-upright. But I am absolutely determined I won't cry. I have whispered my battle cry and so I swallow down the crying and lift up my chin and stare at her with all the strength I can muster.

I know none of this is her fault. I know she knows it isn't her fault. But she is the only person that can make this happen for me, so it is on her that I must focus everything I have left. I am sorry, I think, but this is your karma, so let's just get on with this and fight to the bitter end. To my bitter end.

We wait while she picks up the phone and, reluctantly, dials the number. It is obvious this is uncomfortable for her – he is a hospital god after all, and no one wants to disturb a god on his way home on a Friday evening. This whole situation is probably harder for her right now than it is for me. I know what I want, what I need, what I am prepared to do to get my way.

She slips over her words, in deference, holding her hand over her mouth as she talks quietly into the phone. And I realise that I am going mad. This surgeon, this specialist who is world-renowned for his work with pancreatic ailments, will never turn his car round in the Friday-night rush-hour traffic to come back to see me. The idea is laughable!

By the time the receptionist puts down the receiver, my heart has sunk like an anchor, deep into the seabed of my soul. I wait for the polite refusal. I brace myself and prepare mentally to leave, to come back another day. I know I am condemned to a three-hour drive home, sinking in my own rage and disbelief until the next time.

As my thoughts collide with my feelings, I feel suddenly tired. The fight has drained from me. I barely hear the words framed by the receptionist's astonished mouth.

'He's coming back,' she says.

She looks as amazed as she tells us this as I feel. I thank her too much. I say too much. My gratitude spills on to her desk as she begins to pull off her coat and wait, like me, for the consultant. He is turning his car round on a Friday night to come back and see me. I must look worse than I realise.

By the time he arrives, I am cringing with gratitude, practically wringing my hands in tearful joy like a character from Dickens. I am pushed out of the empty outpatients room and into his consulting room. He is charming, erudite. He asks me my entire back history: when the attacks started, how regularly they come, whether I drink, smoke, eat fatty foods. I laugh in my wretchedness. No I don't smoke, I don't drink, do I look like I eat fatty foods?

I tell him about the jolt which I feel in my stomach each time an attack starts. He listens and I wait.

He tells me the first thing we have to do is take my gall bladder out because the most likely cause of repeated acute pancreatitis is gallstones. I tell him I had a scan (it is in my notes), and it showed I don't have gallstones. He says that the scan may well not show gallstones, but the first step in any case of unexplained pancreatitis is to take the gall bladder out. I say again that it is definitely not my gall bladder and I get this jolt every time an attack comes.

He says again patiently, like he's talking to a difficult child, that I need this operation to rule out the possibility of gallstones.

By now, I am half-fainting from weakness and retching bile in slow tremors into my trusty sick bowl in this small consulting room. I suppose a scan may not be sensitive enough to show up microstones and I am so tired, so feeble that I cannot fight him as well as everybody else and so I murmur my agreement. I am told he will call me on my mobile when the first slot for the operation becomes available.

I shake the surgeon's hand and thank him again. The receptionist has left by the time my Adrian pushes me back to the now deserted waiting room. The sound of his footsteps and the wheels of my wonky chariot are the only noise apart from the low buzzing of computers, humming into the night until tomorrow's onslaught.

I am past feeling and past sense. I hurt. The pain is coming fast and strong, pummelling through my back and into the top of my abdomen in vicious hot waves. By the time we get back to the car park, I am doubled up and shivering with cold and weakness. We scrabble through the bags and retrieve the bottle of OxyContin. Adrian measures out my missed dose and I take it gratefully, pulling the sickly, bitter-sweet liquid into my mouth, running my tongue round the inside of the measuring cap, desperate for all the pain relief I can get into my sickened body.

I am lifted out of the chair and placed in the car. I drop my sick bowl on the ground; Adrian leaves it there, saying it is our gift to the hospital which took us to the edge of our coping skills. I watch it, buffeted slightly by the evening's breeze, as we drive back down through the car park and on to the road. As it disappears from view, I wait for the drug to do its work. To take me away from the pain and into a dream world where there is blessed relief, treasured escape from myself and my body. I dream in the half-light of my soothed mind, in drugged serenity, until eventually, finally we pull into the drive of my parents' home.

CHAPTER 6

# Last Resort

*March 2007*

I was right. I had no gallstones. My lowly gallbladder has been ripped out of me, dumped in a chemical waste bag and is now halfway to heaven in the curling smoke of the hospital incinerator. I, meanwhile, am halfway to hell, in the rip-roaring, broiling flames of acute pancreatitis set off by the operation. Instead of being cured, I am pushed yet again to the brink of madness by the sensation of a million red-hot maggots eating away at my insides.

That is how I feel as I lie here in the white starched bed of a ward in the London hospital. I am rigged up to a series of bleeping machines and drips which are keeping me alive. Coming round earlier, I knew I had survived when I felt the gnawing, writhing sensation of restless agony in my abdomen caused by the trapped enzymes digesting my tortured organ from within.

This time, I know they are worried about me. I have a dedicated nurse, I am in a small ward with only three other beds and I have a monitor which is pulsing IV fentanyl – a powerful synthetic opiate similar to, but a hundred times stronger than morphine – into me every five minutes. It is hard to focus, hard to think. I am woozy. The room sways, then there are burning feelings, then I am gone again. I struggle to listen when the nurse comes round. I struggle to hear the doctor who is telling me my surgeon was on call overnight because my condition was so serious.

When I manage to crawl my mind out of the strange, slippery place it goes to with each jerk of the IV, I see there is a pale blue curtain around my bed which is positioned alongside a long window. I move my right arm a little, to feel something, and note the familiar sensation of the cool plastic tube which penetrates my skin, into my vein, and is held to me with large, clear sticking plasters. The plasters wrinkle within a few hours, resembling the skin of the old lady I am one day hoping to become. The odds don't look good right now, though.

The plastic tube running into the inside of my right arm connects to a saline drip which is running empty. As the pump tries to force the last droplets of liquid into me, the pressure turns the motion outwards and suddenly, there is a jolt as I feel my blood being sucked out and up the tube. Panicking slightly, I move my arm to press the buzzer, and wince slightly as the line pulls on the soft skin of my arm. As I wait, I turn my sluggish attention to my left arm. There is a plastic tube running via a needle into my wrist. A huge purple and yellow bruise is flowering around the top of my hand, and I am guessing they needed several goes to get it in properly. Must have been a rookie doctor, I think, as I inspect it with objective interest. Now it feels sore, sensitive, as I shift my body slowly on the mattress. Connected to this tube is a large, bullet-shaped machine which contains a clear liquid. There is a complicated panel on the front of it with a set of flashing numbers which must represent the quantity and timing of each fentanyl dose as it is delivered intravenously.

To the right of that is an obs machine, which mechanically checks blood pressure and pulse. All the machines are on, bleeping in unsynchronised regularity, a mismatched symphony of hospital noises.

The nurse comes quickly. She brings another weighty saline bag and lays it on the blanket as she unscrews the empty one. There is a small spurt of blood which stains the sheets, and she apologises before screwing on the new bag of liquid. This one has glucose in it – my blood sugar must be low. I try to recall the last time I ate anything and I really can't remember.

My mouth feels dry, my head is thick and slow, and the pain stays beating at me, throbbing into me, underneath the heavy, lethargic slug of the drug.

Visitors come and I try and sit upright. I can barely move, and I sink back into my pillows in a kind of indolent invitation. Grace comes. She sits by my bed, holding my hand, trying to make me laugh. She tells me about her latest boyfriend and her upcoming trip to Cuba. We met ten years ago when we were both reporters on a local newspaper. We hit it off immediately – fused by our passion for travel. Grace is a travel writer and editor specialising in Cuba.

Over the years, we've made trips to Havana and most of Spain. She makes me laugh now with memories of our travels. Like the time we were in a bar in the back streets of Havana – a crumbling old building lit by candles, with an old guy playing guitar in one corner – when two members of the British band Morcheeba came in and started buying us drinks. We giggle, remembering how we thought we'd nearly made it to fame and fortune, our one night mingling with the stars.

Then, when she is finished talking, I remember where I am, and how that whole part of my life and soul is now missing, probably not to return, and so I cry. Grace wipes away my tears with tissues, soothing me with platitudes like, 'You'll get better one day', and, 'This won't last forever'. And the love she fills them with does soothe me – even though I don't believe them.

My sister Laura and her boyfriend James also come to visit me from Cardiff. Despite my senses being slugged by the bulldozer opiates, I feel a mixture of anger and joy as I see their slurred shapes enter the ward. Laura is looking around, trying to find me among the shapeless, formless sleeping patients rigged up to drips and machines in this acute-cases ward.

Things keep coming in and out of focus. I try to keep with it. I try to look pleased, but the insistent anger keeps seeping up, fighting against the blurred edges of my waking. Laura has called me throughout all this, always the loving sister, ready to listen to my woes and struggles, but she has not really been here, in the flesh. She has her own life in Wales, but even so, I have sometimes felt abandoned by her in my moment of need. But maybe I'm being unfair. Seeing her older sister so ill and frail must be bloody awful for her, so I can understand why she may not have come to see me as often as I'd have liked. Maybe she feels abandoned too, like the illness has taken me away from her. The thoughts slide away with the next jolt of the IV and I smile – a wispy, fragile welcome.

They sit beside me for an hour. We talk. They talk. I reply with a thick tongue. They bring in the smell of the outdoors. I have forgotten what air smells like, what cars and roads and fields smell like. I am used to the cloying lilt of the disinfectant and other, worse, unmentionable smells now.

Then something is said. Vague. Hazy. Small flashes of meaning among the bed pans. James is saying something. I try to lean in, to hear properly. He's saying he doesn't buy into this. This isn't the end for me. He's saying it isn't the end for me. It seems a funny thing to say. A weird thing, but a good thing. The words slip in and out of my mind, but the memory of them stays; it stays, and it feeds the hope that is still buried so far, far away from here.

Eventually, they leave. I didn't ask why Laura doesn't visit. I couldn't – she looked so scared; maybe that was my answer. It doesn't stop me feeling alone, though.

*

Days pass.

The heavy hangover of the fentanyl hovers like a persistent fog now, even though my dose is being gradually reduced. At times, the fog lifts a little, just enough that I can see more clearly, blink and focus, then it all slips away again, back into the pleasurable blurring of my senses that is fentanyl.

I shift in restless discomfort as the ratio of blood to drug becomes smaller each hour, bringing with it the all-too familiar thud of the throbbing, burning sensation that has accompanied me for so long. I even dream about being in pain, in the brief moments I manage to slide away from consciousness.

One morning, the doctors come round to my bed. It is early, about 8.30 a.m., and I am surprised to see all these intense, suited males around my bedside. They've had a meeting about me, one of them says, and they want to perform another procedure. I groan my response. I can't bear to think about another operation, another round of hurt and helplessness.

'This is a risky procedure,' he continues. 'We want to measure the pressures in your pancreas.'

'Ok,' I say, my face contorted by a grimace that speaks of fear, new fear. My voice is reticent, hesitant.

'We'd put you to sleep. We'd feed an endoscopy tube through your mouth and down into your stomach, and from there into your pancreas,' he says, watching my response.

'It sounds gruesome,' I reply. 'What will it achieve?'

'We don't know. It's the last chance of finding out what's causing your pancreatitis,' he replies with as much honesty as his position allows. He is a young doctor, but they all look young to me now at the grand old age of thirty-six. His face is tanned and healthy, he wears glasses and has a line of black Bic biros hooked over the pocket of his white coat. I don't know why I notice these, but I stare at them as he goes on.

'It's not pleasant', he says, 'and there's a risk it will cause severe acute pancreatitis.' Then he adds, 'We've lost people after this procedure.'

I don't look at him. Part of me wants to laugh and say, 'Well look for them, then.' But the giddy denial is so fleeting that I am instantly back in the room. The white room, in the London hospital, with four surgeons standing round my bed and a decision to make.

They tell me I'm booked in for tomorrow. I have twenty-four hours to digest the news and the implications. I have twenty-four hours with the fear which mugs my senses, which hugs me in its cold embrace, contracting my heart and rendering me caught like a rabbit in headlights. I am trapped and frozen.

The doctors leave and the rest of the day confronts me. I call my mum, I call Adrian. I don't tell them of the terror which chokes my breath from me, which widens my pupils and renders me insensible. Instead, I ask their advice, keep it practical. They both say the same – it may be my only chance. It may be the missing op, the answer to some of my prayers. We all agree that I cannot go on as I am. I must grab whatever I'm given like a piece of fraying rope slung to a drowning person.

And so I sit and wait. I wait. I sit and listen to the sounds of the hospital. I hear the soft, muffled hum of the nurses' conversations. I hear the clanking sound of the lunch trolley as it's wheeled into the ward. I hear the dim screeching of traffic, beeping, driving, braking, somewhere outside of the parameters of this building. I hear the chatter between patients, desperate for company and to pass the interminable time. I keep listening, frozen and accepting, until the day finally gives up and draws to a close.

Then the fear finds me and eats me. As the light fades, as the sky blushes indigo then black, and the clatter of the medicine trolley leaves the ward for the last time, I am struck by my powerlessness in the face of this operation.

It has held me in paralysis all day and now it blinds me, fights me, beats me. I pick up the phone. I have so many things I want to say, then suddenly, I can say none of them. I have so much life left unsaid, so many apologies to make, so many people to call and tell them I love them, yet I cannot say a word.

The frozen hands of my fear clasp my throat now. I want to say hello – or is it goodbye? Is this my last evening on earth? I don't feel I am exaggerating when I finally face what has been stalking me all day: I might die. There. That is it. I might lose my life. I might never see my parents, my friends, my sister or my boyfriend ever again.

It is funny how I've spent most of this illness feeling desperate to die, to escape from the daily grind of pain and frustration, but now it comes to it, now the truth of death hovers before me, I suddenly realise I want to hang on to the life I have, however meagre. It is contrary and a bit twisted, but there it is. I want to live and I want to get better, and I absolutely, categorically don't want to die. I feel almost giddy at the realisation.

The phone sits heavy in my hand as I start to dial. Then I stop. Then I start again. Each time, I punch fewer numbers in. Each time, I get further away from the people I love. I am so scared. That is what I want to howl. I am really, really terrified and I am so completely alone. There is no one else to go through this with me. Tomorrow I will be wheeled down to endoscopy alone. I will sign the consent forms alone. I will lie back on the slab waiting for the drugs to take effect – alone. Then I will undergo this treatment alone. Alone, except for the spell of forgetting that is the anaesthetic.

And it is then that I pray. Properly. For the first time in my long, short life. I put my hands together in the universal sign of surrender and I ask for help from an invisible, unknowable entity which is the last hope I have left. I pray for the first time because there's nothing else left for me to do.

I pray first for my family and friends, that they won't suffer if I die. I pray for tomorrow. I pray that what will be will be, and I will accept it. Please help me accept it, I ask. Then, in the back of my mind, I find I am asking questions about this procedure. Do I need it? Is it necessary? I see my mind contort in endless rhythm, twisting into truth with questions and lies which lead me off into exhaustive internal debate. And I see that it's just my denial. The denial of my frightened mind, which doesn't want to do this. To face it. And by the time I finish my prayer I feel spent, drained. At the end of a wobbly line. I am finally at the full stop. It has all been done or said. It is time to sleep.

I turn off the side light which was throwing a pool of steady white light on to the sheets. I pull the blankets over my thin shoulders and lie back, settling on my right side as the left is too painful with the legacy of the last pancreatitis attack.

Seven a.m. I am woken by the wheezing, hacking cough of the patient in the next bed to me.

For a moment, I forget that today is coming. My saline drip is replaced, I use a couple of baby wipes to make me as clean as I can and smear deodorant under my armpits. I reach for my hairbrush and slowly pull it through my hair. The brush feels weighty, my arm struggles to keep aloft and soon I am exhausted. I can't bend my arm properly anyway because the drip line has been switched to the vein on the inside of my elbow.

Yet another doctor in another white coat comes in just after seven, saying I need a new line put in for the procedure. It is almost not worth their breath telling me: I know I have to lie back and yield to their ministrations without complaint or issue. I am used to all this now, but still I hate the cannula being put in. At just the thought of it I clench my jaw, grind my teeth. I bare them as he pushes the needle into the soft place on the inside of my arm. I look away, holding everything tight, taut. He pushes the line in, holds the needle flat as he unwraps the sticky back of a large square plaster. The plaster is shaped to fit round the needle entry point with a slit which has to be guided round the open vein. As he works he nudges the needle, causing me to wince aloud. He says sorry, it won't be much longer now. I stare with ferocious intensity at the obs machine.

'I'm just going to test the vein,' the doctor says, returning a minute later with a syringe filled with saline. He unhooks me from the main line and squeezes down the vial, the cool liquid hitting my hot blood.

'It works, you're good,' he says with a smile and is gone.

And now I wait.

At 8.45 a.m., a nurse opens my curtains and tells me it is time to go. Standing alongside her are two orderlies, who smile briefly. I am pushed through the ward, along the shiny floors and into the lift. Several corridors and another lift later, I'm finally entering the Endoscopy Department. It seems quiet. I must be the first patient of the day, testament to the seriousness of my case.

I hunch in quiet appeasement as it all begins. A doctor wearing a green coat and a green face mask appears at my side. He has a clipboard and papers to sign. I see the risk of severe complications and death writ large and clear in black Times New Roman font. I can refuse to sign. I can give up, demand to be wheeled out, leave hospital, probably die anyway some time in the next few months. But I am almost indifferent to the risks now. Bring it on, I say to myself, as I sign with as much of a flourish as my cannula will allow.

And, again, I wait. I wait for almost an hour. I chatter in prayer continually inside my mind, or is it my head? I never did really understand the concept of prayer – it seems so close to mental illness, involving talking away to oneself in internal thin air.

I see my specialist. He comes over and shakes my hand vigorously. He is charming, remembering my name, asking how I am. It calms me, reassures me. He sees me. I feel seen. And that alone is enough for me today.

He says this procedure is the reason his hair has gone white. It is the Wild West of surgery. He says fewer and fewer surgeons are prepared to do it because of the risks. Apparently, no surgeon wanting a high-flying career wants to take on pancreatic patients as we might bring down their survival figures.

It is the harsh truth. And it sits like a stone in my stomach.

'Don't worry though,' my specialist laughs. 'We'll do our best for you. You're in good hands.'

With that, I am wheeled at the hands of another of the surgeons into the endoscopy room. There is a large metal slab where the op will take place. I feel like we are in a butcher's shop and I am the meat. I climb up on to the table with some difficulty. The room is filled with equipment, monitors, wiring. There are small trolleys with disturbing-looking articles, all metal and shiny. There is a huge, thick black tube lying to one side on a trolley which looks like it has been scrubbed clean enough for a lifetime.

I'm moved on to my side. In the recovery position. I try not to notice this. I am lying on my left side, the side which hurts the most. My left arm is out to the side and my right is positioned behind me. A drip is attached to it. There is the bustle of intense activity and I am shaking all over. There are wires and tubes running like electric cables into and out of my body. I am shivering in cold and fear. I have no knickers or bra on underneath my robe and so I am feeling exposed, naked and vulnerable.

I pray for the last time before it starts.

One of the nurses, who is wearing green scrubs, a green face mask and has her hair hidden under a green plastic cap, asks me to open my mouth. Another nurse is now holding my jaw still and has a tube near by which makes a furious sucking sound. It feels like the scene in *E.T.* when the alien is surrounded by FBI medics and scientists in a medical vacuum. I open my mouth as wide as I can, then something large and cold is being pushed in. As the endoscopy camera hits the back of my throat I gag and I am held down by firmer hands.

This is like the worst blow job ever, I think to myself. I would laugh, but a fucking great big black penis tube is navigating my tonsils.

'Swallow,' the nurse says. I have heard that one before.

Someone is now stroking my hair. There are perhaps seven nurses in here. I don't know how many are holding me down, stroking my hair, pushing the sucking machine inside my cheeks to clean out the spit and sick which rise as soon as the tube enters my gullet.

So I swallow. I try to swallow. The camera hurts. It is too big for my throat. I panic, feeling caught and frightened and I don't want to do this any more.

'Swallow, darling,' says the nurse again. So I swallow and swallow and I gag.

This time vomit comes up into my mouth, starts dribbling down the side of my face.

'Swallow,' says the nurse again, as I feel the tube move, its rigid fat length going further down my throat. My mouth is open, my eyes are wild. I am gagging constantly now, trying to struggle and move. The tube feels far too big for my body as it slides down, going further and further like an erotic nightmare.

I will never give a BJ again, I vow as it slides deeper still. The surgeons are watching a fuzzy black and white TV screen as the tube moves. I feel like my insides are being scraped raw and I can't cope with another second of this.

'We're going to put you out now,' says a voice, somewhere from the side of me. 'Count down from ten to one,' it says, and as I do, I feel a cold liquid slip into my vein. Then I say nine, then eight …

At some point in the blur of the procedure, I start to wake up. The sedation is nowhere near strong enough for someone who has been taking the most potent opiate on the planet. I feel I am moving. There's a sharp command, a scrabble of activity by the nurses, then I am gone again.

The first thing I see when I come round is my boyfriend. His lovely face peers over me, half smiling in relief, I think.

'You've been singing,' he says and smiles.

'Singing?' I reply in a slurry, thick voice, smiling back.

'As you started to come round you were humming, then as the sedation wore off you were singing away to yourself in a little voice.'

I don't know whether to feel embarrassed. Come to think of it, I have a half memory of asking the surgeon to be my surrogate father. 'I think the drugs made me go a bit funny in the head,' I say, blushing.

Adrian rubs my hand. I feel like I haven't seen him in weeks. I'm really grateful he's here.

'When we get married, I promise I won't sing,' I say.

He nods his head, looks away, as if the ward is suddenly interesting.

'If this works, can we get a ring and make plans?' I ask. I know I sound like I am pleading and I know I am hardly in a position to get married, but I just want to hear some reassurance about the future. I am surprised, though, when he doesn't answer. I notice the pause, the way I suddenly can't find his eyes. I want to think I have shocked him, but I am not so sure.

Eventually, he looks up and says, 'Wait a little longer. You need to get well before we can talk about that.'

I am mollified. Lulled by his gentle voice. He wouldn't lie to me, would he? But I am fed up with waiting. I want to start living again. I know I am not even in a fit state to walk to the loo, let alone down the aisle. And I am hardly a great catch right now, but I want it so badly that I push these troubling thoughts far enough away that their emotional threads stretch so thin, so taut that I can almost ignore them. Almost.

'We'll see,' he says. 'Let's get you out of this hospital, then we'll see.'

Later, I am taken back to the ward and deposited in my cubicle. A couple of hours pass before the team of doctors and surgeons arrives.

'We have good news,' says the young doctor who explained the procedure to me yesterday. 'We measured the pressures inside your pancreas and they were massively raised. The condition is called Sphincter of ODDI Dysfunction.

'Basically the band of muscle around the mouth of the pancreas is too tight, so we cut it. Hopefully, this should help your pain issues.

'We have to warn you though that it doesn't work in 40 per cent of cases,' he finishes. And they all look at me for my response.

I don't understand most of what has been said, but they all look happy. It's hard to leap with joy when I'm prostrate and have wires and machines attached to various parts of me. But it looks like hope. So I say thank you and smile back.

'We have to monitor you closely for the next twenty-four hours as the procedure has been known to cause very severe pancreatitis in a small number of cases,' says the doctor. Then he adds, 'There is a risk of severe complications; I believe you are aware of that.'

This time, the smile has gone and he looks as if he is the one to blame.

'I understand,' I say. What else is there to do but to wait? To fear. And to wait.

The twenty-four hours are the slowest, scariest of my life. Every twinge, every surge of burning pain in my stomach and back is treated with alarm and suspicion. What if I die? What if I die ... what if I die?

I don't die. I do, however, have an attack of acute pancreatitis. My meds are increased in the middle of a hellish night. I wake at 2 a.m. after dozing fitfully, pain building, ejecting me from my dreams. I press my buzzer and within half an hour a woman in a white coat is fiddling with the IV fentanyl, increasing the amount given to me every hour. She changes the settings on the amount I can click and receive every five minutes. In all, my dose is doubled.

Bloods are taken and a new saline drip is put up. She tuts when she leaves, saying I should never have been on such a low dose as my body is so used to opiates now.

CHAPTER 7

# Good News

*April 2007*

The sound of the phone is shrill, cutting into yet another groggy afternoon lying in bed, watching the shapes of the shadows make their epic slow dance across the room.

It's been a week since I was discharged from the London hospital. It is now a case of 'wait and see' to find out if the procedure has had any effect on the repeating, continual pancreatitis. Forty per cent of people experience no change in their pain symptoms, but that leaves 60 per cent who improve. I am desperate to be in that percentage. Determined.

I have been terribly weakened by the last acute pancreatitis bout. One of the surgeons, who visited me during a particularly painful night-time pain attack, told me each pancreatitis 'episode' was the equivalent to having a heart attack. And over the last few years, I have had forty or so. I am unable to walk, as I am too feeble; and I'm in such searing pain from my internally burned organ and the surgical cuts that the fentanyl lozenges I have been sent home with barely do a thing.

I am stricken, low in spirit and at the end of a very frayed tether, compounded by the overwhelming exhaustion and muscle cramps of the fibromyalgia. I feel sick all the time, due to the condition, and the combination of severe illness and medication has made me hyper-sensitive to light and smells: the TV is too loud, the air too cold and cooking smells make me reel with nausea as I lie here. Sometimes I feel I should be living in a big glass bubble – away from the harshness of the modern world.

So I am back here, in this strange, quiet room in my parents' home, waiting endlessly to get better. I reach for the phone. The movement makes me feel sick again. I see my sister's number flash up on the display and decide against pressing the off button.

'Hiya,' I say, attempting to sound happy, pretending that all is ok, when it blatantly isn't.

'Good news,' Laura screams into my ear. 'You're going to be an auntie.'

For a split second, the demon within me, the bit of me that feeds on my own loneliness and despair at being so very ill and for so long, wants to end the conversation, wishes I hadn't picked up, after all. It is a momentary jolt of – what? Is it anger that life is good and is moving forwards for others? Is it that horrible, lowliest emotion of self-pity? Or is it plain jealousy that it isn't me having a baby?

I hear myself saying, 'That's amazing. Oh my God, I'm so happy for you both.'

I hear her happiness, her excitement for this longed-for pregnancy and, just as quickly as it came, the demon disappears, slinking back into its own venom, and I find myself talking, crying, laughing at this ordinary miracle. Any residual feelings I had about my own yearnings for a baby and a settled, married life, vanish into my sister's good fortune. If I can't be happy and positive for me, then I'll damned well do it for my sister.

By the end of the conversation, I am exhausted. We say goodbye, I wipe the tears away, and as she disappears into her life, I sink back into mine.

The sultry hush of my sick room feels unbearable. The absence of life. I look into myself and see the grief of unrealised motherhood. My primal maternal instincts are still there – raw and untouched. And I see that I have to live through others these days. Instead of fulfilling my own desires, I must rejoice in the blessings of others. And this will simply have to be enough.

I call my boyfriend, he is at work and busy, but he listens as I howl bittersweet tears down the phone. He promises to come to my parents' later to sit with me, comfort me, whisper promises about the future to me. Some of which may even be true.

I look around the room – I see a small TV in one corner with a pile of DVDs to fill the achingly lonely hours. I see a chair, empty now, but where either of my parents will sit in the evenings to keep me company. I see my dressing gown slung over the end of the bed, my bedside table piled high with books, tissues and boxes of tablets, and I see a window which looks out over the fields and into the skyline. I can't turn my head any further as the movement produces such intense nausea that I am reduced to retching uncontrollably.

Half a mile down the road, there is a small cottage with wooden beams and whitewashed walls and a tiny, sweet garden filled with wild flowers. I know about this cottage because it is now mine. While I was at the London hospital, my parents put my apartment on the market. It sold, at a loss, but it sold. Throughout my illness, that flat has been a millstone of lost hope, of crushed dreams and also practical problems, and it was finally abandoned to the tenant I had found to help cover my mortgage payments. Knowing my predicament, he had bought it at a knock-down price. I was glad to be free of it, and the proceeds were put straight into this cottage in the heart of the village my parents live in. Close enough to them for comfort and help, far enough away for me to live for myself in some small way. And now I am waiting till I am well enough to be moved in to my new home.

Adrian is moving in with me, not so much a romantic gesture as a practical one. I cannot live independently. I need help getting to the loo, washing; I cannot cook for myself or walk. So he is now my carer. He hates the term – but it is our reality. He will work part-time and Mum will help when he's not able to. He is graceful and gentle with my physical dependency, telling me never to take my multiple diagnoses too seriously. He tells me every day to hold them lightly, not to be defined by them, but it is hard. It is so hard.

The thought of the home that is waiting for me, brings me back into the room I am in now. My pyjamas are clean, freshly on today and the bed is warm. I have a single candle burning in the window as a talisman, a symbol of hope. I watch it for hours, marooned in pain and nausea. My abdomen is swollen and sore, so that even touching it gently threatens to induce vomiting. I have to stay still to prevent this and also because the fibromyalgia is really taking its toll on me now. The muscle spasms tighten my whole body with an exquisite pain which is hard to explain to anyone but other sufferers.

My body hurts, my stomach burns and my mind wanders between abject fear of another acute attack of pancreatitis on top of the chronic pancreatitis I have at present and apathy – an apathy so deep and swollen it threatens to carry me away for ever.

The light is already leaching from the room, the candle's flame glows brighter with each passing minute. I lie and watch and think. I remember the life I now realise will never be mine again.

I'm transported to that bar in Havana, where a candle is burning on a table. I see Grace laughing in the dark glow of the bar as we sipped mojitos before deciding which club to go to. We were both working, but we did it together, exploring the bars and clubs of the magnificently crumbling city and dancing salsa with charming strangers until the early hours.

I remember another candle in a room in Reykjavik. We were

there to write features about the inaugural flight of the Iceland Express airline, which we did, as well as spending hours in the steaming, salty blue lagoon, watching street theatre, visiting art galleries and discovering the secret DJ bars of the Winter Festival.

A candle burned in Alicante, as we drank scalding bitter coffee in a bar outside the ancient city walls. And another in Venice, as we tasted Prosecco in the flamboyantly expensive tourist café during a trip to record and research carnival – I remember flirting with the dark-eyed, olive-skinned beauties who were waiting our tables in their black trousers and white shirts. We skipped through that most troubling of cities with a kind of decadent abandon, wearing our masks with huge burgundy feathers and exploring the weaving pathways and waterways.

There was a candle burning in a cabin in the centre of New Zealand where I rested – this time, with another great friend – after a long trek.

Those candles seem to light the path back to my past and, as I think about the life I once lived, my throat forms a lump of grief. In my mind, I am still hopping on to planes, dressing up in heels and glitzy clothes to dive into the nightlife of wherever I happen to find myself, or pulling on hiking boots, lugging around a rucksack I can barely carry. And I am just not facing this new reality: this half-life, spent in hospital wards and beds that are not my own. There is such sadness that the things that made me 'me' are no longer a part of my life – no travel, no social life, no dressing up, no going out, no deadlines, no languages to decipher and learn, no galleries to suck art into my soul . . .

And if the things that made me 'me' are no longer here, then who does that make me?

The question remains unanswered as the door edges open and Mum comes through it, carrying my dinner and my next dose of fentanyl: two lozenges to be taken slowly after eating. The meal consists of steamed spinach, kidney beans and potato mashed with salt and water, which is as much as I can take these days. My food still has to be very low-fat and easily digested to avoid triggering another acute pancreatitis attack. I have been living off meals like this for almost three years now.

I try to look enthusiastic. Mum looks weary and tries hard not to show it. This is a dance of gentle lies – each untruth built on a carpet of them, as we attempt to protect each other from how we really feel. I thank her. She smiles as brightly as she can manage and disappears down the corridor to her dinner with Dad. They offer to eat up here with me, but the smell of their food makes me feel nauseous, while their forced, bright chatter leaves me exhausted and feeling claustrophobic.

My head spins off to strange places these days. Too long spent by myself, I reckon. Lying on my solitary bed for weeks and months on end, with only the terrible, frantic trips to A&E to break the monotony. Waiting, hurting, screaming inside my frazzled, demented head. Trapped in my own body, like that moment before waking when I try to claw myself out of sleep, except I cannot get out. I am stuck in this place of fear of pain, of endless days and worse nights, immobile and forgotten. I certainly feel lost and alone.

My fentanyl doses carve up my days: two lozenges in the morning, one at 8 a.m., the other at 10 a.m. to cope with the breakthrough pain of eating breakfast, however pitiable. The next two lozenges are after lunch, which I eat tentatively and in fear of the pain which starts about half an hour later. I brace myself, hoping and praying it won't lead me back into hospital. I dread mealtimes. The pain after lunch is generally the worst of the day and so I have both lozenges within an hour or so of each other. At 4 p.m., Mum or Dad brings me another, then I have two after supper and one for bedtime. Eight lozenges every day – each one keeping me this side of sanity, or so it feels.

My body is weak, stick thin, and my mind feels deranged from starvation. It is a wasteland in my head. Sometimes I am unsure if my thoughts are real or not – whether the things I am remembering ever happened at all. I think I have called someone and then they tell me I haven't. I experience strange, dislocated thoughts. Time stretches on and on and takes me with it in a tumbleweed trail.

The weeks go by, then months. The residual pain of the pancreatitis still eats away at me as my continual companion, but the acute attacks seem to have stopped. Does that mean the surgery has been a success? I feel like I have been burned alive inside my gut, which is, in effect, what has happened: all those digestive enzymes that were trapped by the muscle spasms in the neck of my pancreas burned me from within, causing an agony it is still hard to describe.

There are strange sweats which come on suddenly, where I shake and vomit and cry out. My mind strays into dark places at these times and I find I am confused, my head littered with the ghosts of the wards and the surgeries. I cannot move except to write short bits in my diary. I have being writing through all of this – even asking the nurses to put the cannulas into my left arm while in hospital, so that I could write with my right. At times, the exhaustion has been too much and I have managed only a spidery scrawl which drags off the page along with the fatigue that goes so deep into my bones. Sometimes it is despair which leaves my letters trailing as, once again, the abyss in my spirit beckons. And other times I feel I can get through this and I feel a bliss and an excitement which I cannot explain – at these times, I call old friends, laugh and joke that I will be up and salsa dancing again soon. But the silence seems much thicker, much deeper after these calls. The momentary high gives way to this low place and nothing has changed. Nothing.

*

It is a warm September morning when the call comes. I have been back at the London hospital for a couple of weeks with ongoing pain issues. It hardly seems worth mentioning, as I yo-yo in and out of the same wards, with the same nurses, the same doctors and even the same poor bastards in the beds every few weeks or so. The pain is the main issue I have now and I am finding it hard to manage at home. Every now and again it peaks to a point where I have to be taken back in for blood tests and more IV relief.

I answer the call gingerly, as this time the on-call doctor put the cannula in my right elbow, just at the crease where I bend my arm. I can barely lift or bend my arm to brush my hair, answer calls or pick up a book.

'Laura's contractions have started. We're going straight down to Cardiff, so don't expect to hear from us for a few hours,' says Mum at the other end of the phone.

I hold the phone as near to my right ear as I can manage, wincing as I try not to jog the needle. 'Oh my God! Give her my love,' I say. 'Tell her I love her, right, and tell her she has to call me no matter how hard her contractions are!' I can't believe I am missing the birth of my sister's baby. While my family rush down to Wales, I am attached to a series of bleeping, flashing machines. Back in hospital, back on the block.

That same morning, I learn that the surgeons have decided to redo the procedure I had last time as my pain levels haven't settled after all. Adrian cannot be here today as he is working, and so I am alone, waiting to go under the knife again.

My bed is right by the window though and we are on the top floor, so I can, at least, watch the clouds properly, see the sunsets and sunrises. There is nothing worse than a hospital bed without a view of the outdoors. It has always felt to me like there is nothing to aim for if there is no view of a life outside.

Later, I am wheeled down into the now-familiar ERCP department. ERCP stands for endoscopic retrograde cholangio-pancreatography – it is a very useful procedure as it can be used both for diagnosis and treatment. There is a queue of lost-looking patients, sitting or slumped in wheelchairs, but I am pushed in first. I climb up on to the operating table and my mouth is moving with a simple prayer which I repeat over and over again: help me, please help me.

The big penis tube is pushed into my mouth once again, the cool liquid of the sedation hits my warm vein and I hear a nurse tell me I'll be asleep soon: ten, nine, eight ... Then it is much later.

The sky is dark outside and I'm back in my bed in the ward. There is a needle in my left hand which hurts – it is sitting uncomfortably and I feel irritated because of it. I have a top-of-the-range plastic catheter which is filling nicely and I realise I will have to crap into a huge steel bed pan as I have a multitude of bleeping wires attached to me. There is a saline drip shooting cold water into my bloodstream via my elbow. Basically, it is business as usual.

I have been given another fentanyl IV which is a very impressive cylinder with lots more buttons and a pump which sends a steady stream of the good stuff into my body.

My tongue feels thick, like I've had a heavy night out on the tiles. My head – which I can hardly move for fear of launching spectacular projectile vomit from my swollen belly – is a beating, pounding mashed-up mess. But it is all ok because something amazing is happening: my sister's baby is being born. I try to stay awake for the next phone update, but it's almost 11 p.m. before I am nudged out of my drugged sleep by its insistent ring. My dad has tried a couple of times to get through to me.

'How's it going?' I slur.

My dad's voice sounds panicky and breathy.

'It's good. She's ok. She had a bath and then the contractions started coming faster, so we brought her into hospital.'

'Where are you now? I wish I was there,' I answer.

'I'm standing outside maternity. You won't believe how many people smoke outside hospitals.' He sounds indignant.

'Forget the others, how's Laura?' I say urgently, half-cross at him for going off the subject.

'She's fine. They gave her pethidine. She said she understands a little of what you must be going through,' he said, before adding, 'Look, I've got to go, I don't want to miss anything. We'll call you later.' And with that he was gone.

Feeling isolated, feeling a million miles away from where I should be, I shut my eyes as the tears come. I want to be with her. I should've been her birth partner. I should've thrown her a baby shower and treated her. Instead, all I can do is a big, fat nothing. Illness has robbed me of the love I so want to give other people. It's taken everything away.

I turn my head, trying to ignore the jolt of nausea. I can't bear to watch the clouds any more.

Weeks later, and I am allowed out of hospital for a brief couple of hours to meet my new nephew. Taking the tiny swaddled boy, Freddie, in my wasted arms, I can only marvel at how perfect he is. How small and fragile, but how lusty and alive.

Through the haze of the pethidine dose I've been given to tide me over until I return to the ward and get back on the drip, I feel a pull of protective love so fierce it almost knocks me back. I would do anything for this little boy. I want to get well again for this precious baby.

I look at the cannula sticking out of my hand, bundled in bandages, and I know I have to fight again. I have to get better, if not for me, then for him. I want to be a real auntie, not an invalid to be pitied or a burden to be cared for. Leaning into the fuzzy hair on the top of his milky-smelling head, I promise him I will recover.

But the hope is short-lived. Within two weeks of being released from the ward, I am back on death row. I collapse at my parents – and I finally hit rock bottom.

CHAPTER 8

# Suicide Watch

*December 2007*

Looking up at the five men standing around my bedside, clutching clipboards and pens, I abandon the shreds of my dignity and vomit into my lap. The nausea rises in waves, swelling and breaking as my mind descends into a distorted, sickening madness. As I throw up on the sheets, the floor, I clutch the metal sides of the bed and see the shapes and the faces of the people watching me as if from a rollercoaster. Nothing really makes sense, nothing feels real. Reality distorts and shrinks around me. I have no anchor, no framework, only a vast vacuum separating me from them, patient from doctor. The ketamine which was injected into my frail arm a couple of minutes ago is still freewheeling around my brain and body. A voice from far, far away tells me not to worry, that it only lasts a few minutes.

The chamomile tea I drank earlier has given the vomit a sweet herbal fragrance. My sheets are stained yellow, my sanity is in tatters, worn threadbare by each fresh humiliation and my body is out of control. It is all I can do to cling on to the bedsides in raw terror and it feels like forever before the strong pull of the drug subsides. Finally, the stretched-apart feeling that pulled my mind wide open dissolves, bringing me back into the present and to Ward 11 in my local hospital.

I look up and five men – the very aptly named Pain Team – look back at me, blankly, like I'm an experiment. I *am* an experiment, like one of those bunnies in a lab you see on Animal Rights posters, except that this is all being done in the name of trying to help me.

The Pain Team are trying to find me a new painkiller as they are worried my pain levels are so high. I suppose they *are* helping me. I suppose I am being churlish and I am probably hoping that they won't stop the fentanyl, as it is the only drug I have had which has ever come close to coping with the pain, but even so, I can't find it in me to be ok about this. Somehow, it feels like the last straw. I am not even sure why they need to find me another drug as the fentanyl is the most effective one I have been given so far – and, believe me, I have been given pretty much everything over the course of the last three years. This time they have given me ketamine and it seems they didn't weigh me just beforehand as the dose was too strong for the weight I am now.

'How was the pain?' asks one of the men. He has a row of three pens lined up in his breast pocket. He is wearing glasses and has his head cocked to one side.

'No different,' I say truthfully. I almost want to tell them otherwise, as they now look so disappointed.

But then my head is shaking. Things seem to be breaking down. I seem to be breaking down. I have found the edge and am tumbling over, going faster and faster downwards. My hands are shaking. The tears are pouring from my eyes and I don't have the strength to wipe them away. They flow, I shake. The men leave, saying they'll ask someone to clean me up, but something in me has cracked open. The frayed edges of my life have unravelled and stretched so far that they snap. I can almost hear them break, one by one.

The only logical thing to do now is find a way to die. I cannot do this any more.

I cannot lie looking frail, being ill, watching life move past me without me in it. I cannot be with this terrible burning, haunting, wretched pain any longer; it has fried my mind as well as my body. I cannot go on looking positive in the face of adversity and shitty luck. I can no longer be grateful for a kind nurse or a prompt dose of painkillers. It is over. I am done. I am through with all of it. I have taken the first step over the crumbling edge of an emotional cliff top and I no longer care if I live or die.

I have felt what it is to be depressed several times before and I recognise this feeling – when suddenly, nothing matters any more. The first time I suffered depression was on returning to England after spending three months living in Moscow during my art degree. I remember the assault of bright lights, busy modern life and all its sounds and smells when I arrived back, minutes after getting off the plane. I remember seeing the shops screaming Christmas at me, stacked high with colour and light. And it was all too much after the bleak months in a cockroach-infested block of flats, living four people to a tiny one-bedroom apartment in a mafia-run suburb. I remember retreating back into myself to try and escape. I had left something of myself in Russia, abandoned it as part of the wreckage of the brutal and awe-inspiring city which I loved and hated in equal measure. I could not find my way mentally back to the UK.

I dropped out of college briefly, sank further into myself until a course of anti-depressants and a college counsellor drew me back. I never felt quite the same after that episode, though. I always felt something of me had gone missing – and I could never figure out what that something was. I stopped going to the student union bar, stopped hanging out with friends on my fine art course. Instead, I buried myself in working for my degree.

The second bout of emotional paralysis came when I was living in Barcelona. Despite loving the city, despite the privilege of being in Spain studying for my MA, despite the international feel of the course, with all the richness that brought to my work, I fell again into that dark place – that deep pit, the inside of which is only familiar to anyone who has walked through the shadowy lands of depression.

This time, it came after my first semester. I found out, to my horror, that I was not invincible, I didn't always bounce back and I was not always ok: I failed. And with that failure, I swooped back down into the place where life felt a terrible burden, where friendships and family existed only on the other side of the invisible prison walls of my mind. I stopped eating. I stopped sleeping. I became a ghost walking the streets of Barcelona at night, trying to come back to myself. Eventually, the feelings of desperation and futility, the deep apathy and the terrible panic subsided and I was able to complete the course and return home. But that old feeling of a wound inside that had never properly healed remained.

I quickly won funding from the London Arts Board and went back out to Moscow to photograph the city. Looking back, I was probably looking for that part of myself I had lost in that city of concrete monoliths. I stayed there for six months this time. I delved deeper and deeper into the frayed fabric of the city, watching it edge into the future, watching as the bright lights of strip bars and Prada moved into town. I knew that after six months it was time to leave – no mysteries recovered, just a set of pictures as evidence of my frenzied search.

I returned home, put on an exhibition of the works, then left art, convinced it had given me nothing, led me nowhere. Instead, I embarked on a career in journalism. I pushed myself to the limit again, loving the fast-paced life of deadlines, each one moving me inexorably through a life filled with glamour, celebrities, travel and money – towards the illness which first struck in 2004.

And here I am now, back in that place of desperation and finality. I am back at that point beyond the edge of sanity, and am heading for the point of impact, of oblivion. Well, this time, I may as well end it completely. I may as well reach the bottom.

In my muddled mind, things start to make sense. I haven't hit the bottom yet, but I can do that now. I can see that the window in my small side room – just off the main ward – is open. No nurses should be able to see or hear me. I know what I have to do.

As I lunge to grab the saline drip which is attached to my arm, I have a momentary jolt of guilt. I see my mum's face in front of me. I see my tiny nephew and my sister, my friends Grace and Francesca. I see my dad and Adrian, though his face seems fuzzy these days, as if he's not really with me.

But it is not enough. The jolt lasts for a moment before the pain roars back. Leaning into the drip pole, I grab the wires which run into my veins and twist them into a rope, holding them all in one hand as I stand upright. I wait for a few seconds, as the small ward spins around me in dizzy circles. Then my little body hobbles and judders in impatient spurts to get to the window. I can already feel the sharp air on my skin where the tears lie in salty saturation. I have been crying for years now. It has to stop and I don't know any other way of doing it. I shuffle up closer to the window. I peer outside, just to check it is as high up as I thought. I laugh grimly as I think that it would be my luck to be on the ground floor after all. But it's ok. We are at least four flights up. That should do the job.

As I reach up for the lever to drag it down and open the window wider, I feel a strange sense of peace. The present moment slides away from me and I finally feel hope, almost a kind of serene excitement. Any minute now, it will all be over. Any minute.

The window opens upwards which is difficult, but not impossible to negotiate. I realise it has probably been designed to stop people like me doing exactly this. Luckily, I am so thin now – weighing barely six stone – that I am sure I can wiggle through the gap. The breeze hits me with a freshness I haven't felt for a long time now. The outdoors. It thrills me, and, still clutching the drip pole, I hoist up my gown. I laugh again as I realise I must look a sight. A sick-covered gown held on with just one tie at the back, leaving my back and bottom exposed . . . For a moment I think, oh God, the gown might slip up when I fall, rendering me naked and dead at the same time and everyone will see me. I'll be famous for being naked and dead. Then I realise I don't care and I lean into the air, pulling my pole up with the strength of the determined.

My eyes are closed, I am sucking the air into my body, hoping it is the last time and then, nothing.

I don't remember what happens next. Maybe there was a gentle hand on my arm, pulling me back. Maybe the pole got stuck in the window frame and stopped me from falling. I simply can't remember.

A red light keeps flashing, bringing the world back to me in a slow, woozy dance. There is a blanket around me and I appear to be in a bed, swaddled like a baby, back in the bigger, brighter of the two wards. Lying in a row of beds with a red light flashing, flashing. It makes my head hurt, so I turn away to find a nurse sat in the chair beside me. In all the years I have been in hospital I have never seen this. I feel surprise and ask her why she is there and why there is a red light.

Her face is impassive. She says the light is for me.

'Why me?' I say, astonished.

'Because you are on suicide watch,' she says, matter-of-factly. She looks at me for a moment then adds, 'The on-call psychiatrist has been bleeped. He is on his way. You are lucky; normally on a Friday evening they have gone home by now.'

All this information is too much to take in. Suddenly, I am really frightened. They think I am mad and I am going to be committed to a mental hospital.

'I'd just had enough,' I say, trying to sound normal. 'It was a perfectly logical thing to do. I'd had the worst reaction to the ketamine and I was bloody fed up with being prodded and scrutinised by the medical profession.'

I sound angry and misunderstood. The nurse just nods, but stays sitting there, like I am going to try and do it again. I feel mad at her, for her calm manner, for sitting there. It sparks rage within me. The anger is at myself, obviously. I fucked up the chance to be free of all this. I don't know how I fucked it up, but I did.

'What happened?' I ask her, nicely this time.

'Don't worry, darling, you can speak to the psychiatrists. They can help you with this. In the meantime, try to rest.' Then, 'It does get very lonely in that little ward, a bit isolated for you, maybe,' she says, not exactly answering my question, but clearly determined to say little more. 'We've called your mother,' she adds.

I groan and settle my head back. My thoughts churn round my head and chew me up. This is the worst-case scenario. My poor mum is going to be distraught. She won't sleep for weeks for worrying about me after this. They will all think I don't love them when I do. I really, really do. I just cannot take it any more and the combination of strong drugs and the pain distort and shift my thinking. I can't grab hold of anything in my mind. Now I'm wondering if I really tried to get out of the window or not? Was it real or was it part of the fever of opiates, simply a desire so strong I made it real in my mind?

I don't know. I don't know myself. My personality changes minute by minute, from scared and little to angry and difficult. Sometimes I even feel calm, but I am either in pain or drugged up. That is my life and my sanity, somehow buried between the two. And awful as it is to admit, I'd still rather be dead than living through this unfolding nightmare which never seems to end.

An hour later and my mum and sister arrive. Laura left Freddie with my dad, so she and Mum could come together. Mum's face is white. Laura is wide-eyed, somewhere between fierce anger and fear. I can hardly look them in the eye. Shame fills me to the brim.

'I'm so sorry,' I croak, unleashing the tears which have been waiting to fall since I woke up.

'What happened?' my mum asks. Her hand is cold as it holds mine, her skin soft and fragile. My sister rubs my arm. Every time she does this, it jogs the needle in the cannula, but I don't care. I just want my family here with me. It's dark and the ward lights seem lower tonight. The psychiatrist is due to arrive at any minute.

'I couldn't cope any more,' I reply. 'I'm so sorry, I've hurt you so much.'

My mum cries. I think it is only the second time in my whole life that I have seen her weep. She never cries. Even when her beloved dad died she held herself together. This fact drives the guilt and shame of my actions straight to my heart. I cannot bear to see her upset. It is a worse pain than all the operations, pancreatitis, everything mixed together. It is the worst agony. I would take back my actions, step away from the window, endure the ketamine, if I could. But I can't.

Guilt and confusion engulf me. I still don't really know what happened and everything seems so vague. Was any of it real? Even the red light, which is still flashing, feels like an extension of my drugged-up, crumbling sanity. Again, I wish I could die, so that everyone is relieved of the burden of my life. But the wish dies as soon as it comes, replaced by the sight of the shadows under my mum's eyes, the worry written on my sister's face. They both look like I have stabbed them in the heart, which, of course, I have. When will it all end?

When the psychiatrist arrives, the soft, low voices of my mum and sister are halted. He asks them to leave and, reluctantly, they do so. He sits beside me. He is a large man with glasses and a straggly beard, but a straight-forward, plain-speaking manner. I like this.

There is an awkward silence, before he asks me what happened.

'I don't know,' I say, my voice trailing off as I search his face for any sign he might be compassionate. I am so used to the hard, disinterested faces of some of the nurses and doctors here.

'You told the on-duty nurse you wanted to commit suicide,' he says, looking at me, waiting calmly for my answer, as if we're discussing the weather.

'I tried to jump out of the window, didn't I?' I say. My voice sounds feeble and quiet. I don't want anyone overhearing this.

'Did you?' he says, then waits again, patiently.

'I wanted to,' I say. 'I really wanted to jump. I made it to the window, but I can't remember what happened next. I wanted to jump though, that I can remember. Does that mean I'm mad?'

The psych takes a few seconds to reply. His words are measured, carefully drawn for me. 'You are in pain and you have been in and out of hospital for several years,' he says, slowly, deliberately chewing over each of his words.

'Yes,' I reply.

'You told the nurse you wanted to die.'

'Yes,' I say, more firmly this time. 'I must have done, because I did want to.' There's no point me lying my way out of this.

'Some would say it was a perfectly rational decision to want to end your life after years of agony,' he says, 'but it now matters what my team and I think.'

I nod, in silent reply.

'Tell me about yourself,' he says and leans in to my bedside.

Here we go, I think.

I tell him about my life in hospital. I tell him the continual compromise of my dignity and privacy, the humiliations and frustrations of being a patient for so long. He listens as I tell him about my old life. How I loved being active, how I travelled the world, living as though I was immortal – and how I loved every minute of the thrills and adventure, from white-water rafting, to parachute jumps to jungle trekking.

And how this is so different – so vastly, unbelievably different – that it hardly matters if I'm alive or dead because what I have now is no life.

As I speak, treacherous tears start to run down my gaunt cheeks. I know I could not kill myself because it would destroy my family. I tell him this. I say it may have been a moment of temporary insanity, a fleeting fantasy of an escape route, however drastic. He watches me cry, sees the honesty, the anger at being so ill, the desperation and the boredom of my days and how it is driving me truly crazy.

I tell him I have been seeing a counsellor to help me cope with the illness, with the panic attacks which come in the night, every night, at the fear of going back into hospital. I tell him how she diagnosed me with post-traumatic stress disorder as a result of how I was – or wasn't – treated for the cause of the pancreatitis. I tell him that for a long time I was simply left to die.

And he listens. He actually listens. At the end, he tells me he doesn't think I am insane or a danger to myself any more. He says I sound like someone who has experienced too much and has had a breakdown as a result. This makes sense.

I am breaking down – in every way. It is a relief to hear it.

'I will advise my colleagues not to refer you to the psychiatric unit here, but you will need to be seen by a consultant psychiatrist when you leave hospital. I will write to your GP and get that under way.

'If, by any chance, the Psych Team do commit you, and I doubt they will, but just a warning: go without kicking and screaming. Don't make a fuss, and you are more likely to get out quickly.'

I nearly choke in response.

'I'm sure they won't. The course of action I'll recommend is to refer you as an outpatient. Hang in there,' he says, smiling as he takes his leave. 'Until then, good luck, and I really mean that.'

I'm not sure I like him any more, and I am unsettled by his last bombshell. I smile weakly in response then he leaves. Seconds later the curtain is pulled back and my family, who obviously heard every word, came back in.

'Oh my God, you might be a mental-head,' my sister cackles with glee. It is clear this has amused and frightened them in equal measure. Best to laugh about it, I suppose.

'Oh bloody hell, what have I done?' I say, and we all look at each other's scared faces before bursting into laughter.

'You might be carted into the loony bin,' my sister shouts.

'Don't be so un-PC!' I reply, so glad we're joking about it.

'We always knew you were touched,' Mum concludes, and it is suddenly so good to be together, sharing this crazy secret of mine. It feels like it is us against the world and, for the first time in ages, I am happy. Truly happy.

My phone goes and it is Adrian on the line. He sounds frantic.

'What happened? Are you ok?' he says.

It is so good to hear his voice. He has felt like a stranger in the past few weeks. There have been fewer phone calls from him, shorter texts. I can't blame him though. How can someone who is in hospital possibly hope to keep a relationship with a fit, healthy person in the 'outside' world. He has been a tower of strength and support and I couldn't have done without him, but deep down, I know he is starting to leave. Call it instinct. I can't honestly expect someone to find me remotely attractive while trussed up with catheters, drips and horrible gowns. It still hurts though, this sense that he is going. So it is wonderful to talk and, selfishly, I am delighted that he sounds so concerned for me.

'Don't worry, it is all ok now. I had had enough, that's all. I did something stupid which I now regret and I've seen the psychiatrist and I might be sectioned.' I gabble the last bit quickly, hoping he won't notice.

No such luck.

'You what?' he shouts down the phone. 'A psychiatrist. Oh Pip,' he sighs, using my pet name. 'You are not mad. Don't let them tell you that you are insane. You have put up with more than most people could bear in one lifetime. Don't believe a word of anything they tell you. You have your family, you have your friends, your counsellor, your interests and intelligence, don't ever believe you are mad,' he says firmly.

'That is so lovely, thank you,' my voice is quiet as I absorb his words. They mean so much to me.

'I'm coming to see you tonight. I'll come straight from work. We can watch *Northern [Exposure]* together on your DVD player and snuggle up. I'll look after you, lovely.'

I tell him I love him and put down the phone. He is coming tonight and I am so happy. He has been so busy recently, working late, and I almost feel this was all worth doing, just to spend some time with him.

But still, I have a nagging feeling that he doesn't feel the same way about me any more. Nothing I can really put my finger on, but it is there all the same. I try not to dwell on the feelings though and instead look forward to him coming. I tell Mum and Laura. They are pleased. They know I have been having doubts about his feelings for me. But it is also time for them to go and I can see they are worried at leaving me. Despite the fact that I'll have a visitor within the hour, I am still moved at them having to go. I cling on to Mum's hand just a second too long.

'Don't worry about me. I'm absolutely fine now,' I say. There is a tear threatening to roll down my face but, thank God, it hangs back. Mum stands up and looks at me, her face half-lost in shadow now. She hesitates, and I feel a lump in my throat.

'This too shall pass,' she says. 'I will hold the faith for you, as I can see you have none left. I can carry both of us,' she finishes, smashing my fragile exterior into smithereens which, in turn, carry shards of grace into my heart. Then she goes. I hear the muffled sounds of their boots as they leave the ward.

Lying in the semi-darkness, hearing the coughs and moans of the patients crammed within the sickly yellow walls, the groans of 'Nurse, nurse', the sounds of the ubiquitous blue curtains being pulled back, then drawn again, I still cannot even be sure what really happened. Or whether anything happened at all? I may even have dreamed this nightmare somewhere inside the depths of my sedation.

CHAPTER 9

# The First Happy Feeling

*May 2008*

Wrapped in blankets, I am lying on the sofa in my cottage (which I finally moved into at the start of the year), while Adrian makes tea in the kitchen. I can hear the chink of the cups as he pulls them from the cupboard, his clumsy movements echoing through my listlessness. I haven't been back to hospital since the suicide attempt, and there is the faintest seed of hope spawning inside me that the last procedure may have arrested the disease.

The pancreatic pain is with me all the time though, and so I am still living on a cocktail of pills and potions prescribed during my last stint as an inpatient: fentanyl lozenges, 200mcg, eight a day, plus tramadol (another opiate drug), 100mg, three times a day, and paracetamol or ibuprofen, as well as the anti-sickness drug ondansetron, which is usually prescribed for cancer patients because it is so strong.

Suddenly, there is a bleep and Adrian's phone vibrates, a green light flashing the message. I wait for him to run in and retrieve it, but as the seconds pass it is clear he hasn't heard it. Sighing, I reach in a slow, cumbersome gesture and pick up the phone. It is then that my stomach swoops into my bowels, in a short, sharp judder of intuition.

I have never looked through his phone before. I have always judged those who read other people's texts or letters as violators of privacy, unwelcome intruders, but today I don't feel that. I feel cold and scared and I know I have to read that message. And more than that, I know I won't like it.

Holding still for a moment, I check the sounds from the kitchen. The kettle is still making its slow way to boiling point. I'm safe for a moment. I click on the message and the words shift and move in front of me as I register what my trespassing eyes are reading: words like 'Darling' and 'Dear' and 'Can't wait to see you today'. Today? He told me he's going trekking today. With one of his mates. And it's signed by V. His old flame. The girlfriend who never quite went away.

My heart slips out of my body and my throat goes dry. I'm frozen in the spotlight of this deceit. I know I don't need to ask questions. I know from that small message that he's seeing her behind my back. And looking down at myself, I can't blame him. How can I possibly compete with the long-limbed beauty that she is?

There's a second's pause when my world starts spinning, when the wave of emotion slams into me and engulfs me with oceanic force. Then comes volcanic anger – the kind that reaches down into the depths of your gut and wrenches the feeling up in hot, molten lava. Even so, it's tempered by something. I can hold it in for the sake of more time to remain as we are; safe and cocooned in ignorance and lies. Because I don't want him to leave me. If he goes, I'll be heartbroken and alone. If he goes, I'll be just a sad, ill woman and no one will ever want me again. I'll be stuck here by myself, dependent and vulnerable.

So the fear pushes the anger back down inside me and seals it up with a tight smile on my face. I put the phone back on the table and gather my thoughts. He probably won't notice I've opened the message. I'll pretend nothing has happened.

He brings the tea in and I take mine with shaking hands. He says he has to go soon and dashes off to take a shower.

I pass the day in a state of shock and can't settle to anything. There is too much whirling around in my mind. What are they doing together? Why does she have this hold over him? Is he going to leave me? Who will want me – a disabled, broken wreck?

Yet even as the self-defeating thoughts shred my peace, I sense that I'm not as wretched as I think I am, that there's a part of me that's starting to stand up and face this. It's his behaviour after all, and I have the choice of being victim or survivor.

It's dark when I hear his key in the door, breaking the silence. I sit, still and waiting. There must be something about my face that tells him I know. He moves closer and I'm hit by the sweet, cloying smell of her perfume. My man really has spent the day with another woman.

My pent-up rage bubbles only just beneath the surface now. My voice is harsh as I ask him if he loves me. There's a moment where he steps back into the still-open door as if to escape. His eyes focus somewhere else, away from me. He looks defeated and for a moment I almost feel sorry for him. Almost.

'Cathryn,' he says, and his voice is soft against my brittle judgment. Hearing him, I crumble inside, sink into the sofa and bow my head, so the tears don't show. I feel his warmth as he sits beside me. He holds my hand tenderly, but his words cut me to ribbons. 'Cathryn, I don't think I ever loved you. I'm sorry.'

Those words, those awful, hideous, soul-destroying words, shrink me back, tear my insides down into a big black hole. He doesn't think he ever loved me. What could possibly be more upsetting, more cruel, more hurtful to hear? Though stunned for a moment, slapped with the full force of his disinterest, the words soon become a battle cry.

Sorry? With this apology I feel as though I have been struck. It takes me a moment to recover my breath – and then I realise it's time to hit back. I pull my hand away, as if his touch scalds me.

He shakes his head and looks away, as if I am encroaching on something private and valued. The hot bile fills my throat and I gag.

'You bastard, you owe me an explanation at least. I love you,' I shout, the sound of my anger veering sharply into pleading.

He shakes his head again, his eyes turned away, his silence becoming more unbearable by the second.

I stagger from the room and out to the bathroom where I am sick, very sick.

The next few weeks are a blur. I can't sleep or eat. I lurch from angry tears to impassioned begging; desperate for him to stay with me, despite what he's done – is doing. There's no dignity in desperation. I know that it's over and he loves someone else. The rational moments come and go, the hurt rages last longer, stay longer.

We set a date for his departure later in the summer. The weeks leading up to his leaving are an uneasy calm as I wait for the tornado to hit. We are polite. He still rings me three times a day from work to check in, to make sure that I'm ok, that I've eaten, that I don't go too crazy on my own in my sick bed.

Each call brings an assault of emotions again. I treasure his attention, but I can't bear the thought that he does it for friendship and not love. My pride hurts and howls after every call, but I take them all. The sound of his voice is becoming more precious by the day.

A week before the date set for his leaving, he tells me he's found a place. It's a studio flat on the other side of the village. Too many emotions to identify collide and tussle with each other, but the hardest to face is the sadness. The anger and the tears are all surface stuff, covering up the truth that I am about to lose the love of my life: this kind man who has slept on hospital floors for me, who stroked my hair as I threw up in beds, in cars, on roadsides. This man, who all along loved another woman, but wouldn't leave me so ill and so alone. Thinking back on this makes it all so much harder. He knew I loved him and so he stayed to protect me.

One day, absorbing the impact of another of his phone calls, my mind turns to the new prescription of the strong painkillers, which is stored in the kitchen cupboard. I am allowed up to eight fentanyl lozenges a day as that is the NHS maximum, and my daily routine is now two in the morning after breakfast, two at lunchtime, two after dinner and two before bed to get me through the night.

I also wear a patch on my arm – not dissimilar to the nicotine patches you can get from the chemist – which delivers a slow-release form of the opiate. I wear the highest-strength patch available (100mcg), which emits a steady flow of medication into my bloodstream during the day and overnight. The lozenges are intended as top-up pain relief and I have stayed strictly within the NHS limit. But today is different and I don't know why.

I'm suddenly aware of the clock ticking, the birds singing outside, the lack of any human presence in this house. I'm lying in bed, the hushed tones of Radio 4 echoing in the empty room. Empty except for me. This is how it will be, I think. This is my future. Me, the radio, the birds and nothing.

My mind goes back to the lozenges. There are two new boxes of thirty in the kitchen cupboard. It's 4 p.m. My next dose is due at 6 p.m. Two hours to go, except I know I am going to go downstairs and take one now. I am going to snap it off the row of three in the blister pack, tear open the strip and I am going to take an extra one.

This thought fills me with the first happy feeling I've had in weeks. I can feel a giggle in my throat as I ease myself out of the bed, drag a dressing gown around me and slowly make my uneasy way downstairs.

I've been out of hospital for months now, and the thought of changing my dose has never crossed my mind. Until today.

One more won't hurt, will it? I ask myself and smile as I make my furtively contented way down to the cabinet where the meds are kept. The feeling of opening the illicit dose is like opening an unexpected gift at Christmas. I feel giddy, naughty and girlish as I stash it in my pocket and head back to bed.

Settling down, I sigh as I place the medication in my mouth, open a novel and relax for the first time in so long.

It can't be wrong? I feel so much better, like my old self again. I am finally back in charge of my life, making my own decisions and operating under my own rules rather than everyone else's. And it is only one more. What harm can it do?

But the feeling doesn't stay long. Soon the day dawns for my newly-ex boyfriend to leave. I have been in denial about this day. I watch as he packs his last suitcase. Downstairs, the shelves are half empty as his books and papers lie in boxes waiting to be piled into the car. He places his work clothes in last and I watch as these beloved items leave me.

It isn't just him going. It's never as simple as one person leaving. Our friends, our habits, our likes and dislikes, our jokes, our arguments and our families. The links in all those chains are sliding apart.

Suddenly, I am seized by utter desperation and fear. I want to stop him. I want to say, 'Don't go, stay with me even if you love her.' I hate myself, but I know if I had the strength, I'd probably throw myself at his feet and cling on to his legs as he tries to go. I know I'm being dramatic, but I am degraded and hurting.

He turns to say goodbye, but I am too upset to say anything. He looks at me with friendship and this is truly unbearable.

The front door shuts with a deafening click. He is really gone. I look around the emptied cottage. The floor greets my body with a smooth, cold touch. I sink into it like a drowning ship, my dressing gown billowing around me, and I stay there for a long time with my forehead on the cold wood and my hands clutched tightly round my stomach in an attempt to hold in my feelings. When eventually I raise myself, still in shock, tears unshed, I move towards the kitchen cupboard. It's an automatic response. I don't know if I am in physical pain or whether it is the emotional ravages that compel me back to the cabinet. Back to the drugs. This time, I take out a row of three. Enough for most of a normal day. Barely enough for now.

Time stands still. The clock has stopped ticking or so my fanciful mind tells me. The silence has an overbearing enormity which cowers me. The beams and walls seem to moan gently in tune with my grief. My house seems to sympathise with my state, or maybe I am going mad – but that is how it feels to me.

I gently break open the packaging containing the fentanyl 'lollies'. The first I suck then and there on the floor. Back in position. The only place that feels safe right now. As the pellet melts into my cheek, calm creeps over me, stills me enough to shuffle up on my bottom and get myself back to bed.

I know that the fentanyl is not the answer. I know I have taken an extra few lozenges to calm me down and see me through this, the worst part of the break-up. It does not occur to me that this could be the start of something I cannot control. My doctor prescribed these drugs for me, so I assume I am 'safe' using them, even if I am pushing the limits by taking the extra few.

I am already feeling a bit woozy when I take the second lozenge, but I don't care. I would rather feel a little woolly than cope with this pain. I take it all into my mouth and wait as the hurts start to fade away. Then I take the third. There is a different feeling now – a quiet, connected, ok feeling which tells me I can handle this. That I am strong enough to get through it, just as long as I keep feeling this peace. I feel magnanimous for him – like I needed to let him go and I am better for it. The ripped-apartness subsides into a blossoming serenity and I feel love for him again. Not possessive, raging, hurt love, but a gentle connection with his soul. My heart is soaring and I feel ready to take whatever life throws at me. I've got through so much already – why would this be any different?

Eventually, I start awake. I can't remember what time or day it is or whether I've been asleep or musing. I might have been lying here for hours or days, I have no anchor to reach for and it confuses and frightens me a little. The room is dark, the streetlight from across the road is casting an eerie glow, peering unashamedly through the open curtains. I shake myself a little to wake up and check the radio, which is still humming, quiet voices like ghosts, at my bedside.

It is still the same day. Nothing has changed. I am alone here now. Except my sense of place and self is hazy. I feel like I am in a dream sequence. My memory feels disorientated. I can't tether myself to the evening and I feel foggy – almost as if I am hung over from a night out. I've had eleven lozenges today, I think.

It is only three more than the limit, so I'll cut back tomorrow. But as I think this, I am already reaching for the box which I must have brought up earlier. Time for my missed 6 p.m. dose. None of my decisions is making much sense. But I don't seem to care any more.

Several days later, I am back at my GP's surgery, telling him my boyfriend left, that I had a pain episode and that since then, I've gone up to eleven and sometimes even fourteen fentanyl lozenges a day. I hear myself talking and I don't know if this is fact or fiction.

I have a strange feeling of disconnection from my feelings and actions at the moment which isn't altogether unpleasant.

I see him frown, but commend me for my honesty, which confuses me further. He says he'll contact the Pain Team at the local hospital and get me an appointment as it would be better to move me on to something else for pain relief. He explains that although the fentanyl is obviously giving me a quality of life at the moment, it is not a long-term solution to my problem. He says I have to be careful that I am not medicating my emotional pain.

I nod, but inside I'm saying, 'Hell, no.' The last time I saw that particular Pain Team they gave me an overdose of ketamine, the horse tranquilliser. I've finally found something which works, which doesn't leave me sleepless in the agony I live with all day, every day, so no one, not even my GP, is going to take it away from me. Living in continual pain is mentally and emotionally exhausting. It is a battle for every second of sanity. I can't go through that again, especially not now with the break-up so raw still. Maybe he's right and maybe there is some kind of 'hurt' crossover, but that's understandable and totally justified and so I don't care.

I'll cut back down to the daily limit of eight doses once the shock abates. It is more important to me that I get through the next few days and weeks; I'm not worried about the fentanyl – it's what makes my life manageable.

Of course, I say none of this to my GP. I just nod, and clutching my next prescription for sixty lozenges, I say I'll see him next week.

CHAPTER 10

# Lie Still

*August 2008*

*There's movement, and noise and someone shrieking. There's green light, then blue curtains and the sound of a woman crying and moaning. She's hurting. She's me. I'm panting and writhing into a pain I cannot describe. There are the red-hot maggots again and this time they're eating me alive, in a twisting, tortuous, squirming feast. And I'm yelling now. Yelling. I'm crazy, demented. I hear 'Lie still!' It's a command, not a request, must be a doctor. I open my eyes and see a kind face. She looks panicked. She looks as scared as me. She's got a needle and it's going into my arm – the cannula, the thin plastic tube slides into my arm and I don't feel it. It's nothing compared to the billowing, relentless onslaught of this god-fucking-awful terror inside me. Then something else goes into my arm, through the plastic tube, into my vein and the hot red blood flowing inside it. Something takes away the hurt, dilutes the agony and I fall back into the damp pillows which are sodden with my sweat.*

Panting, I'm suddenly aware of the sound of birdsong filtering through the foggy outpost of my head. My breath feels thick and fast, like I've finished running hard. And the pull of the air hitting the back of my throat brings me back to the room: my bedroom, in my cottage in my sleepy village. Eyes suddenly open,

I blink at the soft honey-coloured sunlight streaming gently into the space. It takes a few moments to gather what there is of me and to breathe more slowly, realign my mind back into the present tense.

Another flashback to another hospital admission. They haunt me in my dreams and in my waking now. Hypnotised by terror, I have as many as ten a day. I seem to drift away, back into the worst times, the awful, scary, fraught times, and my body tenses up into it, as if it's real. The feelings are so real. Real, but lies all the same. I drift back into the fear and chaos of the hospital, wandering back into a random memory of any one of my admissions like a stuck record, playing over and over again.

I'm not there, I'm not having an attack. I'm here now and I'm safe. I know I'm speaking aloud and I briefly wonder if I'm going mad or if I'm already there. So I tell myself slowly and calmly out loud that I'm not in A&E, I'm at home in my lovely little cottage. I'm at home and I'm safe.

And this way, I slowly heave myself out of my mental torture. Will I always have these memories? Or will they one day fade away, slip out of my subconscious and become like a faded black and white photograph, too absent to hurt me any more?

My hand reaches out and finds the packet of lozenges which is my constant companion. It lies sprawled and open on the bed and there are two lozenges sticking out; joined together in their plastic casing. I rip off one of them; I always leave one for 'just in case' on the days I need to pick up a new prescription. I live in fear that the delivery lorry will break down, or the chemist will shut early or some other unforeseen disaster might rob me of my prescription. So I keep aside my 'emergency' supply. Not that a single lozenge would last very long, but it's a mental thing, I suppose.

As I place the sweet-tasting (strawberry cheesecake) white

moulded medicine into my mouth I murmur a sigh of relief, of release. Thank God I have these. I can't imagine how I'd cope with the residual pancreatic pain or with the harsh flare-ups of those terrible memories without my drugs. Saying that, there is a tiny thought at the back of my mind. A tiny question I'm starting to ask, which is: are these drugs to blame for the flashbacks? I can't be certain. But then again, I can't be certain of much these days. My life seems foggier, harder to grasp. It keeps slipping through my fingers and I keep letting it go, forgetting and remembering in haphazard symphony.

My mind feels stretched too tightly inside my head, pulled too thin to make sense of things. I am forgetful. I have no idea what time it is or what day. I feel disorientated, so I haul myself up on my pillows which are plumped up all around me, trying to navigate myself into time and space.

I heave myself out of myself and find the comforting familiarity of my bedroom again. The warm midday light is making shimmering patterns of the dust suspended in its pathway, and yet I hardly notice it. Instead, I concentrate on the slow, seeping feeling of the drugs working into my system. The panicky feeling starts to dissolve. I feel my head coming back into place and my mind calming, slowing back to 'normality'; my normality.

I never crunch the lozenge, I treat each one with respect. Holding the white plastic stick firmly, making it last as long as I can manage. Then, as the white lump of medicine finally shrinks and falls from the stick, I reluctantly pull the tube from my mouth, sucking the tiny grooves which screwed the drug on, licking the spirals to salvage any white stuff that is still lodged within its coils.

This way, the dose can last for ten minutes per lozenge. Ten minutes of peace, ten minutes where the pain softens, my muscles relax and I feel 'normal' again.

*

I look at my phone and it's just gone 12 p.m. I have to be washed and dressed by 2 p.m. as the Consultant Psychiatrist from the local mental-health team is coming to check me out. It's the legacy of my failed and vague suicide attempt.

Soon I hear Mum's key in the front door – she's a bit late today. Within an hour she has helped me into the bath, made me a late breakfast and I am propped up on the sofa, held in place by a muddle of cushions.

When, eventually, the psychiatrist pulls up outside and comes to the door, Mum lets him in then busies off. She has her own life to lead as well. We go through the dance, the psychiatrist and me. He looks around the cottage, sees it is clean and cosy, he looks me up and down, sees I am washed and presentable.

He writes small notes in cramped handwriting as I talk about how I am coping. I don't say much. I tell him I am managing. I don't tell him about the flashbacks, the panic attacks, the morbid fear which stalks me day and night. I don't want to sound mad.

'Have you had any more suicidal thoughts or impulses?' he asks.

'I haven't,' I reply, almost truthfully.

'That's good,' he says, making another small note. 'And what are your interests? Are you able to read or pursue any hobbies?'

I almost laugh out loud at this.

'I can see you are an intelligent woman, so it must be frustrating living with your disabilities,' he adds, rather kindly.

Living with my disabilities. What an elegant way of describing this strange, desperate life of mine. Somehow, it sounds like I've almost chosen these disabilities which render me incapable of performing even the smallest everyday things like brushing my own hair or preparing my own meals.

'I read when I have the energy to hold a book. I listen to Radio 4 all day every day, so I know everything that's going on in the world. I just can't join in,' I say quietly. 'Intellectual stimulation is thin on the ground, admittedly, and I sometimes feel I am going mad without it.' I pause then, feeling uncertain as to whether I should've admitted to near madness.

But the psychiatrist just nods and smiles, as if all I can be accused of is being human. And that isn't a crime worth being committed for.

'We need to set you up with a blood test to check you are ok with the mood stabiliser you were prescribed in hospital. After that, I think we can safely see you as and when you need us.' He smiles and gathers up his papers, and as quickly as he walked in, he leaves.

I sink back into the cushions, the upholstered scaffolding which is keeping my head upright. And I know, at least, that one part of all this is going to be ok. I won't be carted into bedlam, not today at any rate.

I collapse back into bed and don't move for two hours, but as 4 p.m. edges closer, I know I have to somehow get up and collect my repeat prescription from the chemist. I always try to hold off going because I know when I pick up my boxes of drugs I won't be able to stop myself opening them, but today it is sheer exhaustion which keeps me from attempting the tiny journey to the pharmacy. I look at the last dose sat innocently on its own, in solitary splendour in the box lying next to me. Can I risk taking it? Can I trust that my meds will definitely have arrived at the chemist when I get there?

I want to take it because there never seems to be the feeling that I've had enough. I am always wanting the next lozenge. The craving follows me around all the time, like a lost puppy. But I stop short this time. I'm worried about looking 'drugged' when I go to the chemist to pick up my new prescription. Still, the feeling is one of ongoing internal negotiation – the sensible part of me pleading with the drugged part to stay, however, shakily, on the right side of myself.

So I hide the final lozenge, pretending to myself that I don't know where it is. I put it underneath a towel in the bathroom cabinet, as far back as I can reach. I know this is mad, but I have to do it. I have to tell myself it's out of my reach or I'll take it. I know I will.

I check my phone. It's 3.45 p.m. I want to hold out till later, but I know I'll be at the chemist at 4 p.m. on the dot. Not sure why I can't seem to get there any later. I reach for my book and spend the next few minutes reading the same line over and over, while watching out of the corner of my eye as the minutes change excruciatingly slowly. The words fidget and move in front of my eyes. My mind feels like distorted shapes and sounds. I think of the recurring dream I have each night.

It is without boundaries or scale, without perspective or orientation. All I can remember is that it is yellow, with sharp black shapes which are sometimes in the same plane as me, sometimes far, far away and sometimes so close to me I cannot breathe. Then the scale changes and the shapes become monstrously large in proportion to me, then shrink to the tiniest microcosm, throwing me mentally and emotionally through spatial loops, where I am rendered helpless and small, disfigured and large. It is the same dream I had as a child when I had a fever and was dosed up on whatever they gave children in the 1970s. It is my sickness dream, my fever nightmare – and I have it now, every night. So much so, that I dread the onslaught of sleep. But sleep is something I cannot fight these days. It reaches me, pulling me down into my subconscious, into the deep, dark slumber that this medicine brings. I wake every morning as though I've been pulled from the depths of a rough sea: I gasp awake, sucked into reality, expelled from my night-time visions and left bleeding and sore on the beach of each new day.

I digress. Did I say that my
I get caught in aimless musings,
memory lanes until I find myself bac
on with my day. Always slightly confus
away peculiar, unsettling thoughts. Even t
mentally through my past, my present an
seems alarming and odd. I've gone off again.
Must get my cardi on and get myself ready for m
the chemist.

It is 3.52 p.m. I'm pleased – it's seven minutes la
'usual' time for leaving the house. Does this mean som
don't know, but I'm pleased anyway. Mostly, Mum either drives me to the chemist or walks me up there, holding gingerly on to my arm as if I would snap in two. Today she can't though, so the daunting journey is mine alone to take.

Wrapping a scarf around my throat, I creep towards the stairs, my head spinning off its centre of gravity as my blood pressure adjusts to my new, unfamiliar upright position. Sometimes I can't even get this far. If I'm really bad, feeling ill and with very low energy, I call Mum and ask her to collect my prescriptions for me. Today, I'm ok. I'm going to try.

Unsteadily, I greet the stairs with an intake of breath. I fear that I'll be so woozy from my painkillers that I'll fall down the length of them. Then it will be like those news stories you hear about people who live alone and are found weeks after they died by a neighbour who noticed the smell of a decaying body. I swallow the fear and tell myself I'm being dramatic, but I don't breathe properly until I reach the bottom step.

My keys are on the sofa, untouched since the last trip to the chemist. These trips are my only outings. I can't walk very far, so I order my food shopping online from my bed – I order the bare minimum, money being a constant worry through all this. And as I

…g, Mum comes in and helps me with cook-… this is done around me, while I lie or sit in … something to change. Waiting for my life to … it's a videotape stuck on pause.

… door clicks shut behind me and I walk my uncertain path …y prescription. I know the drugs are in because I rang before I …eft. I rang to reassure myself, to be absolutely 100 per cent completely sure that my painkillers were at the chemist, waiting for me. I try not to walk like a little old lady. I try not to notice that I'm wearing several layers of clothing, including a cardi, a jumper, a scarf and leggings under my skirt and coat, even though it's a mild day. Passing people on the street, I note their shirts and thin layers, whereas I tremble against the slightest breeze. Even in my home, I'm ultra-sensitive to the temperature and spend a small fortune keeping it heated at twenty degrees in all weathers. I feel so ill; so tired, so heavy and sick.

At the pharmacy, the door is heavy and I struggle to open it. This makes me angry. I wish someone would fucking realise that ill people can't open heavy doors. The pharmacist says hello and I smile weakly before making my way to the chair which sits alongside the tonics and vitamins lining the shelves. I sit patiently among the cough drops and tinctures, the Band Aids and the spot creams while my prescription is made up for me. There's no need to say my name. They all know me. Regular as clockwork, every four days and sometimes even three days if the weekend falls before the script runs out. Each time, I'm here, at 4 p.m. (4.07 p.m. today) waiting for my next lot of sixty lozenges. Two boxes of thirty lozenges, each delivering 200 micrograms of the painkilling opiate.

One of the ladies behind the counter greets me cheerily. She asks how I am and I say I'm struggling. She turns round to me and says, 'You must be in such a lot of pain to be on so much fentanyl.'

The pharmacist nods, adding, 'That's a hefty dose you're taking.'

I am in pain. And I nod back. I don't trust myself to speak as I suddenly feel I will break down and cry in this tiny chemist in this funny little village. I feel like I'm the unluckiest woman alive and I am so angry that my life has been reduced to this decrepit rubble. I can't believe this is me now, that this is my life.

Eventually, a large blue NHS paper bag appears on the counter. I sign the back of my script and I clutch the bag which is bulging from the two large boxes. Thanking the friendly staff, I slowly make my way home, not trusting I have what I need until I can safely shut my front door behind me, crawl upstairs on my hands and knees, holding the bag between my teeth (which takes fifteen minutes as I'm so drained from the journey to the chemist) and collapse on to my bed. Then I let out a sigh of relief.

Ripping open the paper, I free the boxes in joyful abandon. I'm ok. I'm safe from pain for another few days, and right now that's all I care about. I don't realise that I haven't called my sister for two weeks, nor spoken to my nephew or any friends. My world is shrinking to the size and shape of the two boxes now sitting on my duvet.

I know I shouldn't take any before my dinner. I've had twelve lozenges already today and I only have three of my daily allowance left if my script is to last until the next one. But. And there's always a 'but'. But I deserve an extra one or two. I've had a rough day, my stomach has been hurting, it's sore and swollen and I'm exhausted after walking up to the shops, so surely one more won't hurt?

The feeling as I snap off a row of three lozenges from the pack is indescribable. It's excitement mixed with elation, mixed with reassurance and relief. It's like having a treat and feeling that I deserve it at the same time. I decide that taking three more lozenges won't affect my daily tally too much, and I can always tell my doctor I had a bad pain day. It wouldn't be a lie, would it, as I hurt all the fucking time. Except, of course, I've already told this lie before – but my mind doesn't even register it. Acting judge and jury, I acquit myself and award myself the three extra lozenges. I calculate that I'll need to see my doctor a day early this week, if I am to get the next script half a day earlier. It's a complicated balancing act. I have to weigh the GP's surgery hours against the least amount of time I can safely wait before he'll allow me another repeat. I live in terror of him refusing to sign my prescription. The thought fills my waking hours and at night I dream about it too. I dream that I leave without the green slip which is so familiar to me now – and as I stand, confused and dazed outside the surgery, my head flails about. Where should I go? What shall I do without my meds?

So I calculate the time needed for the drugs to be ordered from the depot (how do I know this?) and driven on one of the twice-daily deliveries to my chemist (11 a.m. and 3.30 p.m., except Saturdays when there is only one delivery at 12 p.m. and Sundays when obviously it's closed). Working it out, I estimate I'll need to see my doc in two and a half days' time in order to compensate for the extra dose I'm taking right now.

Soothed by my calculations, reassured by my logic and rational thinking, I tear the paper strip from the first lozenge. This is such a treat. I sigh out loud and settle back into my pillows, getting comfy, reaching for my book and readying myself to receive my illicit extra doses.

Luckily, my prescription falls over a weekend. So on Monday morning I make an appointment with my GP for that afternoon, making sure I sound especially weak on the phone.

Later, Dr M. is silent, watchful, as I sit down opposite him. I've rehearsed this moment over and over again in my mind. In truth, I've spent the weekend worrying and fidgeting, scared he won't believe I've had another pain episode, terrified he'll refuse to give me my drugs.

My voice is shaky as I ask for a repeat script, but I feel I'm fighting for something here and so hold my head as high as I can manage. I stare him boldly in the eyes as if I have nothing to hide.

'You've taken sixty lozenges in almost three days,' he says, looking back at me.

'Yes,' I say. 'I was in horrendous pain this weekend and they stopped me from having to go into hospital.'

'You realise that you are taking too many, that the maximum dose per day is eight lozenges, ten at the very most,' he replies, still staring me out. I feel he is daring me to confess to something.

'Look, I'm in bloody awful, actually, fucking awful pain, doctor. I make no apology for that. I needed the pain relief,' I counter.

It's his turn now. Will he give me the drugs? Will he give me the drugs? Will he give me the drugs?

He picks up a pen from beside his computer and pulls a blank prescription sheet from the printer. On the pale green paper, he draws a rough graph, illustrating the relationship between opiate use and natural endorphin (the body's natural painkiller) levels. His spidery drawing seems to morph into an A-level exercise as he concludes, with a flourish, 'The more your body gets used to the fentanyl, the less work its natural painkillers will do. Your endorphins are on holiday, they're sunning themselves in the Med, while you're sucking your lozenges.

'You have to start cutting down. You need to get your body working properly again. I'll sign your prescription today, but I want you to go away and think about this. You can draw up a chart and we'll work out how to reduce them slowly, week by week.'

I nod. I agree. But in all honesty, I am trying to hide my smile of utter delight. I'm safe again for the next few days. His words don't sink in; they don't even touch the surface of my elation. I'll worry about cutting down next time. Next time. For now, I tell him I really want to cut down. I tell him I'm really, really fed up of being dependent on drugs as I know this is what he wants to hear. I don't mean it. I can as easily imagine my life without painkillers as I can living on the moon. An impossibility. All I can see is the next prescription. My time is divided into three-day chunks and literally nothing exists outside that.

The simple truth is that I am frightened of feeling that physical trauma again, and I'm scared of having nothing to help me escape it when it gets too bad to cope with. The drugs give me a life. Without them, I'd probably commit suicide because of the horrendous pain which stays with me, its grip harsh and tight.

I stumble home, call my mum and ask her to drop the prescription into the chemist. She sounds weary, hassled. I feel guilty, but I can't stop myself asking her all the same.

Later, as the light fades, bathing my bedroom in the soft half-light of the setting sun, I lie in silence, listening to the sounds of the aged cottage as it creaks and groans gently around me. There's a softness to the evening, and I lie in it, alone, the anaesthetic balm of the pharmaceutical rendering me quiet and still. My cure, my tonic, my sedation.

CHAPTER 11

# Doctor, Dealer?

*October 2008*

Dr M. screws up his face in contorted mockery. He grabs a pen and mimics licking it, sucking it, rolling it in his mouth in a revolting semi-erotic swoon. He sways into the seduction, his tongue curling round the pen, his eyelids blinking rapidly in mock Bacchanalian pleasure. In a small, whiney female voice he says, 'Don't hurt me, don't be nasty to me, don't upset me.' Then his head lolls to the side and his too-bright, piercing eyes find mine.

'If you hurt me, I'll suck my druggie sticks and that'll teach you,' he croons in twisted derision. 'If you hurt me, I'll kill myself with my painkillers. I'll kill myself to get back at you.'

I sit opposite my GP in his surgery, frozen rigid in disbelief as I watch him perform his perverted theatricals. I understand that this is me I'm watching. This monstrous, unnatural figure is me taking my painkillers. I can't speak or move. I feel the billowing thump of nausea in my belly, deep down inside. My eyes find a mug on his desk. It is decorated with bright pictures of horses' heads, rosettes and saddles. 'Champion Dad' is printed along the bottom edge of the cup and I focus on the words until the show is finished and my humiliation is complete.

There's silence when Dr M. stops his act, drops his sideshow like an aberrant medieval player. Stunned into silence, I can't bear to raise my eyes to meet his dispassionate gaze. Let's see how she reacts to this. Let's shame her into – what? What am I being shamed into? I need my painkillers as I live in chronic hurt, so why this pantomime? Does he think I take them out of choice?

Still smarting from the pain of degradation, I ask if he's done. I know I should get angry, storm out, write a letter of complaint, sack the bastard for putting me through this, but I am weak, and I need him like an addict needs their dealer. I need him because if he doesn't sign my prescription request then what will I do? I can barely think of the alternative, so I stay there, composed in the plastic chair reserved for patients, waiting for this latest indignity to pass, so I can grab that green sheet of paper and get to the chemist.

The silence drags on. I am desperate to leave. I am desperate to go home and lick my wounds. Lick my wounds. Lick my lozenges. Maybe that is me? Something inside me seems to have shifted and in doing so, a tiny crack in a minuscule door has opened and I'm asking myself. Is that me?

Before I get a chance to expand that thought, the need for my prescription crowds it out. Slams the door shut. Inside my mind I beg, I plead with this slightly overweight man in his late forties with the ruddy cheeks of the well-fed upper classes to fucking sign my fucking script.

He watches me. Drags out the time. We must have long since run over the ten minutes allocated to each patient. Still we sit in uncomfortable tension until eventually, he sighs and returns to his computer, clicking the mouse. Then, miraculously, the printer shudders into life and seconds later there's the green paper in his hand.

He pauses before signing. Sign the fucking thing. Sign it, you fucking shitty, miserable, manipulative wanker, I'm thinking, pleading, praying.

'I'm going to sign this today, but you have to face the fact that you cannot stay on these drugs for ever. You are a drug addict and the longer you leave it, the harder it will be for you.' His voice trails off as I finally find my anger.

'I am not a drug addict. And I will not be manipulated into stopping the pain relief I so obviously need,' I say, my tremulous voice rising above the uneasy quiet of the room. 'Don't you dare treat me like an imbecile. I won't be hurt and humiliated by my doctor. You can't just stop giving me the pain relief the NHS put me on in the first place,' I shout. I actually shout at my GP and he is smiling.

'What the fuck are you smiling about, haven't you done enough today?' I'm furious now, seething, angry, raging.

He watches me for a moment then says, 'Congratulations, you finally got angry. I didn't think you were capable of sticking up for yourself, Cathryn.'

'What kind of smart-arse comment is that?' I reply with a sneer. It feels great giving him back some of the shit he has piled on me today.

'I have just worked Provocative Therapy on you. It's a useful device for breaking through the emotional barriers erected by patients and bringing out trapped emotions,' he says, now serious, now seated again and signing the prescription.

'I think you are now using the opiates to medicate your feelings, as well as your physical pain. Your use of them has gone up sharply since your relationship ended and I think you are taking them to dull some of that pain.'

I hear his words, but they don't go anywhere inside me. They buzz angrily around my head as I watch him in shocked silence.

The main realisation that hits me is that I have just been 'rewarded' for screaming at my doctor. The world has just turned on its head, creating a whirlwind of confusion and shock.

'I must warn you again that taking twenty fentanyl lozenges a day is well over the prescribed dose,' he continues. 'Please draw up your chart for cutting down, by one or two doses a week, starting from now.

'I have also drawn up prescriptions for paracetamol and ibuprofen and I strongly suggest you start using those to supplement your pain-relief regime and help reduce your reliance on fentanyl.'

And with that he hands me the script. Speechless, horrified and delighted in one tumultuous convulsion, I retreat into the relative sanity of the waiting room, clutching the script in hands sticky with hope and desperation.

I am almost unaware of how I got home, and barely recall going into the pharmacy, but by the time I pull my weary body and mind back into bed, I realise I won. I got my prescription. I won the battle, but I know I'm facing a life-or-death struggle to win the war.

I have made some small attempt to have some regular company through t'ai chi lessons once a week. Cameron, the instructor, has been coming to see me since January. Most of the time, he just sits by my sick bed, while I perform small movements with my hands and legs to try to boost my circulation. The exercises are simple, but it is the company I most crave.

My friends Francesca and Grace come and see me whenever they can. Grace comes from London every couple of months or so when she's not working abroad and Fran drives up quite regularly. And my family visit as often as they can manage. But it isn't the same as having a real life. I have always been quite a sociable person and the enforced solitude feels unnatural and isolating.

I watch a lot of DVDs; I have caught up with all the films I missed seeing in my working days. I watch some TV, I speak to friends on the phone but it is all exhausting. After each visit, however longed for, I fall back into barely being able to speak or move, so drained am I of all energy. I don't know if it is the ME or the pain or the combined effects of all the drugs. I suspect it is all three and together they leave me wrecked on an island of pain so intense it leaves me in a swoon.

One day, after I return from yet another trip to the pharmacy, the doorbell goes. It is Cameron. I lean out of my bedroom window and throw down the keys. It is my system for letting in guests as I rarely have the energy to get down the stairs myself, and today I've already taken four lozenges in the fifty minutes I've been home from the pharmacy.

He bends his tall frame into my bedroom a few seconds later, his expression reflecting the feeble sight of me, pale-faced and skinny, lying in my invalid's bed. He helps me sit up. I'm not feeling great today and was sick through the night, but even so, I want to get downstairs.

He carries me downstairs, and although he's a stranger, I feel oddly safe in his arms. He's loud and gregarious, cheering me up with his dating tales. He has a one-night stand in an expensive hotel with a woman he met online to report this week. With laughing pride, he tells me about the date, how he fancied her, but only looks-wise, before admitting with a grimace of shame that he won't be calling her again.

I raise my eyebrows and say nothing. He takes this as it was meant and tells me I need to get out more often, knowing full well how disabled I am. I laugh at that and let him hold my hands in the position he wants me to work with today. I notice he smells nice, fresh and outdoorsy.

I try to concentrate on the movements, but I keep wondering what it would be like to be closer to him, maybe even kiss him. I recall my brain before it wanders into trouble. I'm a weak, pathetic cripple and the last person in the world he would ever fancy, I decide, as I shove all interest in him to the back of my fuzzy mind.

In between our banter he teaches me simple exercises, moving my hands and wrists, feet and ankles in gentle, slow rhythm. Even the small movements make me feel sicker still. I took too many of my drugs before the session and I'm paying for it now. My head is woolly and I feel faint and un-coordinated. My speech is slightly slurred and I'm praying he doesn't notice and think I'm a druggie too. I'm struggling to concentrate and my back hurts just in the act of sitting. I can feel myself slumping into the sofa. The effort of sitting upright exhausts me utterly. By the end of the forty minutes I feel strained, tearful, taken to the limits of my endurance.

Even as he packs up his bag to leave, I can sense he wants to stay and chat. He's so friendly and open – a world away from the place I inhabit now, where I keep secrets from myself and others. Where I lie to myself about the number of lozenges I take every day, where I lie to my mum and dad and sister about the amount of medication I now need. With a guilty start, I realise I'm up to twenty-five lozenges a day. Only my GP, the pharmacist and I know this. The guilty sordidness of my life seems so far away from this tanned, exuberant man that I shrink back into myself, unwilling to let anything of this happy stranger into me or my existence. He feels like a threat now, I feel shrunken and insecure, in danger somehow and unprotected.

He hesitates at the door and I know instinctively that if I offered him a cup of tea he'd happily stay and talk for a while. He seems to want to get to know me. He is relaxed and confident in my company. Despite this friendship or whatever it is he is tentatively offering me, I suddenly feel trapped, claustrophobic in this small cottage with its beams bearing down on me, its creaking walls hemming me in. I don't know him, I think. What does he want? I am suspicious and cowed and I plaster a fake smile on my white face as I hold the door open.

He realises I want him to go and he bounds out, a symbol of health and beauty and life departing. I silently count the seconds before I can wave goodbye and collapse my broken body on to the sofa.

It takes me another thirty minutes before I have the energy to propel myself out of this place and up to bed. I have to go up to my bedroom. The lozenges are up there. I can feel the first shudders of wanting again. The small, grabbing, insistent feeling which is telling me it is time for my next dose. How many have I had today? Too many, probably. I think it's been six, or maybe eight. I can't remember, the paranoia of forgetting wraps up my mind and I stretch my neck from side to side, hoping to release this longing out of me. It won't work, but I try anyway.

This yearning feeling is something I can't control. When the itch starts in the back of my brain, when my body starts to ask for another dose, I am utterly in its power. If I leave it too long between doses, then something else starts. The longing becomes a shivery, restless urgency: a psychological, emotional and physical fusion of craving and wanting which soon advances into something more sinister, more frightening. Within hours of the last dose, my body starts to eject the drug with brutal force, shaking and sweating it out. This is the state of body and mind which is starting to greet me each morning now.

After eight hours' sleep I wake feeling raw, cramped and flayed bare for having less of the fentanyl inside my cells. It is starting to feel like a battle now, between feeling normal and feeling indescribably wretched. I have to keep my body dosed up correctly, at the right level, in order to function. I know this. It scares me, but what can I do? The pain is so awful when I wake up every morning that I instantly reach for my medication. I never want to face coming off these drugs. How would I cope without my pain relief?

CHAPTER 12

# First Dates

*December 2008*

The smell of the sea air is like whiplash of the senses. The salt spray is strong, fresh and it rips the fog that hovers over me into oblivion. The sun is shining; it's a clear, bright winter day – sharp, yet warm enough still to beguile, a heady enchantment. The sea and its blueness, the sky and its arching copycat blues are a revelation of a world forgotten.

Cameron has brought me in his car to Bexhill, to the De La Warr Pavilion. We are on a date. The thought of it makes me laugh with disbelief and pleasure. It is not a very big date. This strange, yet endearing, man who seems to like hanging out with an invalid, takes me from the car in the wheelchair I was bought by a local charity. He sets me at the edge of the pebbled beach, I can go no further as walking on uneven ground is simply too much effort, costs too much in pain and energy. And so we sit, with the last of the summer sun on our faces, and we smile into the radiance as the sounds of the waves keening the shoreline wash clean our souls.

This must be the third time we have been together outside of Cameron's role of t'ai chi instructor. The other times were simple and sweet. Cameron asked if he could come round and cook dinner and watch a film. He brought the film and the food, and he helped me down on to the sofa where we watched together in companionable silence. The second date was much the same, only this time I made it downstairs myself and wore a dress and some make-up. It was odd feeling feminine again, even for such a brief time, having felt almost sexless, 'other', for so long. But after two hours, I was spent and he left. It was also as long as I can cope without needing a top-up of my lozenges.

Cameron knows I take pain relief. I told him when he was just my instructor. He doesn't know how many I take though. That is a secret, carefully guarded by me, my doctor and the pharmacist. I keep trying to tell him I take a lot, as if I subconsciously feel guilty, but I can never find the right moment. Maybe I am ashamed that I need it. Maybe there is a small part of me which doesn't buy into taking this much, every day – a part of me which doubts myself and my motives. I don't know – and neither does he.

Today I can relax. I have a new prescription – collected this morning – and so I don't have to ration them out yet. Tomorrow I'll count what's left and work out when to go for my next appointment with the GP, but today I can enjoy being outside, carefree even. I have six lozenges in my bag, which also contains a small sample of all my medicines: the mirtazapine mood-stabilising anti-anxiety drug I take every evening, the anti-sickness drug, extra tramadol for breakthrough pain, paracetamol, Buscopan for abdominal cramping – practically an entire chemist shop hidden away. Just in case. I don't trust the world any more, you see.

I don't trust that I won't fall ill with an acute case of pancreatitis again, I don't trust that we won't break down and be left stranded with no medication. I don't even really trust the man I'm with, who is becoming part of my life. My trust, my naivety, my innocence were robbed from me, stripped away from me in the course of the four years I have just endured. I can no more trust my body than I can the universe, which feels to me like a frightening and harsh place, tempered only by the company of friends, family and, of course, my fentanyl. My drug keeps the fears at bay along with the burning hurts which still haunt me day and night.

But for now I can sit back, watch the seagulls cry over the white-tipped waves as they fly into the heavens on this glorious day.

It is while we are sitting, chatting quietly about nothing in particular, that Cameron reaches for my hand. I feel a warmth envelop me as he does it, a feeling that maybe something is ok in the world. I can't look at him, or his hand, I feel too self-conscious; and so I just feel his hand there, enclosing mine and I realise I feel happy again. Like the emotion never really went away – and it was just left unused instead.

Eventually, the wind whips up and the sky turns grey and it is time to go. As Cameron takes me back to the car, gently lifts me out of the chair, I feel a kind of amazement that he is doing this for me.

We drive back. I'm tired now, so I lean back against the head-rest and Cameron puts a CD of classical music on. As the blue turns to green and brown, the landscape swallows up the expanse of sky and sea, turning it into close-knit fields and woodlands. For the first time today, I have a sense of claustrophobia as he pulls up in front of the cottage which hugs the main road and which is my home. Suddenly, it seems very small, very quaint, to the point of being stifling. I am surprised at my reaction as it has almost always felt like the only safe place in the world, a haven which may be becoming a prison. I shake away the thoughts, I'm tired to my bones and struggling to hold my head upright as Cameron helps me inside.

He asks to stay, make me tea, watch something with me, but I shake my head, smiling. If I don't take the next dose of fentanyl, I will start to get shivery and the sweating will come. I'm already feeling the deep pull of the drug, calling me back to it. I make my excuses, as they say in the press, and he leaves, squeezing my hand and looking into my eyes. It is the seedling of something and I am content to take its growth slowly, with caution and something else – respect for my unholy condition.

As the door shuts, part of me breathes with relief. We had a lovely day, but the cravings have started: the prickles of sweat creep over my whole body and I shiver. The shaking has begun, the trembling hands and stretched feel of everything; the withdrawal pangs are with me and I have to fumble in my bag to find one of my supply of lozenges. I have to take one in order to calm down so I can dig out the rest of them. Using these painkillers is becoming more complicated by the day – calculating the times I need to take them before the awful symptoms of them leaving my body kick in, calculating when I need to collect another prescription. Running out is unthinkable. I would dissolve into terror and unimaginable pain.

I have to keep telling my doctor this as his calls for me to detox off them become more and more frequent. He rings me at home, telling me I have to come for appointments twice-weekly now. We have set goals for me cutting down – and I try, I really do. I go from my daily thirty lozenges and sometimes I manage to cut down by half – but the symptoms of withdrawal are so horrendous, so all-encompassing, that I cannot cope on my own any more and I always, always go back up. It is a constant battle. It is like giving up smoking which I finally managed at the age of thirty after several attempts – but it is much, much worse. Smoking is a doddle. The cravings were mental, emotional even, but they were not physical. Stopping an opiate though, or cutting it down, is like swooping into a physical dungeon where the body freefalls and every sense is pushed to its limit. I hover between sated calm and sensual disintegration daily. As the drug starts to leave it takes everything: my body, my mind, my soul. And I cannot do it alone, I cannot detox by myself. I am scared. I am more scared every day of dying, of trying to come off them, of everything. And it is only the drug which takes the fear away. So I am stuck, between a rock and a very hard place, and I don't know what the hell to do. I cannot tell anyone. How would they possibly understand? How would they be able to help? I don't understand myself, so how can anyone else fathom this pit I am in and how can they possibly help me climb out?

A week later and Cameron texts again, asking if he can take me on a drive. I have spent the entire week in bed since seeing him, exhausted by the day spent at the seaside. At first, I think I should decline; it is too much for me and I am scared of his interest in me. I don't know why. But as I reply, I surprise myself by saying yes and, a day later, he is helping me out of my secluded cottage and into his car again.

'Where are we going?' I ask, leaning my head back and sighing at the feel of the last of the day's meagre sunshine warm on my skin.

'It's a surprise,' he says and starts the engine.

'I love surprises,' I answer, then wonder, do I? It has been so long since the good ones, the surprises to relish, have come along that I can't remember if I like them or not. I decide that today I will adore them and smile back at Cameron.

He looks handsome today – he has just come back from a few days in the sun and the tan suits him. He looks healthy and he's wearing a blue top which mimics the colour of his eyes. I sit back and watch the green roll past the window as the day fades. After half an hour, Cameron pulls into a lane which leads over a rough track upwards to a hilltop.

The car wheels crunch on the uneven surface and we pull to a standstill. From this viewpoint we can see miles across a valley, across the weald in a swooping arc. As if planned, the sun blushes orange streaked with a magnificent pink which colours the sky as far as the eye can see.

It is a wonder, Mother Nature at her resplendent best. I gasp, at Cameron's thoughtfulness and at the spectacle of the sunset. It holds such promise, such hope, that I look over at him and there are tears in my eyes.

'I didn't mean to make you cry,' he says, half in jest, half serious.

'I'm not crying, not really. I'm just happy,' I reply and take his outstretched hands in mine.

At that moment, he leans in to kiss me and my tears smudge his cheeks. Then, as the last radiant glow of the leaving day finally relinquishes itself, surrendering into night, Cameron tells me about himself, his life. I already know he has a son of seven, but is separated from the boy's mother. That's about as much as he's told me, but from little things he says now and again, I can sense this is a source of incredible and ongoing pain for him.

'My boy,' is all he says at first, and he wells up. The sunset must have got to him as well. 'His mum left when he was two years old. We moved down to the coast because of the cheap housing, but she never settled. I didn't know what to do. She kept saying it wasn't working for her away from her friends and she wanted to go back, and there was nothing I could do to stop her.

'We'd been married just four years when she moved away, taking Harry with her.'

His voice chokes on his emotion, but he carries on speaking into the blackness. I sit in silence, listening to his heart telling his story.

'So now I see him every second weekend and have him for holidays. It isn't enough – it isn't nearly enough, but it's all I have now. He's the centre of my world. I'm his dad, I should be with him every day.'

There is nothing I can say to this. This is his truth, his pain, the kernel of which is carried by him every second of every day. A bitter harvest.

He is silent for a long time and I watch his profile, set hard by promises unkept, until, finally, it softens and he turns to me. Gently, he puts his arm around me and I lean into his warmth. I feel safe with this man. We stay like this, remembering our solitary hurts, consolidating our loneliness together and I know somehow that this is my future. This is the path I will tread. Our fates are entwined and there is no going back.

Cameron drops me off and it is late. We joke that this has been a big night out for me. We both know something has changed and the present is, perhaps, merely a map of what is to come between us. I kiss away his sadness for a brief moment and then he is gone, and I realise I am no longer alone.

CHAPTER 13

# Patient, Junkie

*January 2009*

The phone rings and rings. I try again, this time putting the phone down too harshly, dialling too quickly. The insistent drilling noise of my call is still uninterrupted.

No one is at the pharmacy. It's 9.30 a.m. and they're usually open at 8.30. Outside, the trees and pathways, roads and lanes are a blank, quiet white. It snowed overnight. Logically, I know the chemist might not open at all today but I have to keep calling, I have to keep trying because if I don't get through to them, I don't know what will happen. It's the day to collect my prescription. I should be there, picking up the next batch of fentanyl lozenges.

I have only two doses left and I'm going into some kind of detox. Every part of me is shivery and uncomfortable. My nose is running like I have a head cold, my muscles are aching and twitching like it's the flu. My skin feels itchy and too sensitive – to the cold, to the touch of the air itself. I can hardly bear feeling the temperature on my skin, so I'm wrapped in a blanket, huddled up and rocking from side to side in my chair by the telephone.

I am finding the symptoms of the drugs harder and harder to conceal from my family and friends. I know this isn't right, but I haven't a clue how to solve it. I know, in the small part of my 'normal' brain which isn't clogged by the nullifying effects of the opiates, that spending my time chasing away the delirium tremens (better known as the DTs) isn't a great way to live, but I am too ashamed and frightened to tell anyone.

I have been calling the chemist since 8 a.m., knowing he wouldn't be there, but calling anyway. I have to do something to pass the minutes which feel like hours as the last traces of last night's final dose leave my quivering body.

Every morning I wake up like this now. It's awful, absolutely horrendous, and yet I can't do anything about it. I am in pain, I need pain relief to have any quality of life, yet this constant battle to top up the drugs in my system leaves me exhausted and scared. Plus, I have to hide it all as well. I can't possibly let on what a state I'm in.

Unwanted questions start forming in my muddled mind. What if the pharmacist doesn't come? If he doesn't, then the assistant can't issue the meds and what will I do? I'll be in full detox on my own here. I'm frightened. I rock into my terror and pick the phone up again. I feel like Arthur from *EastEnders* when he had his breakdown over stealing the Christmas Club money. Same wretched pallor of the guilty.

One last go, I say to myself, knowing I'll keep going as long as it takes. The two lozenges I have sitting in the box, taunting me, will barely last me ten minutes, let alone the next twenty-four hours. He has to be there. I have to get my meds. I am at the point of despairing as the phone rings and rings, when the sudden click of the receiver being picked up makes me jump.

The voice is the pharmacist's. I silently thank God and say hello in my brightest voice, hoping he won't realise how crazed I feel. I can hear myself talking in this sickly sweet charming way, asking about my script, as if it's of hardly any consequence, like I'm asking him if he stocks haemorrhoid cream. The reality is that I am clenching the phone tightly while sweat pours off me, soaking into the invalid's blanket around me.

My voice is careful, polite, as I ask when my meds will be ready. I know I'm being extra nice because I need that prescription so badly. I need it like I need air to breathe, food to stop starvation and water to hydrate. I need it like my life depends on it. And this need, this all-encompassing need renders me the most charming, affable, compliant patient in the world. And the sound of my near-pleading disgusts me.

'Your prescription is here, Cathryn. I knew you'd need it today, so I came in. You can pick it up in about half an hour. I've only just walked in the door,' he says, before putting down the phone.

I would skip through the house if I could. Thank God, thank God, thank God, I trill. If I thought about things for just one moment, then I'd realise that this man, this kind, caring pharmacist, has travelled along fifteen miles of icy country roads to get to the village, knowing that my prescription was due. I'm sure it wouldn't be an understatement to say he risked his life skidding through virtually impassable roads and hilly lanes to get here, but it doesn't occur to me. I don't think about him at all. All I can think and feel is that they're there. My meds are there. I'm saved.

It takes me a moment before I realise I'm too sick to get to the chemist. Then, without thinking, I pick the phone up again. My mother answers.

'Hello?' She always says it with a question mark.

'It's me,' I say, and without pausing for breath, because I know we'll have to have an actual conversation and I'd have to ask about her, and I'd have to lie about me, I add, 'I need your help, Mum. Would you pick my prescription up for me, as I'm not good today?' I say it quietly, clutching the blanket around me.

There's a small sigh at the end of the phone and I can't tell if it's for me or her. Then she says yes, because she always says yes. Because she's an amazing mum and whatever I ask of her, she always says yes.

I know I'm sending her out on a snowy day. I'm sending my retired mother out in the cold of mid-winter on a snowy day to pick up my prescription. But the craving for the drug is so strong it knocks out everything unconnected to it, like the needs of other people. I know I'm being selfish, but I really am in a state. I hate myself though. I know I am on a path from which there may be no turning back and I can't stop. I really can't stop.

Huddled, with a hot-water bottle at my feet, I sit and wait on the sofa. I luxuriate in being able to take one of the remaining lozenges. I know that a single dose will hardly smooth the roughest edges of this horrible, insistent insanity of craving, but it's better than nothing. I sit and suck. Suck and sit. Some of the sweating stops as the dose enters my bloodstream, but not all of it. I barely notice the individual lozenges any more. I only get any painkilling effect from them when they're taken in batches of three or six.

I watch the path leading up to my cottage. My eyes never stray away from those ten metres of white gravel. At every small movement or shadow that lurches from the roadside I start and then sit back. Waiting. Furiously waiting.

An hour later and she still hasn't appeared. I don't for a moment wonder if she's ok, if she might have slipped on the icy pathways and hurt herself. Instead, I feel an intense fury with her for making me wait so long. That last dose has worn off again, so weak was its effect and I am itching, shaking and starting to puke up my breakfast as the drug withdraws again from my body.

Shuffling over to the phone, I call again. Ringing through to my parents' home with manic intensity. Again, the phone rings out. I pick it up again. Dial the familiar numbers again. I repeat this four, five, more times, until I'm openly swearing into the phone, leaving angry, scared messages on the answerphone.

'Where are you?' I keep asking, as if the silence will curl up into a mouth and tell me. 'Where the fucking hell are you?' I shout, getting louder with agitation and twisted fear. Then I see something from the corner of my eye. I swing round and see Mum's red duffle coat swoop low under the snowy bough covering the end of the path to my door.

Thank God. Thank God. Thank fucking God, she's got a bulging blue and white paper bag with her. A bag with the NHS logo on it. She's got them. I shuffle to the door and open it.

'I need a cup of tea,' she says, pulling off her coat and gloves.

'Mum, thank you so much. I'm so sorry to make you go out on such a crappy day,' I say.

'That's all right, just make me a cuppa and we'll call it quits,' she replies, giving me a kiss on the cheek.

As I pour the steaming water into our mugs I remember my phone messages.

'Oh Christ, Mum. When you go home, please don't listen to your answerphone. I left some awful messages on it. I didn't know where you'd got to,' my voice trails off weakly. I can barely look her in the face.

Why did I go so mental? Am I mad after all, or am I just a vile bitch?

'I'm really sorry,' I say, as if that helps. She looks at me, and I see something in her gaze I haven't seen before, like she's looking at me for the first time.

'Promise me you won't listen,' I plead. Then the moment is gone, the suspicion erased by my manner which is now calmer, quieter, because I know the drugs that my body so clearly can't function without are sitting in a paper bag on the sofa, waiting for me.

'It's ok, I expect you were worried,' she says. She probably wants to believe that.

'Where were you, anyway?' I reply.

'I just decided to do some shopping while I was out getting your meds,' she says, like it's the most normal thing in the world. Well, it is the most normal thing in the world, but to me this feels like a betrayal. Like she deliberately kept me waiting.

I find it hard not to feel angry and a frosty tone comes over my conversation.

She doesn't stay long. My dad picks her up, and she wades back out in her moonboots, lovingly kept from the 1970s. I feel deep pangs of guilt. I keep hurting her, I don't mean to, but I do. And I know she'll listen to the answerphone, and I know she'll be shocked at the voraciousness of my temper. And there's absolutely nothing I can do about any of it.

I ponder this for a moment before the blue paper bag pulls me back to my reality. I drink the last dregs of my coffee, then grab the bag and make my slow path back to bed. The relief is incredible. I know that soon I will feel normal again. With six doses one after the other, the sweats, the shakes, the itching, the cravings and the nausea will fade away like they were never there in the first place.

Later, I'm back on the phone. This time calling the surgery. I have my first session of electro-acupuncture today. It's my GP's way of starting to wean me off the fentanyl. He has been talking about getting this machine which sends electrical currents through acupuncture needles, inserted into various points in the body. He has told me that this method kick-starts the endorphins and has proved useful for people in pain and people on high doses of painkillers who are trying to cut down. I'm hoping the session will be cancelled due to the snow, but no, my doctor has walked in as he lives near by.

Fucking hell. Bloody typical that Mr Healthy walks into bloody work when everybody else enjoys having a day off. I've got to go. He signs my prescriptions, after all.

This is my second attempt at slowly weaning myself off my meds. The first attempt was a disaster. I drew up a chart with Dr M., cutting down by one lozenge per week, but the withdrawal symptoms and cravings became so alarming and the physical convulsions so terrifying that I discarded it. My tally is now thirty a day.

I know this is too much, but my body seems to have adjusted so fast to each increase in dose that I need more and more to achieve the same painkilling and symptom-reducing effect. In the back of my mind I'm wondering where this will go, but the thought scares me so much I squash it with full force. I don't want to think. I just want to be given the drugs I need and to try and get on with living some kind of life. After all, I have a right to pain relief. I buck myself up with this argument and get myself to the surgery.

Once the needles are in place and the machine switched on, my GP has a captive audience in me. I'm propped up on an NHS pillow, lying on some thin white paper sheets on a trolley as he talks.

'I should just stop your prescriptions,' he says with a flourish.

'What!' I emote, barely able to sit up and fight my corner before he launches into his own counter-argument on my behalf. This doctor confuses me, one day playing devil's advocate, the next supporting me with angelic patience.

'If I cut you off, I would be acting like a stern parent and you would then be the naughty child. Do you see?'

I nod with a compliant smile. He signs my prescriptions. I'll do anything, agree to anything, as long as he carries on signing.

'I want you to learn to be an adult and to make your own

choices,' he adds as he turns to leave the room with theatrical timing. Leaving me alone in this room, surrounded by medical equipment, and with steel needles vibrating in my feet and ankles, feeling rather bewildered. I don't know if I'm meant to agree with him or not. And as I don't know that, I'm now not sure if I'm being a child, adult or parent, and what does it matter anyway as long as I keep getting my meds.

I sit and wonder for perhaps half an hour. The needles finally stop shaking. I don't feel any different. In fact, I'm starting to get the first inkling that I need another dose, so I want to get going as soon as I can.

But I need to wait for Dr M. to return, so I sit in silence. The clock ticks, the doors open and close in the corridor and, eventually, he walks back in.

'I'm drafting a letter to the Substance Misuse Service (SMS) to book you an appointment,' he says, staring at me, waiting for my response.

Now I'm really confused. What was he saying about being parental?

'Ok,' I say. If it's anything to do with the NHS, I reason with myself, then it'll take weeks or months for an appointment to come through. That gives me some time to think about cutting down. Yeah, I might even have started doing it myself by then, I decide, so I smile and agree.

My GP looks pleased, which means getting my next prescription from him shouldn't be a problem. I can always start cutting down myself. I'll do it tomorrow. I'll cut down tomorrow.

And I believe it, I really do.

CHAPTER 14

# Saying No

*September 2009*

The concrete walls are lined with posters which shout from the walls: End Domestic Violence, Stop Rape, AIDS: Don't Die Of Ignorance. The shock of being greeted by their graphic messages almost makes me turn round and walk out of the Substance Misuse Centre. I hesitate, then step through the glass door which has those municipal cross-hatched panels, and walk with increasing unease into this most unfamiliar of places. The appointment came as expected, months after the referral, although I admit I deferred it twice before finally being told I could no longer put it off. Even so, I am not ready for this. Nowhere near ready.

The centre itself is in the basement of a council-owned block with its regulation faceless windows looking down in austere disinterest. Outside, there is a crowd of ten or so people, mostly men, shuffling in the cold morning air, dragging hard on rolled-up cigarettes. I have just walked through them, my gaze held downwards, not wanting to make eye contact with these people, these druggies.

Fear pounds my soul. There is nothing in here for me. I clasp my designer bag and wrap my expensive winter coat, bought on a working jaunt to Las Vegas in my days as a reporter, tightly around me, as if to protect me from these hostile surroundings. Inside, there is a counter to the right which is being besieged by a densely packed queue of people, perhaps twenty of them in total.

They all appear to be shuffling, fidgeting or jerking their way to the front where a young woman wearing a white coat is pouring out a frothy pink liquid into plastic cups. She looks hassled and she keeps pushing back her blonde hair with her free hand. In front of her is a man wearing a hoodie and tracksuit bottoms. He has one of the cups they are all being given, and swallows the contents in one gulp. Another man, this one wearing a scuffed winter coat, tied round his waist with string, pushes to the front.

The scene looks pitiful, pathetic in the true sense of the word. I find myself feeling sorry for these poor men who have to be here, taking that nasty-looking stuff – until I realise that I'm here as a patient too, though I feel I absolutely don't belong here. I shuffle nervously on the spot for a minute, thanking God that Cameron is in the car outside because some of these men look really downbeat and scary.

As I walk hesitantly up to the counter, some of the men look me up and down. I wonder if they think I'm a new member of staff. Ignoring the stares, I ask where I should go as I have an appointment with one of the team. Glancing round the room, I see there is a lift to the left and a door which must be where I have to go. There is a line of scratched plastic chairs against one wall which is also lined with posters. I am told to sit and wait and so I choose a chair under a poster saying, BE SAFE BIN DIRTY NEEDLES. Against the wall opposite me, next to the door, are three yellow plastic sharps bins for heroin addicts' needles. This is like some kind of stinking bad joke – I half get up to leave, but the door opens and a man's head pops round it.

'Cathryn Kemp?' he says.

I nod my response. I literally can't speak. Shock and disbelief hold me mute. I go through the door, away from the concrete walls of the desperate-feeling entrance and into a brighter office, with magazines on tables and even a pot plant. I relax – a little. My heeled boots pad softly on the orange carpet. My head swims a little from the lozenges I took in the car and I already feel tired and overwhelmed. I don't belong here, I keep saying in my head. I can't possibly belong here, can I?

We walk into another room – small and sunlit, with a desk and two chairs either side of it. The walls are blank. On the table is a red file. On the top right-hand corner is my name. I have a file? The sick feeling in my stomach doubles in size and I want to run away. I have a file.

I open my mouth to tell the serious-looking man in front of me that there's been a terrible mistake and I'll just go now and do another reduction programme with my GP, when he speaks.

'We should probably start by you telling me your history,' he says, without smiling. He adjusts his glasses then sits back, waiting for my response.

'Erm. Ok,' I reply, before gushing, 'well, I became very ill very suddenly in 2004. I was in and out of hospital for years, on morphine the whole time.

'Then I nearly died, sorry, a couple of times after procedures I was seriously ill and nearly died and the pain was just inconceivable. I was sent home on fentanyl patches and lozenges. At first I was on a 100mcg patch, the strongest one, which I wore on my arm for three days, then as I started cutting down the patch to 75mcg and 50mcg, I started to use more of the lozenges.

'Then my relationship broke down. I was devastated and somehow the lozenges got caught up in that. I was taking twenty or so a day by then – this is about a year ago. Then my body needed more and more to get the same painkilling effect because it got used to the increased dose so fast.

'Then it went up from twenty to twenty-five, then thirty and now I'm on about forty lozenges a day . . . ' I hear my voice trail off. I look up quickly, trying to gauge his reaction. Should I be telling him the truth? What if this is much more than he has been told by my GP?

He doesn't flinch. Instead he says: 'We don't judge in here. This is why we see you alone and not with your family because we need you to be completely honest.'

I nod. I feel like I want to cry and curl up somewhere dark and warm. I feel scared. I don't know what is going to happen to me. I don't want to be here. I feel panicky. Why doesn't he realise I don't belong here with those people who probably take heroin and crack? He is taking this all far too seriously and that frightens the hell out of me.

'How long have you tried to wean yourself off the fentanyl?' he asks.

I pause. Thinking about it, it has been quite a while.

'About nine months or so – give or take a few weeks,' I say. I now have to concentrate really hard on what he is saying and how I respond because I can already feel the craving starting up again and my hands are a bit shakier, a bit sweatier, even though I had three lozenges in the car during the hour-long drive down here.

Although Cameron has brought me here today, he still has no idea how many lozenges I am really taking every day. Most days, I am taking somewhere between thirty and forty. It is hard fitting them in, in truth, and I find that most of my time is now spent chasing the dosage, trying to keep the amount of opiate in my bloodstream steady, so I don't go into detox too quickly. Even so, I could see he was surprised at me taking so many in the car, but he didn't say anything.

We have been spending more and more time together. He is

very sweet to me, especially as I still can't do much as I'm mostly in bed with the zombie-like fatigue of ME and the pain, of course, the bloody, relentless, all-consuming pain. He took the morning off work to come here today which was so kind. He always makes me laugh and for those moments I forget about all of this, and I forget that my stomach hurts and I can't walk very far. He is a gentleman and the thought of him sitting outside is so comforting, it gives me strength to carry on.

'I know I've got to come off the drugs,' I say and shift uneasily in my seat.

The serious man greets me with silence and a half-raised eyebrow.

'Your GP is very concerned about you,' he says, 'and frankly, looking at your level of painkiller use, so am I.'

I feel a nervous jolt in my belly. My hands are sticky and I have to stretch my neck to hold back the tight feeling of tension.

'Ok, I accept I am struggling to come off the fentanyl, so what can you do to help me?' I say, trying to lead him towards a solution because I desperately don't want to look at my own behaviour too starkly. I know it doesn't look good either way.

'The course of treatment we will recommend for you is methadone. There is another, easier way with opiate substitute Suboxone, but because of your history of pancreatitis, we can't do that with you.'

'Methadone!' I spit out with revulsion. 'You are joking? Isn't that what they give to heroin addicts? Isn't that highly addictive as well?'

'Yes, we do have to warn you that methadone is an addictive opiate and can cause long-term health problems. It is a serious drug, it causes bone cartilage to break down, among other things; but we would have you on a strictly controlled programme of reducing doses to wean you off safely,' he replies.

'Methadone.' I just can't believe it – my head is bloody spinning out now.

Methadone – highly addictive – rots bone cartilage.

You must be fucking joking, I think.

The counsellor takes my silence for agreement. He adds: 'The dose is given at 10 a.m. each day. You will have to get here at about quarter to and line up to be given the dose. You won't need anything else during those twenty-four hours, the dose will be sufficient to take you through to the next morning.'

Slowly, my brain starts to work again. 'So you're expecting me to drive an hour here every day for 9. 45 a.m. to queue up for my daily methadone fix? For a start, I am too ill to drive, secondly, if what you are saying about me is true, then I'll just be addicted to something else and not fentanyl, so in effect, I'll be swapping one addiction for another, and thirdly ... well ... no.'

'Sorry?' the serious, bespectacled, clean-shaven counsellor man says.

I look down at my tote bag, my nice coat and boots and I draw courage. I find a spark of my truth and I say, more firmly this time: 'No.'

I continue, 'If you think I am going to fall as low as those poor bastards out there, then you are very much mistaken. Thank you for your time, but I absolutely won't be needing your services. There must be another way and I am going to find it.'

And with that I get up, grab my bag and I walk out of there, my head high. Once the door shuts beside me and I am safely inside the car and out of earshot, I collapse, trembling and crying. I cry howls of anguished weeping.

When the crying calms down and I can finally wipe the last tears on to my expensive coat sleeve, I realise something else needs sorting. Not caring whether Cameron sees or not, I lunge for my bag and crack off a line of three lozenges. Ripping open the paper

I feel a heady, giddy sense of expectation. Nearly there. Nearly there. Then I free one of the milky white lozenges and draw it into my mouth in sensual reverie. The tears dry, the gasps for air slow, the world spins back to a gentle shudder and my normality is resumed. For now.

We drive home in silence. I am uncomfortable that Cameron has seen me so emotional, even though he is also adamant that methadone is not an option.

Methadone is the kind of thing we read about in the papers, and never in a good way. A burglar who is being treated with methadone for heroin addiction, homeless people dependent on their daily M script. I just can't tally myself up with that kind of desperation, that helplessness. It doesn't occur to me that opiates, whether painkillers or the street kind, are all the same thing and that addiction to one kind is no different from addiction to the other.

Mine is a more respectable fix, I reason; what could be more appropriate than painkillers to treat acute-on-chronic pancreatitis, widely believed to be the most excruciating pain known to human beings. The thing is that for me, it has all got mixed up. And now I don't know if I'm medicating pain or the withdrawal symptoms as they are both so similar. Nausea, weakness, sweating and mood swings are all symptomatic of both conditions, plus the pancreatic pain swoops back with a vengeance the minute the fentanyl starts wearing off, but my GP keeps telling me that ultimately it's made worse by painkillers because the body's natural painkillers (endorphins) simply stop working. Whether it is pain or withdrawal, they both stalk me twenty-four hours a day, and so I keep chasing round inside the wheel, trapped in a place from which there is no clear way out. I just wonder how long I can keep doing this. Neither of us knows what other options there will be for me, or even whether any exist at all.

Two days later, I receive a phone call at 8.20 a.m. It is Dr M. He has been sent an email by the SMS telling him I declined their services. He is angry. I can hear it in his voice. I don't blame him. I have tried many times since I got home to call the surgery and make an appointment with him to tell him what happened, but failed. Every time I started dialling the number, I panicked and put the phone down, calculating it would be at least a week before the counsellor contacted him by post. It seems I was wrong.

Dr M. tells me to please make an appointment to see him today. He has left a space for me in his surgery this afternoon. Now I feel crappy – guilty and ashamed and stupid for not facing this. Of course, he is going to go mad at me and now I have to wait almost eight hours until he does.

Later that day, Mum drops me off at the doctor's. My stomach is tight with agitation. I'm so nervous I can barely say my name to the receptionist. He's going to go frigging mental at me – and the worst thing is, I know I deserve it.

My bravado of the other day has completely vanished, leaving only an echo of feeble pride in its place. My name is called and I have to remember to breathe as I walk into the GP's consulting room. I sit opposite him, dragging my eyes up to his face, reluctant to meet his gaze. I am thinking about the time I lied about my prescription only a couple of weeks ago. Maybe he knows about that as well?

I had told him I was going to Cardiff and needed an extra prescription as I would be away. But I didn't go. I collected the extra prescription and stayed huddled and hidden in my house with the curtains drawn until the day I had said I would be back. I know this is odd behaviour, but I had intended to go. I just didn't make it because I felt ill. I didn't tell him though, and I didn't return the lozenges either. I just sucked them in semi-darkness in visceral illicit pleasure, tinged, as always, with the fear of being found out.

My shame confuses me and everything feels all mixed up

together right now. One crime melts into another and the way forward is strewn with foreboding.

The doctor sits quietly. He freaks me out when he does this. He doesn't speak until I become so uncomfortable with the silence that I blurt out what it is I went for. This time I don't crack. I'm too wary. I want to know what that counsellor has said and what will happen next.

Then the universe turns upside down. Instead of boring into me with his steely doctor eyes, instead of the fight I expected, instead of the justified anger, he says this: 'Do you remember I told you about Provocative Therapy?'

'Erm, yes, I think so,' I reply, still wary, still unsure what to say or do.

'It's a form of therapy where the practitioner plays devil's advocate,' he reminds me, with a kind of sublime detachment.

'Yes, I do remember that now, you did that on me once before . . . ' I say quietly, scared to say more.

'Yes,' he gathers pace with this affirmation. 'And in this situation it means that I'm going to play along with you. I'm going to give you what you want.' He says this with a flourish and turns round to his computer screen.

I can see my name on there. He appears to be writing a prescription.

'How many lozenges do you want?' he asks, warmly, like he is asking me what I want for Christmas.

'I'm taking somewhere between thirty and forty a day,' I tell him (slightly tempered, though I don't know why, as he can do the sums, see how many I'm really taking). 'So it would be good to have enough for a whole week, rather than having to come in every other day to see you . . . ' This sounds weak, I know. It *is* weak, as arguments go. I want the drugs. He knows I want the drugs. So he is giving me the drugs. It just doesn't make any sense.

He doesn't flinch. He writes in 180. I can see it on the screen. For the first time in two whole days, I feel a smile coming on. I can't show him this. I don't want to look pleased, in case he changes his mind. Stunned by his reaction, and my immense good fortune, I try to look serious, like this is perfectly normal and I am allowed forty lozenges per day, no sweat.

The printer next to his desk clanks into motion. A ream of green sheets is expelled by the mechanical chug and I am handed a prescription for six boxes of lozenges as a repeat. Six whole boxes – that is 180 lozenges in total, which is three times my normal repeat prescription. I can hardly believe it. I don't want to breathe or say anything, in case this is a big joke and he is about to take it off me and rip it up furiously.

'Thank you, I'll see you next week then,' I say and back slowly out of the room. Feeling that any minute he will march up behind me and whip the prescription out of my hands.

I take it up to the pharmacy. I hand it in. Again, I wait to be reprimanded. Nothing happens. The prescription is accepted and we chat about the weather.

'It should be here by tomorrow afternoon,' says the assistant and I stumble home, hardly able to believe what has happened. I still divvy out my drugs though, to last me through, in case there is a problem with the script.

The next day, at 4 p.m., I'm back in the chemist where I wait in agonised expectation for my meds to be given to me. The boxes are so awkward to carry that the pharmacist gives me a black bin liner to carry them all home in. We pile them into the bin bag, I hoist it, literally, over my shoulder and I shuffle my slow, decrepit walk back home. Once in, I tip the boxes on to the floor. I feel like I've robbed a bank and got away with it, all at the same time.

All thoughts of giving up the drugs are lost, thrown into the chaos, submerged into the decadence of this glorious moment. There's enough to last almost five days. At least there should be. It won't hurt if I take an extra three tonight as a reward, to celebrate this glorious victory, I decide.

The SMS centre seems a million miles away. I don't need to come off the drugs, I just need to cut them down a bit. After I've had my little extra celebration, of course.

CHAPTER 15

# Going Crazy

*December 2009*

Crouched on the toilet seat, clutching a towel around my shaking body, I rip open a strip of three lozenges and cram all of them inside my mouth. It's 7.45 a.m. and I am sat in my bathroom, trying to be as quiet and as quick as possible. Cameron is sleeping in the next room, my bedroom, my bed, in fact. And even as I suck furiously, trying to get as much of the opiate into my bloodstream as I can, I know that I should be lying there with him.

I can't though. My body is in free-fall. I am sweating hard, the moistness penetrating the towel, which is there partly to soak up the sweat and partly to keep my shivering body warm. I have until 8 a.m. to get six lozenges inside me before he wakes up and discovers my shame. I haven't told him how many I need before my body becomes 'normal'. He is sleeping, far away from this, my stark, painful reality. Six lozenges. I need to take them every morning the minute I open my eyes. I wake every day with the violent craving, the screaming, crazy urges which wrench me out of my sleep and into the cold, wet bed which I have soaked overnight with the sweat of the withdrawing drug. Six lozenges. That's what I need to stop the shakes, to stop the early-morning sickness and diarrhoea, the feeling of grinding my teeth and the desperation. It's the desperation which is the worst. It's like a monster has barged into my brain, demanding the substance, creating utter chaos and havoc until its needs are met.

As the three chalky white pellets melt into nothing, I feel the first signs of calm, of peace. I can feel the moisture on my face, my back, my legs start to dry up, leaving a salty trace on my skin. Three more and I can chuck the towels into the washing machine, then slip back into my bed, our bed. Then at 8 a.m. I can pretend to wake up with him, as if I'm ok and everything's normal and right.

Three more, which I tear open more slowly, the harsh urgency having dissolved with the medicine. I have to take them together again, I haven't got much time now. It must be five to eight. As the seconds pass, a warm sweetness seeps through my mind, my skin, my body. The pace of existing, of living and breathing slows right down, like I was moving on fast-forward before. It's like stepping into a hot bath, a sigh of pleasure escapes me and I come round and back into the present where I notice the light from the window hitting the back wall, making angular shapes on the whiteness. There are birds singing in the trees, inches away from the rooftop room which sits level with the treetops. It's going to be a nice day and I can finally begin to appreciate it.

My musing is stopped by the sound of Cameron shifting in the bed. I crunch the last part of the dose and quietly unlock the door. The towel finds a new home in the washing basket, along with several others from last night. I have a strategy for all this: I have a towel under my head, on top of my pillow as my head and hair are saturated every morning. I have a towel under my sheet and one wrapped around me, whatever the temperature. If I don't do all this, I wake throughout the night in the cold, dank, sweat-ridden duvet which entwines my legs in its tortuous, serpentine clutches.

I have just enough time to creep back into the room and settle back into bed, this time with neither towels nor shakes nor any of that torment. I place my head back on the pillow which hasn't yet touched my skin and I wait. A minute or so later his alarm goes. He moves, then yawns, then an arm stretches out from under the duvet and reaches for his phone. I move against him, pretending I have just woken up, thanking God – or whatever – that I made it back to bed in time. In time to get warm again; in time to be convincing.

The mental games involved in co-ordinating all this deceit don't escape me. I know I am a fraud, but I don't know what else I can do. I could not bear for him to see me as I was only half an hour ago. I can barely admit my condition to myself, let alone to another person, especially someone I have been in a relationship with for the past year.

Cameron rolls over with a grunt and puts his arm around me, then resets his alarm for an extra half an hour to cuddle up in bed together. My first feeling is one of panic – how will I be in half an hour? Will the convulsions of the drug leaving be with me then and will he see me as I really am? I pretend I am pleased, I kiss him back when he moves on top of me. I concentrate on not sweating, on trying to forget that the clock is ticking until I can get my next dose. Always the next dose.

My mind feels like it's constantly whirring, assessing when I can top up my fentanyl, when I can sneak away or hide in a room to take my next dose. I have no choice though today. I am not alone as I normally am and I have to stage-manage this waking-up ritual. I know I should be concentrating on this gorgeous man in my bed, but I can't; well, not completely anyway. I still haven't worked out when to tell him, and so I feel guilty and criminal, but also strangely pleased with myself for managing to get thus far with my deceit intact.

By the time the second alarm goes off, I am starting to feel the itch, but it's a distant echo still, so it's not too distressing . Even so,

I am thinking, Please go, please go. What time will you go; the next dose is calling me and I have nowhere to hide.

Cameron throws back the duvet and pads into the bathroom. I can hear the sound of the shower starting into life. I get up, slowly, pulling on my kimono, checking myself quickly in the mirror before heading downstairs. I put the kettle on, feeling feeble. As I sit and wait for it to boil, I stare with increasing longing at the cupboard next to the back door where my drugs sit waiting for me. I pray silently that he leaves quickly. I pour boiling water into my cup, then drag the teabag out, add sugar and stir absently, thinking I have twenty minutes maximum before the craving becomes too much to cope with and I need my next fix. It should be a joy waking up with Cameron, being in a couple – I hardly thought this would ever be possible again – but, honestly, I just want him to go.

Still, I smile as he lopes into the kitchen, my face a masquerade. He kisses me before settling down at the table. I'm starting to feel nauseous again and wonder if I'll throw up. Please God, don't make me vomit this morning. I normally throw up several times each morning; it's become so normal now I barely notice. But today I do. I can taste bile rising in my throat and I swallow it down, praying it will stay there.

I spread Marmite on my toast, but can barely manage a mouthful as even the smell of it sends contractions to my stomach lining. My foot starts tapping with the renewed sensation of wanting, the insistent feeling of needing more which is building slowly inside me. More meds, more drugs, more. My head is buzzing now, like there's a whole nest of angry bees trying to get out. The kitchen starts to disintegrate into my mind and I realise it's begun. The inevitable has begun, and I can do nothing about it. My leg is now shaking softly, but I smile over the breakfast table. Cameron is talking. He's telling me things about his day and I can't hear any of it. In truth, I don't want to hear any of it. Just go, just go, go, go becomes a mantra, invoking the gods of time to speed this up, get him out, bring me back to my meds which are screaming at me from behind the cupboard door.

Eventually, he drinks the last of his tea, oblivious to the internal monologue which shouts into every crevice of my battered brain. It is so loud, I'm surprised he can't hear me. He kisses me swiftly on the mouth, says he'll call me later. I spread a thin smile across my face in response, hoping I look convincing.

He picks up his keys. Any minute now, any minute. My leg is shaking and I can't control it. My body is spiralling into the madness again and my head is way out in front. This is all wrong. It shouldn't be like this. I know that. The truth has dawned, slowly and surely over the months. I know now that I am helpless in the face of the surging tide of craving which is curdling my insides, rushing towards me and washing me away.

I'm panicking now. Cameron says something else and I nod, hoping it's the right response. Fucking hoping he'll fucking go because I can't fucking take any more. Can't wait any fucking longer. I'm boiling with rage now, angry at him for dawdling. I can see he wants to banter a bit more, is reluctant to leave me and I should feel pleased about that, but I don't. I don't care. I want him out now. I hold the door and wave, slamming it shut before he gets to the end of the pathway outside. I know he'll turn his head in slight surprise, but I'm long past caring either way.

My hands a fumbling, juddering mess, I get to the cupboard as fast as I can. Open the door. The packet – the last of the six boxes prescribed less than a week ago – falls to the floor. I sit, slumped on the cold tiles and pull it open, ripping the cardboard package and snapping off three lozenges. Thank God, I mutter to myself, knowing this is deranged, knowing my life is becoming insane and demented. But the sound of the package opening is bliss, second only to the feeling of my tongue curling round the plastic stick with my druggie lolly on it.

It's no wonder that Cameron doesn't take my drugs seriously. He never sees me like this. Out of control. Can't stop, don't want to stop. It's far out of my command now and I have no choice. The drug pulls me to it then spits me out, so I have to keep chasing, keep running with my meds towards the winning line, except that the line never actually appears, and I never arrive. I am alone in the isolation of my chase for the peace which eludes me. But I know that if I keep running, I will get there some day.

And it's ok, I can calm down. I have a doctor's appointment today which means I should get my next prescription tomorrow. And that's as far ahead as I want to plan. As long as I'm careful with my meds today, I should be able to pick up the next 180 lozenges at 9.30 a.m. tomorrow. That means I can have another twenty-two today which leaves me with five doses to get me through tomorrow morning until the delivery. I'm a bit short, but it's ok. With that thought I settle down into myself again.

Heaving myself up into a standing position, I click the button on the kettle and watch as it glows red until, spluttering and quaking, it throws out steam and spits boiling water. I make myself a coffee and pat the pocket of my dressing gown. The two lozenges are there, safe and sound. I can just chill out now, get myself back up the stairs and prepare for the long, slow shuffle up to the doctor's. I have an hour before I have to leave. Enough time to finish the extra doses and gently pull on my clothes. I don't have the energy to wash today; if I try to do it alone, without Mum's help, I'll be knocked out with tiredness for the rest of the day.

Most of my time is spent recovering from the smallest, most pitiful activity. Brushing my hair is exhausting, bathing even more so as it involves standing up, undressing, getting into the bath, washing, pulling myself out, drying myself off and then dressing again, all of which leaves me nauseous, exhausted and thoroughly defeated.

Mum still comes round every day to cook for me. She fills a flask of tea for me to keep by my bedside as there are days when the stairs defeat me almost entirely. She puts biscuits and fruit on my bedside table with my bottles of Creon – a digestive enzyme without which I would be unable to eat at all. The capsules digest my food for me and I will need to take them for the rest of my life. It hardly matters; I am just grateful to have them. Part of the reason I got so thin is because my pancreas simply couldn't digest my food and so I couldn't absorb anything. It took three years to get this wonder medicine prescribed for me, but I got there in the end.

If I haven't washed, Mum runs me a bath, helps me in and washes me, like a baby. I have to ration what little energy I have to complete the simplest tasks. Each time I manage to get up, get dressed and get to the GP's, I end up in bed for days afterwards, trying to recoup the lost energy of exertion. I am frustrated most days. In silent isolation. Alone in my bed. Until now, that is.

Picking up a novel now, I take a sip of the coffee. It's hot and bitter and feels good. I lie in bed in contented silence, reading and sucking. Letting the slow, soft call of the drug bring me back into myself again.

Later, I'm dressed and ready to go. Unsteady on my frail legs, I hobble out of my door. The surgery is close by, literally around the corner from me, but it's too far, way too far. I have to stop and sit down several times before I finally reach my destination and when I get there I am spent, drained, wiped out. I will have to ring Mum to drive over and collect me.

The guilt is always there – I am a burden to my mum. Her life stopped the minute I got this foul disease and she has been at my beck and call ever since. Unpaid. Unassisted by the NHS. She doesn't complain – she just gets on with it, but I am sore for her. I would be dead without her daily care, without her feeding me, and a rage blazes within me at the fact that in these modern times, in the twenty-first century, there is no help for me, for us. The unfairness sears me, licks hot flames of anger which never burn out.

The door to the surgery clicks open mechanically which I am grateful for, and as I tremble my way in, one of the receptionists looks up and smiles. It's the smile of pity which follows me everywhere I go now. I see the look on the faces of family, friends and strangers alike. It's a kind of embarrassment at being confronted with someone so young who is so ill, and has been for such a long time. I can see my presence is unsettling, it provokes the thought that there but for the grace of God ... It reminds people they are fallible too, they are mortal and as vulnerable.

There is an awkward silence and I say my name, gripping the high shelf behind which the receptionists sit in a bid to keep myself upright. There is almost a sense of my illness being a moral or emotional failure on my part.

There are so many theories now about illness, the most fashionable being that repressed emotions create disease, and this irritates me intensely. I am saturated with painful and uncomfortable emotions and cannot help but express them violently and constantly. At home my moods veer between anger and futility, despair and depression, fear and despondency until my family are so scared of upsetting me that they keep a dignified distance.

Then there is the more spiritual theory that illness is God's way of slowing us down, forcing us to take stock and reassess life. While this may be true, there is no glory or peace in dependency, there is no inherent value to suffering per se. It is suffering, nothing more or less. And I abhor every enforced second of it.

The receptionist tells me to sit down and I struggle to a chair. The world is spinning and shuddering, and I have to wait for my balance to catch up with the movement. When my name is called, I heave myself off the chair and push through the surgery door, where my GP is waiting for me. He motions to the bench-like bed and I drag my reluctant body on to it.

Dr M. taps acupuncture needles into the most sensitive parts of my ankles and feet with what feels like unnecessary force. He's talking as he moves, telling me this treatment has proved successful in clinical trials in rehab in America for helping patients to withdraw more easily from their drugs.

'So that's why you've been sticking pins in my feet for the past few weeks,' I say. 'And by the way, they're really sore.'

'They're meant to be,' he replies. 'This is to get your endorphins working again, remember?' Then he adds, with a flourish, 'Electro-acupuncture,' and I realise I am meant to be pleased.

'As usual, I will attach electrodes to each needle, then you will have control of the machine. This helps to empower you as you will be in charge of the strength of the vibration,' he says, as if this means anything to me at all.

All I can think is that I'll do anything to please the man who signs my prescriptions. I say great, which is what he wants to hear. He hands me the black box with solemnity and I turn the dial. In an instant, the needles jerk into life, vibrating with a low humming sound. The sensation is unpleasant, sore and tiresome. I'm only doing it to please him. Anything to keep him happy. And if that means I have to sit here in enforced surrender, with pins sticking out at odd angles from my feet every week, then so be it.

As the needles hum, he talks. He stands by me and I watch him with eager attention, wanting him to think I'm really listening. Keeping him happy. He says I have to think about going into rehab to get off my meds. I nod, hoping he'll talk and talk and then sign my next script. He says that as I won't go on to methadone, we'd better try and get me into a facility for people like me. People who are addicted to their drugs. I don't fight him. I nod again, I smile and look like I will really consider it.

'Good,' he says, handing me my next green slip, my next 180.

No arguments. No having to fight for it. He just gives it to me, like it's the most natural thing in the world.

Then he tells me he's got other patients to see and he'll be back in half an hour. He leaves and I stare at the yellow walls of the room, holding my pass to the next few days' worth of drugs in my hand, feeling a huge sigh of relief gently escape me. The memory of the time spent with Cameron the previous evening has already sunk deep into the outer reaches of my emotional universe. I have my script – and that's all that matters.

Later on, at the pharmacy, I hand over my prescription and start to walk off towards the door. The chemist calls me back.

'We didn't expect you to have another lot of fentanyl so soon. I'd better call the surgery and double check this is the correct dose,' he says and picks up the phone.

My heart freezes, I stop dead in shock.

'Yes, yes, ok well, if that's what the doctor has signed. Thank you, anyway.' The chemist puts the receiver down and looks at me. For the first time, I can see it – the seed of suspicion is sown.

'Everything ok?' I say, gulping down the tremors in my voice.

'Your meds will be ready at 4 p.m. tomorrow,' he replies, before adding, as an afterthought, 'I thought it was a misprint.'

Before he can say any more, I turn round and pull open the door. If I could sprint home, I would. Something has changed, something isn't right. They are looking at me, not as a patient who needs compassion, but as something else now, something I cannot bear to name and something I know I can never face.

CHAPTER 16

# Secrets and Lies

*New Year 2009/2010*

'You are an addict. You are addicted to your drugs. You are a drug addict, Cathryn.' The GP's voice rises to a crescendo and I hear someone who sounds very like me screaming back.

'I am not a fucking drug addict. I am a desperately ill person, I am in fuck-loads of pain and I need these drugs. That does not make me an addict. How dare you, how bloody dare you.' I am definitely shouting. As my voice gets louder and louder, I am aware that there are people in the next room waiting to see the doctor, but it's as if they are in another galaxy. A universe where things make sense and normal life exists – because it doesn't in here. But actually, I don't even care that they can hear every word I'm yelling.

It is the end of December 2009 and the surgery has sent out a double prescription of everyone's medication to cover its closure over the Christmas holiday. Except they didn't double my fentanyl prescription, so I rang up in a panic, demanded to see my GP today, filled with the fear that I'd be left with no painkillers over Christmas. The idea of the surgery being shut for any length of time terrifies me, anyway. I hate the thought there will be no one there in case I get ill, have a pain episode or need more of my meds.

I hobbled in to the surgery seething, barely functioning I was so upset, and by the time I was ushered into the consulting room I had lost my sense of self. My pride and my dignity were somewhere deep inside my box of lozenges and I really didn't care what I had to do to get what I needed. Things had gone a bit wrong, though.

I remember standing up, holding my head in my hands and pulling my hair out in rage. I remember standing, then walking a frenzied path round and round the room, past the trolley covered with its thin layer of paper and NHS pillows, past the computer and printer and the pile of green prescription slips ready for printing, past the obs machine and shiny kidney bowls and sachets of plastic tubes and strange spatulas and cotton wads, then past the locked cupboards, back to the two chairs facing the doctor's desk and then round again. I was walking and pulling my hair and shouting. Then I was crying. I definitely cried in there – and all because I was not given an extra dose of my drugs.

'You have to get off these drugs. You are taking more and more and your own efforts to wean off have all failed. When are you going to realise you are addicted to them?' He does shout this time. He is standing up. His face is almost as red as his jumper. Part of my brain, one of the bits that feels light and woozy, even though the rest of me is in a fight to the death, thinks that he should try wearing different colours. I'm sure the red doesn't suit him; maybe it even fuels his anger. I can see his rage and not my own. Mine is mercurial, shifting in intensity, moving in and out of focus, until I latch on to it again. I find it, and I ride it home to victory.

'I am not a junkie. I need my meds and you cannot leave me to go into detox on my own over Christmas.' It is my trump card. He's signed the Hippocratic oath; he can't just leave me in the state I know I would be in without my drugs. I might even die if they are taken away too quickly, though this is speculation on my part.

'Ok,' he says, his voice deflated in defeat. 'I will sign this prescription for 240 lozenges. That is eight boxes of lozenges, eight boxes, Cathryn.'

I nod. The room spins. The floor shakes underneath me. I grab for the chair and sit down. So, eight boxes, I think to myself, that's just over five days' worth – just enough to see me through the holiday, though I will need to make an appointment early on the first morning the surgery reopens. Still mentally making notes, I watch as the GP changes the amount for my repeat to 240. This sends a thrill through me, undershot by sheer relief at having secured enough to last me through the dreaded festivities.

I am taking forty-five lozenges a day now and have been for a month or two. We have already gone through the process of applying for NHS-funded rehab and been rejected. Now, as the printer churns out yet another of my slips, Dr M. pulls out a letter from his desk. He hands it to me in silence. I take it, but the words are fogged up and keep dancing in front of my eyes. I blink and take a second before reading the word 'refusal'. I don't have to ask. This means I have lost my appeal against the NHS rejection. I am shocked, then within a split second I am relieved. I didn't want to do it anyway.

I just can't imagine living without my fentanyl and now, surely, I won't have to. If I can be helped to cut down then maybe, but I just couldn't live without it, at least that's how it feels right now. My moods change and swell round the confines of my cottage with oceanic force. One minute I am determined to face this crisis of terrible dependency which is wearing me down, and the next I am lurching into fear of the drug being taken away.

I ask the doctor why I have been refused. He says it is because I am not offending and I am not homeless. We look at each other and a sharp shard of truth pierces my blurred vision: I'm in the shit and I don't know what to do. The glimmer dies.

I reach for the green slip – my beloved, my hated green slip, my path to sanity and insanity – and get up. Slowly, I walk to the chemist and deliver it. He makes no comment this time. He tells me he'll have it ready tomorrow in one of his larger black plastic bin bags. I go home.

The key turns in the lock and the shaking starts. The appalling DTs which begin in my hands and shimmy in cold waves through my body. Have I eaten today? I can't remember. I feel sick and cold, so maybe not. I haven't had a bath for days now either, so maybe it's time to do that as well. I can feel my hair is a mess and I'm not wearing any make-up. I'm wearing the same jogging bottoms that I wore at the doctor's three days ago when I collected my last prescription. I hope vaguely that no one noticed, but the stares and feelings of others are like droplets of rain on a duck's waxed back. They don't penetrate; they hit, they slide and they vanish into the sea of my despondency and disconnection.

My mind wanders. I haven't spoken to Grace or my sister for a while. Are they ok? I muse. Then the thought vanishes and I reach for the cupboard which is reassuringly full of lozenges. Just looking at it gives me comfort, even though my waking and sleeping moments are a symphony of misery, chasing the withdrawal symptoms of the opiates with increasing and constant regularity.

Come to think of it, I haven't spoken to anyone outside of the chemist, surgery reception and my GP for days, apart from my mum, who still comes in daily. I haven't even had the energy to speak to Cameron. I am hiding away inside this intricate mess of a life which I have somehow fallen into. The strands of my soul which should weave together to create a life have shredded and ripped into fragments so tangled up that I have no hope of setting them free.

I have strange dreams. Sometimes I feel very far away, even

though I am aware of my body's physical parameters, and sometimes I am too close, too raw, too large and pumping this temporal visceral heat which scorches everything it touches. I get migraines which beat inside my frayed skull; hot, pounding headaches which render me motionless, stranded on my bed in a pool of exquisite torture. And sometimes I get moments where the good feeling comes back to me, the connected, blissful, mellow feelings which I have missed now for so long. Now and then they come, they stay for a few moments and then they leave me, leave me to chase after them and keep chasing and keep wanting and keep needing more and more and more. It goes on in endless regularity.

In another of my fevered dreams, I am swamped by huge tidal waves which chase me till I turn to face them in all the drama of their horrifying intensity. I wake up panting, tears on my cheeks, heart pounding as the wave starts to fall, to fall, down on to me, to overwhelm me completely, to drown me. I used to dream about bombs when I was having the repeat attacks of pancreatitis. I shudder when I remember those because I always knew an attack was coming if I had one. I would dream that an unknown assailant had managed to hide a bomb inside the bank or café or whatever location I was in – and every time I heard the bomb go off, felt the force of the explosion, I knew the attack was coming. Now the dreams are all of waves – maybe they're cooling the burning, dousing the flames, or maybe it's the drugs.

I can't keep hold of memories or plans at the moment as they slip from my mind. I lose things and don't find them. I find socks in the fridge, where I have mistakenly put them, and I even tried putting the kettle away in the oven before realising what I was doing. These momentary lapses of concentration – or sanity – really scare me. I feel much of the time like I am going mad. Crazed by the illness, the drugs or a combination of the two.

I hear voices in the house telling me that Adrian is home, but he hasn't lived here for almost eighteen months now. I hear my nephew's voice, as if he is playing downstairs in the lounge. Sometimes I even feel like the house is talking to me. There are strange draughts which appear from nowhere and the beams make peculiar groaning noises, like they're saying something to me. The worst thing though is the devil above my bed. I know it's a knot in the oak beam which is the exact clear shape of the devil. I lie in bed staring up at it, willing it to speak, feeling haunted and cursed and frightened in the night.

I'm up early now every morning because the drugs leave my body after four or five hours' sleep. They wake me by crunching the muscles of my thighs, calves, arms and the length of my back. I come to in a bath of my own cold sweat, sheets and duvet drenched by the overnight detox. I still wear a slow-release patch on my arm, but that does nothing – it gives out such a small amount that my body does not even notice it.

My day is now punctuated by eight lozenges on waking, eight at 11 a.m., twelve at around 3 p.m., six after dinner, then eleven at bedtime to see me through until 5 a.m. when the whole, horrific nightmare starts again. One nightmare into another.

And of course, I can't tell anyone about all this. I am ashamed of it. I lie to my mum, my dad, my sister and Cameron about how many lozenges I am taking. They think I am on fifteen a day, which they worry about constantly. How can I tell them it is edging ever closer to fifty and counting? It would break their hearts.

I carry this great shame every second of my waking moments and it overwhelms me in tidal waves when I sleep. I am hurting everyone I know and love – and they have no idea of the extent. I am in the loneliest place on earth.

If I know I'm going to see a member of my family, I make sure I have had enough fentanyl beforehand, so I won't need to take my meds when I'm with them – although I don't see them much now. I have virtually become a recluse; sat in my empty cottage with the lozenges, my books and the television for company. So sad, so solitary. I even ration my dates with Cameron. He comes over once, maybe twice a week. I rarely let him stay the whole night because it is getting harder and harder to hide the effects of the drugs from him. He is confused at my withdrawal from him – he probably thinks I am about to dump him. I cannot tell him the truth though – his rejection would kill me. So I lie and cheat and deceive all the people who love me.

I get through Christmas – but only by spending just two hours over at Mum and Dad's and making sure that Cameron leaves early on Boxing Day. I know my family were hurt and confused at me spending so little time with them, but I cannot bring myself to explain. I would rather them be hurt than admit this black secret of mine. In my addled mind, I feel I am protecting them, but that is probably a lie too and it leaves me sore and wounded.

It is not until New Year's Eve that it all catches up with me, when my meds are running low. Cameron is staying here with his son, Harry. I am privileged to have his boy staying as it is still relatively early days in our relationship, but even so I spend most of the day itching to take the drugs which I have secreted around the house. I don't for one moment think what would happen if Harry found one of them; instead, I can only concentrate on getting through on the few fentanyl rations I have left.

Cameron falls asleep on the sofa after our supper and I take the opportunity to sneak upstairs to take my dinner dose. I am relieved, and feel the stress of the day easing as I climb each stair. I settle down on the bed, enjoying this luxury time with my evening ritual. I slowly tear off a strip of three and use my teeth to rip open the first lozenge. As I put it into my mouth, I suddenly become aware of eight-year-old Harry standing at the end of the bed. How did I fail to notice him?

He looks at me a while. I freeze, wondering what the hell he is going to say.

'What's that you've got? Is it a lolly?' he asks, all innocence with his questioning gaze.

'It is my medicine,' I reply. 'I am very poorly. Do you remember Daddy told you?'

He nods, and as quickly as he locked on to me, he's off. Artlessly absorbed by something else, something he is colouring in downstairs.

And at that moment, the facade, the denial, the theatre I have carefully constructed to justify all these painkillers cracks in two. Splits wide open, leaving me naked and vulnerable in the prison of my dependency. The horror of my existence is exposed in the face of this childish curiosity, and I realise I cannot lie any more – at least not to myself.

My cravings for the drugs, my agitation until I get them, my bullying anger at the doctor and his receptionists, my lies to my family. It all unwinds and settles at my feet. Suddenly, I know this has to end, but that I am trapped – all at the same time. The purity of this child's trust in me has shown me to myself in all my corrupted pride and vanity.

I need help. I desperately need help.

CHAPTER 17

# Rock Bottom

*January 2010*

The ink smudges and smears across the paper as the words, scrawled in spidery trails, bloom in the fresh tears I am weeping. I am writing a note which I will keep hidden under my pillow from now on, just in case.

Just in case I overdose in my sleep. Just in case my beleaguered liver gives up the fight to detox this powerful drug out of my system. Just in case I don't wake up. I know I am stretching my body to breaking point as I am taking such massive doses of fentanyl – somewhere between fifty and sixty lozenges now each and every day. That is many times more than the upper NHS limit in twenty-four hours. How the hell am I still alive?

I hate these white lumps on their plastic sticks. I hate them with a vengeance because they rule everything – and without them, my physicality becomes a shivering, puking, craving mess within hours. They rule my life, my thoughts, my fears and worries. I permanently shake now, my hair is falling out in clumps of thin, bedraggled tangles, my skin is grey and my eyes are dull and desperate. I can barely walk at all and am completely confined to my bed except for the slow, painful walk to the surgery and the chemist every few days to get my prescriptions (although mostly now my mum takes me there as I am so frail). My repeat has been set at 240 lozenges per script for a couple of weeks, and as I lug them home each time inside a bin liner, the cycle continues.

Day in, day out. I have nothing except for the drugs. I can feel nothing, see nothing, do nothing. Only the drugs and the withdrawals: the turbulent dementia of memory loss, the itching tremors, the slurred speech and the demons which hover and crouch around me.

Sometimes I see them out of the corner of my eye. They look like a knot in the wooden ceiling beam, but they leap out at me, claw at me. They are there. Sometimes I can hear them breathing, when it is quiet and dark, when the traffic noises outside have stopped and everyone is in bed or watching TV. I can sense their long, spindly fingers reaching to touch me and I cry out to stop them. My voice breaks the delusion, but they come again before long.

I have to suck on a lozenge pretty much all the time now; I am chaining them like I used to chain cigarettes, but that was a long time ago. The tears roll down as I keep taking the drugs, one after another, because I hate them and I want to stop, but I know I cannot. Their grip is too strong, too powerful for me. This opiate is taking me to my death and I can do nothing, except let it.

And so I cry tears of self-awareness and the revulsion that brings. I cry tears of terror because I simply do not have the strength to stop, so cowed am I by this drug, beaten into diabolical submission. Yet, in spite of knowing this, I must take them still, as I lurch between morning and evening, at once praying it will all end and desperate, in case my drugs are taken away. I am paralysed by conflicting emotions and thoughts. One after another. On and on and on.

My hand shakes as I write. The tears have started again, but I barely notice them as I am always crying these days. I look at the note. It's like the script of an old lady whose hands have been ravaged by time and illness. It says, simply: 'I love you all, and I'm so sorry.' It isn't much. Pretty brief really, for what could well be my suicide note. It would not be intentional though, this time.

I can't write any more because the guilt and shame have risen like bitter-tasting bile to the back of my throat and I have to stop so I can breathe. I sign my name, then fold the note in half. I slip it under the pillow, so that if anything happens, it will be found by someone. I know that someone could be Cameron or, more likely, my mum.

I am so scared I am going to die. I know that the amount I am taking could easily kill me, could easily lead to the situation where my family would find me dead in bed. Yet even knowing this, I cannot stop. I love my family, but I *need* my drug. It is the dark, horrifying truth. It sickens me. It tortures me. Yet I have to keep taking the painkiller because the effects of not taking it are so severe, so frightening and so all-consuming.

I don't want it to end this way, but I can't see how I am going to get out of it.

Tonight I am alone as I ease my legs on to the mattress. Pulling the duvet over me, a lozenge in my mouth, I pick up a book. It has been weeks since I could read a word though, and instead I stare blankly into space, grateful that for once there are no shadows from my demented psyche, no wretched visions to torment me.

Tonight I am calm. I am, at least, prepared, in case anything goes wrong. I stare for a while longer, but the weight of staring, of being awake and alive is too heavy. And so I turn, switch off the light and lie back on the pillow. The pillow which holds my love underneath it. The pillow which holds my head until tomorrow. Please God, until tomorrow. I pray I will see it.

Then sleep comes.

CHAPTER 18

# The Cut-Off

*February 2010*

'You're an addict. I am cutting you off.'

I glance down at my expensive boots, as if to check that I am still ok, still 'normal'. In the silence that follows those words I hear the end of the line. The closing scene of this worn-out dance is being played out now between me and my GP.

I feel sick. I bend over, retching with shock.

'I'm cutting you off,' he says again. Then the curtain falls and the stage goes quiet.

I have been fighting savagely for the past year at least, but I am too tired and defeated to fight any more. Instead, I surrender. I give in.

It is the end, and my head spins, so I clutch it tightly, rocking slightly, my lips wet and parted to allow the spit to fall in slow abandon to the carpet. A blue carpet. The same pattern as Mum's.

Then I realise where I am and what is happening and all I know is that I've fucked up big-time. I've fucked up so hugely and I can't for the life of me work out how I got here. I feel sick again, but even as I heave forward once more, I am calculating how many lozenges I have got and how many more I need and how long till my next prescription, and then I retch again, covering one of the blue swirls with foul-smelling liquid.

Dr M. tells me I have one week left of my prescriptions, then he's stopping them. No more fentanyl, no more painkillers. 'I cannot justify your use of these lozenges to my partners in the surgery any longer. February the seventh is the last day I will ever sign a script for fentanyl for you,' he says. He is looking at me kindly, but his voice is firm.

This is the end. What the hell do I do now?

I stumble home. If I could run, I would, not caring what people think. I shut my front door hard behind me and lean into the reassuringly solid wood. My head is burning and I feel giddy and weak. Grabbing a strip of three lozenges from the cupboard, I head upstairs, lie back on the soft pillows, a novel in my hands, a lozenge in my mouth. I close my eyes. My mind is a blank. I cannot see the way ahead. I wait for the drug to calm me a little before opening the book, settling into the afternoon, hoping it will all go away.

It doesn't.

Instead, time starts ticking down. Each day will bring me closer to oblivion.

I have to find a rehab clinic and book it today. I have to put my cottage on the market to raise money to help pay for treatment. These things that seemed so outrageous, so outlandish are now the only obvious solution. I have to sell the cottage – the home I have spent my entire working life earning money for. It is the sum total of my old career – and now it has to go. I cannot afford to be sentimental though, to wail at the gods at the unfairness of it all. I have to get on.

Opening up Google, I type in residential rehab. A brutal-looking place in Kings Cross comes up first. It has a mental-health unit and specialises in domestic violence and rape. I start again, this time putting 'private rehab' into the search engine. I click on the top entry. I scroll through pictures of a farmhouse, a nice-looking bed and rolling countryside and I see the word 'secluded' – but none of this matters. What matters is that it says they deal with prescription addiction. I read more, save the search, then go back, typing in more words, checking out more places. The rest are all about crack and heroin though, street drugs which have nothing to do with me, I think.

I go back on to the site. There's a phone number, so I dial and leave a message for the director of the London branch, Elaine. Half an hour later, she calls me back, quotes me a price and books me in.

The seventh of February 2010. I am to arrive at the rehab clinic headquarters in London at 8 p.m. on 7 February. This gives me time to pick up my last prescription, have a leisurely drive to London and start my detox with a full bag of fentanyl. Does any of that make sense? Not at all. But it's booked. I know that if for one minute I actually start to think about all this, I will freak out, lose my heart and mind. So I don't.

Instead, I calmly pick up the phone and call the local estate agent, making an appointment for the next day, then spend the next few hours tidying up as much as I can and absolutely not letting myself think about losing this place I love so dearly. This little home has been my sanctuary throughout the worst of the latter stages of my illness. It has sheltered me inside its 250-year-old walls and helped me hide the ravages of the drugs and the debility from the outside world. It has harboured my secret life, and now it has to go. How symbolic.

Then it happens. The feeling that I am losing everything grips my stomach and drags me down. I crouch like an old sage in India and trace the marks through the wooden floor with my fingertips.

I have to say goodbye to most of the things I hold dear and I do not know how to do this with any dignity.

For the next few days, after the estate agent has been and gone, I retreat back into my TV and my drugs.

Finally, I break the news that I will have to go into rehab to Mum and Dad. They are agog. They sit opposite me at the kitchen table, staring at me like they've never met me before.

'We had no idea it had got that bad,' is all Mum can say.

Dad looks like I've just stabbed him in the chest, so wounded and frail all of a sudden. 'But I've never touched a drug in my life, why would you?' he manages, eventually, looking at me in naked disbelief.

I don't know what to say, how to answer. But before I can summon up a reply which might make any sort of sense to this proud man who made good for himself and his family, and who has never done anything illegal in his life, my mum starts speaking.

'Actually, Cathryn, I knew,' she says, not looking me in the face. 'When you left that awful message on our phone. It was then I realised you were in far deeper than you were admitting to; you sounded like a druggie, you were out of your mind.'

Her words slice me in two. She knew.

She listened to that message. She heard my screaming-banshee words which still send chills through my soul every time I remember them.

I have hurt them so much. I want this to stop now. I can see my hands are all shaky and trembling in my lap, and my back is beginning to droop. I want to be fit and strong again. I don't want to be a cripple any more. Selling my house is the least I can do – I must get better because I cannot bear seeing the look of pain, of hurt, of strangeness on my parents' faces.

She listened to that message. And I will go to rehab for that, and that alone. To purge this demon from me, to slay this beast which has devoured my pride and my love for everything that is good in my life.

I am crying, Mum is crying, even Dad is tearful and together we hold each other. They could so easily have judged me and turned me away, thrown me out of their lives, but they don't. Instead, they hold me like I'm something precious, to be saved and loved, and my heart bursts out of my chest, breaking over and over again in the deep swell of my love for them.

I call my sister that night and her reaction is much the same. Then I call Grace and my ex and lastly, I pluck up the courage to call Cameron.

I am convinced he will dump me at the end of the conversation, but I know I have to face whatever music he chooses to play at me.

'I have to go to rehab,' I say, not wanting to prolong the moment with small talk. I want to be clear and truthful and tell him things as they are. I have to start coming clean.

'I cannot get off these drugs by myself, and my GP has said enough is enough. He will stop signing my prescriptions on February the seventh and so I have booked into a rehab in London and I am selling my house. I will have to borrow money from my parents to pay for the treatment in the meantime.'

There is silence at the end of the phone. I should've done this face to face.

The silence goes on, and I wait, wondering how much longer before he says goodbye forever and puts down the phone.

'I knew something was up,' he says finally. 'You're always sucking those bloody lozenges and I keep finding them hidden in places around the house.'

His voice sounds relieved, like he has been worrying or not

wanting to confront me about this and he can finally be truthful too.

'Yes, I've been secreting them everywhere, in all the little hiding places. You're going to have to help me flush them all out and get rid of them all before I go into treatment,' I say, thinking he's going to ditch me any second now.

'Ok,' is all he says.

'Ok?' I say, my voice rising with the question. 'Does this mean you're not dumping me, or you're just going to help me and then you'll dump me later?'

'I'm proud of you,' he says, quietly. 'It takes a strong woman to face what you are about to face, after everything you've been through so far. It makes me love you more.'

He has told me he loves me. Having just heard the worst possible admission to a boyfriend ever, he has told me he loves me. I think he is the greatest man to have walked on this earth, and I tell him so.

'This will be hard on both of us. I don't know what state I'll be in after the detox. I may be in terrible pain or distress. I may not be myself at all . . . ' My voice fades off into uncertainty and the fear of it.

'I'll be with you whatever happens, even if you are a junkie,' he jokes, knowing he is saying the previously unsayable.

'Will you move in with me today?' I say. Suddenly, I know I want to be with this man and not be apart any longer. I have been holding him off, keeping him at arm's length emotionally because I was so ashamed of who I was becoming and everything I was hiding.

Soon, I hope, I will be free to start learning how to love him.

'Please move in, I don't want to not live with you for another day.'

'Ok,' is all he says, and that evening he arrives with two large bags filled with socks and pants.

And it couldn't be more perfect. When he knocks this time, I make it down to the door. We look at each other for a few seconds, and I am still wary, not ready to believe he really means it about us staying together.

Then he hands me his bag and simply says, 'Put the kettle on, then.'

I smile as I put the bag down on the sofa and head into the kitchen, telling him this is the first and last time I'm being his servant, while he ducks into the house – and into my life.

## CHAPTER 19

# The Girl Who Takes Too Much

*7 February 2010*

The car headlights swoop round the corner, onto an expensive London street. Cameron stops the car and puts on the handbrake before slowly turning to me, or the wreck of me. I am rocking in the passenger seat; I am whimpering a soft sound of terror with a lozenge lodged in the side of my mouth.

'I can't do this, I can't do this, take me home.' I chant the mantra in hostile bursts, barely pausing for breath.

'You have to,' is all he says and I know this to be true.

Reluctantly, grudgingly, I get out, wrapped in my warmest coat against the bitter cold. I knock on the door which has no sign outside to indicate this is a rehab clinic. It is all very discreet.

All very expensive, I should say. I tear away the thought of how much this will cost my parents because I could use that thought alone to justify running away, even at this late stage, as I stand on the threshold of the clinic.

The door opens and we are ushered into a pleasant lounge where we are asked to sit and wait for the admissions counsellor, Anne.

Anne arrives in minutes. I am grateful, as soon the pinpricks of the sweats will start and I will need to think about when and where to take my next dose. Cameron squeezes my hand to reassure me, then leaves the room. Once he's gone, Anne asks some routine questions, clarifying my age and address, then asks how much fentanyl I am currently taking.

I gulp back the nerves and tell her it's somewhere between fifty and sixty lozenges a day. I see her hand falter as she writes the numbers in her notebook. She doesn't comment though – she just tells me which room I'll be in and where to find it.

Gratefully, we make our way to my room which is on the first floor. There is no lift and already I feel beaten – on the verge of collapse. Cameron half-carries me and brings the luggage up and we both drop on to the double bed which sits in serene, plush splendour in this most strange place.

He looks at me, and I can see he wants to go. He's as uncomfortable as I am in here. I don't think he can really believe what's happening – I certainly don't. I tell him to go, but I can't quite let go of his arm. We look at each other in anguished silence before he unravels himself from my grip and gets up. I want to demand that he stays, but the words won't come out and he kisses me for the last time. His footsteps are heavy on the wooden stairs, each one confirming his departure.

Then I really do collapse, on to the floor, sinking into the carpet where the sobs come for what seems like hours. Eventually, the last shudders – of what? – of grief, a little loneliness and a lot of fear leave and I wipe my wet face.

Opening my suitcase, I find a poem tucked between the layers of clothes. Cameron must have written it just before we left. It is a sweet, yet fortifying piece, praising my courage, my steely nature. I almost think he must be talking about someone else.

I put my clothes into the wardrobe, then I take out one of the three boxes of lozenges I have with me. I open it and pull out a line of three. That will keep me going for now, I think, sinking back on to the bed, desperate for relief, for that courage Cameron so lovingly saw in me.

An hour or so later, there is a knock on the door. The woman who let me in is standing there and asks me to give her the drugs I have on me, so she can lock them away in the safe upstairs. She says it is for my safety as there are no locks on the residents' doors and anyone could try to come in and take them, but it feels like control to me and so I only show her the packet I have already opened. Amazingly, she takes my word for it and I give her the box which now contains twenty-seven lozenges. She thanks me and says goodnight.

It is gone 10 p.m. and I should try to get some sleep. I have no idea what is in store for me tomorrow and this uncertainty sits heavily on me. Clutching my illicit lozenges, I hide most of them inside a Boden washbag and take out three more. At least I have these. At least.

As I crawl back into bed, I hug the white duvet around me as tightly as it will go and, despite my best efforts, the tears come fast and furious, soaking my cotton pillow into the night.

After only a couple of hours' sleep and a shivery, frightened night, the dawn comes. With it, the need to get up and get showered and dressed. This takes me an hour as I have to crawl across the carpet and sit on the shower floor as the water hits me hard, waking me into this nightmare.

Wrapped in towels, I crawl back to the bed and wait another hour for the energy to dress myself, feeling weak and pathetic like a small kitten. Eventually, I make it downstairs and force down some cereal. I am told that we will be having a meeting before I attend the 9.30 a.m. meditation group.

Several people arrive and seat themselves around me. I am introduced to the clinic owner, to Elaine (who I'd spoken to on the phone), Anne, the counsellor I'd met the previous evening and one other person – a young woman, whose name and position I miss. It immediately becomes obvious that the owner of the clinic very nearly didn't take me on as I am taking so much fentanyl. He is scared I might die during my detox; either through overdosing on my existing meds or from the effects of the withdrawal symptoms.

When Anne tells him how much I confessed to taking daily, he thinks he has misheard. He looks so earnest (they all do, in fact, with such concern on their faces) that when he turns to me to clarify this, I can only whisper, 'Sixty.'

'Sixty?' he asks, one eyebrow raised – whether in shock or horror, I don't know.

'Sixty,' I say again, with more emphasis this time. If I'm going down, I may as well do it with courage.

Sixty. There's a finality about it. And I have the feeling the stunned silence is hiding their urge to laugh this time. Someone whistles. A low whistle.

'Jesus, it's a wonder you're upright. That amount would floor an elephant.'

It's the clinic owner. He's looking at me like I'm an alien from another planet. I stare back. Too late for shame. I've admitted how profoundly I've fucked up. Suck it up like I have to, I think. It's not as if I'm hiding anything or lying to them.

Actually, I feel that some of the group don't believe me and I don't know why. Later, when they start organising my drugs for the next few days before I go down to the treatment centre in the depths of the English countryside, I realise they think I'm lying to get more drugs out of my GP. Elaine rings him and they have some difficult conversations. He refuses to supply the drugs, saying it's up to the clinic to pay for whatever I'll need during my detox as they're charging me nearly five grand per week.

He may have a point.

Elaine tells me there's nothing she can do and I'll have to pay for my drugs.

This amounts to nearly a thousand pounds which I do not have, so I call Dr M. myself. I apologise for whatever Elaine has said to upset him and ask him direct: will he supply the drugs or do I have to find even more money, borrow more off my parents, throw more of my dignity down the drain?

'It's not as if the NHS is paying to detox me off the drugs they prescribed for me,' I say.

He signs the prescription.

I call Mum, she goes to collect it and then faxes it to the chemist. Job done.

At 9.30 a.m., I am pointed in the direction of the morning meditation group in premises just across the road.

Four people troop in. I am already sitting in one of the plastic chairs which are placed in a circle in the tiny attic room. Anne, the counsellor for today, comes in and says good morning. She's wearing a black suit which makes her look intimidating, corporate even. There's a thin guy with a hoodie on, age indeterminate, a girl who looks Greek with luscious long dark hair and layers of clothing covering her slim frame and an Asian guy in a pin-striped suit. And there's me, huddled and self-conscious in a furry winter coat, trying not to acknowledge I'm here.

We're asked to say how we feel. I have absolutely no idea. It seems others have the same problem identifying their own mood. Anne hands out a chart with a 'feelings wheel' on it. I almost snort out a laugh then, as the man wearing the hoodie picks it up, saying he has an uncomfortable sensation in his stomach/solar plexus area. His name is Will and this feeling apparently corresponds to anger. That feels like it makes sense to me. I don't bother looking at the physical symptoms of suppressed feelings as everything hurts. I see 'joy'. I don't know why I say joy when it comes to my turn. I think I'm being sarcastic, but as each person in the circle introduces themselves by saying, 'I'm ... and I'm an addict', and then my turn comes and I say the words, 'I am Cathryn and I am an addict' for the first time, the tears start spilling out of my traitorous eyes and rolling in floods down my cheeks. And momentarily, I do feel joy. Like I'm not the only fucked-up loser in the world. Like I'm actually accepted by people who are the same as me. They are all nodding and smiling at me, like I've joined some sort of cult and it all feels very odd and unsettling. As quickly as I think the thought it passes though, and I'm just back to being the scared, crying, angry girl again. Sorry – woman. I keep forgetting I'm thirty-nine and I really should've sorted all this out by now.

Today it's Will's turn to tell his story. To start the therapy, Anne tells us that we are all the same emotional age as the day we started using.

Will laughs. 'I'm seriously emotionally retarded then,' he says. 'I started stealing my dad's booze at the age of six.'

Some of the group laugh with him. I just feel pity and sadness – for him and for all of us in this small, incongruous room.

Will goes on. His voice wavers with uncertainty as he speaks. He first blacked out at the age of seven, first smoked weed at the age of nine, then got into pills, coke and smack from eleven onwards.

There's more nervous laughter in the room. He's hit a nerve. And not just in himself. I am a six-year-old boy, he says and he starts to cry. We watch in uncomfortable silence, feeling like we're intruding on something private and secret, taking in the horror of his past.

Will eventually continues telling his story. He tells of his dad lying unconscious on the smelly, lousy sofa. The TV blaring through the night in the dingy council flat that was his home. His mum left before he went to school, just upped and went. He hasn't seen her since. School was a passing phase. He didn't spend much time there, choosing instead to skive off with a mate and a big bag of weed. They'd smoke through the days and nights, the flat blacked out, the curtains shut and his bedroom door locked. Hidden away in an internal world of paranoia, it was the only escape from his grim existence. They'd smoke till the bag was gone. He was still just eleven years old.

His mate would play hardcore house music. Will took to it like a drowning man.

He was a drowning boy. He started DJ-ing, later making it big in the underground music scene. We sat in horrified silence as he described the clubs he went to, filled mostly with men, faces covered with balaclavas or bandanas, eyes glittering in the pitch black. Thumping, banging noise, jagged garage, sharp and frenzied. Scoring drugs, lots of drugs, the music pumping. Scoring pills, coke, smack, crack, anything, anything. Some carried guns, some home-made weapons. Knuckledusters, machetes. There was always someone who got hurt. It was like a jungle, he says. A beating, seething, heartless jungle. Everyone suspicious, everyone paranoid.

My heart beats faster just listening to him. Spellbound and scared for him. So much hurt, fear and pain in one person's life.

He got respect. He became an underground DJ. Machetes, gunshots, knifings – and still he went: for the high, the adrenalin kick, for the thrill of surviving each time he played a set.

Then he plays a tune. Clicks a button on his laptop and the sickening urgency of his world fills the room, like the panicky, racing moments before a heart attack. The vocals are otherworldly, disjointed, pleading for the listener to stay.

Never let me go. Never let me go.

When it finishes, we sit, stunned. Amazed this person is alive, has survived the unhinged world of the grotesque, twisted fantasia he inhabited. How do we fill the space with words, with meaning? We sit. We wait.

The spell is broken by a knock at the door. Someone's asking for me. I step outside, feeling confused. Which world am I in?

There's an urgency growing in me too. It has been two hours since my last lozenge. I'm starting to get the craving, the fidgeting, relentless need as my drug starts leaving me. Never let me go. Never let me go.

'Hello,' I say down the phone. I sound strange, distant even to myself.

It is a man's voice. He is the chemist the clinic uses. Elaine is there with him and has given him my name and number.

'Your prescription is for far too much. Do you realise the NHS limit is eight lozenges per day?' His voice is brusque and it grates against the rawness of the moment.

My humiliation compounded, my nerves jangling in confusion, I choke back some kind of sound, of disbelief maybe – doesn't he know where I am?

I reply slowly. I have to force myself to be calm and polite, measuring each word in my mouth before easing it out. 'Yes I am very aware I am overdosing and I am also aware that if I had stuck to the NHS maximum, I would not be in rehab.'

It's the pharmacist's turn for silence. Elaine's voice, saying something unintelligible in the background, breaks the impasse. Suddenly, I feel vulnerable, weary, hunted.

She takes the phone.

'I just wanted to make sure you understand you are taking too much,' she says.

At this point, I would like to ask her what the fuck she's

playing at, but I don't have the energy. Instead I tell her I'll see her back at the clinic with the medication. Incredulous, I put down the phone and feel a surge of anger I'm unable to express. It turns to tears. I go back into the room. Anne asks if everything is ok. She can see I am in a state.

'I'm the girl who takes too much,' I say. There's a slight pause.

'So am I,' says Anne.

We look at each other and I laugh. I can fucking laugh. I can laugh at that stupid bitch, Elaine, who, as far as I'm concerned, is making such a mess of things. I can laugh at the ridiculous conversation with the ridiculous chemist. I can laugh at myself all angry and victimised. I can laugh at it all. And it feels good.

I drift out of the session on a cloud of revelation. I can be myself, whoever that is. I may have no idea who I really am or what I really like or dislike, but at least I've got some time to find out. The idea that I can actually decide my feelings and thoughts for myself seems utterly, deeply, profoundly revelatory.

The world expands and I move to fill it; the thoughts in my mind start breathing, the feelings inside my battered body shift and swell.

Nothing will ever be the same again.

Within minutes, I'm back down to earth though, as my hands are starting to shake and I'm having trouble holding my mug of tea. It's time to top up. I smile my excuses and make it up to my room. Nausea is coming in waves now. I try to ignore the trembling in my pathetic body as I fumble around in my suitcase for the lozenges I've held back 'for emergencies'. I'm not due for my next dose from the counsellors for another half an hour. Too long to wait. Far, far too long, when each second of craving takes on its own distinct shape and size. The feeling is punching at my brain. Even opening the packet takes too long. Too long. It's a risk, but I take one lozenge. Don't want anyone to get suspicious and realise what

I'm doing in my room. Don't want anyone to twig that I have my own secret stash of lozenges. A secret stash, just like Will had in his ripped-apart childhood home, just like all the others. This is my little secret stash for times like this when it all becomes too much to cope with. I congratulate myself on being incredibly practical and efficient.

Sinking the chalky white lolly into my gums, the world suddenly makes sense again. I'd bury it in there, if I could.

I'm sick in the head. I know these are damaged, dangerous and sick thoughts, but I have them all the same. Sometimes I dream of being on a drip again. Sometimes, at night, I get flashes of the plastic tube which ran from the fentanyl or morphine cylinder into my arm. Sometimes I can even feel the needle still in my arm, permanently keeping my vein open. Receptive. Passive. Submissive. And I know it's fucked up, but I miss it.

I miss the simplicity. The drug that I needed, straight into my body. The drug that killed all the pain and took me out of this realm and into another; a shadowy place of spectral light and undamaged calm. I'm really sick, I'm mentally ill. I just want more fentanyl. More and more fentanyl. Always, always more.

I have to shake the thoughts out of my head, and then I feel sick, really sick, and I make it to the sink just in time. The gleaming white porcelain is splattered with the contents of my stomach. This is so normal to me now, I hardly notice as I wipe away the dregs of breakfast, clean my teeth again and head back downstairs to wait in obedient quiet for my next dose in twenty minutes.

By the time evening falls, there's a new patient. He's quiet and friendly, introducing himself as a chronic insomniac.

I didn't know that was an addiction. I say this and he nods, like no one really understands and he doesn't expect them to. I've noticed here that people introduce themselves as their problem. Hi, I'm Cathryn. I'm addicted to prescription drugs. Hi, I'm so-and-so. I'm an alcoholic, a gambler, a sex addict, a binge eater, a depressive, co-dependent ... the list goes on and on.

'We're all fuck-ups,' I say.

Gillam, the new guy, laughs. 'So what's happening?' he asks.

'I'm not really sure yet,' I say. 'This is my first time in rehab.'

'This is my third time, and I'm guessing it won't be my last.' He laughs as he says this. I look at him with amazement. How do these people afford this, I think. 'This is my first time and it has to be my last,' I say quietly. 'This has to work or I'm dead.'

In the silence that follows, I'm not sure who pities whom the most. Him or me? Me or him?

'Do you want to borrow a DVD?' he eventually says, awkwardly.

Glad he's sidestepped my answer, I nod and we go to his room. It is smaller than mine and doesn't have an en-suite. It's prettier though and has a vase filled with pink flowers on a vintage cupboard. My room feels more like a faceless hotel room.

'It's nice in here,' I say.

He smiles and opens a drawer. It's filled with films, some of which haven't yet been released. This man has proper money, I realise. That's why he keeps bouncing back. All of a sudden, I'm grateful I've only got this one chance. Once I'm done and off, I never want to see these rooms ever again.

I pick a comedy. 'It's been pretty short on laughs here, so far,' I say, grimacing. Gillam laughs.

'Borrow as many as you want,' he says.

He's ok, I think as I head back to my room. Then, making sure the door is shut and there's no one walking around in the corridor outside, I scrabble through my washbag in the bathroom. If anyone comes in now, I'm just looking like I'm about to shower. I feel the hard plastic edges of the lozenges and breathe a deep sigh of relief. They haven't found out.

Thank God. Thank God.

The sneaking around, unwrapping the meds and arranging the lozenges under my duvet in case anyone comes in unexpectedly, only enhances the final pleasure. Everything becomes my slowing heartbeat. The room softens, the edges blur, my focus goes soft and sweet as the drug walks its slow, delicious path through me. I sigh as my hand goes to the DVD player, switches it on. The film starts. My world stops. Night falls.

And I am gone to a place I don't ever want to come back from.

CHAPTER 20

# Sweet Danger

*9 February 2010*

As I'm forcing down a slice of toast with Marmite in the kitchen, a counsellor I haven't met before comes in. He's wearing a pin-striped suit and looks like a corporate lawyer or hedge-fund manager. He looks out of place in here. Next to him, I feel shrunken and ugly. I must look pathetic. He's kind though, asks me how I am. I don't reply. I don't know how to.

He carries on talking, telling me I have an appointment with the clinic GP today to see if I'm physically able to embark on my detox. This makes me nervous. Any reference to my old hospital time or illness puts me on edge. I know I'm very frail and disabled, but I don't want to be told I am. I nod, then make my way back upstairs.

Once inside my room, I quietly nudge a chair in front of the door for extra security. Then I take out six of my saved lozenges. Unwrapping them, I feel the illicit thrill of my secret. I take them into the bathroom, in case someone walks in. Although I hardly care about anything or anyone else right now. I care only that my drugs are safe in my coat pocket. I care that I can sneak up here to take them. I'm a liar and a cheat and I don't care. I just need the relief that these drugs afford.

Cameron rang last night and it was torture hearing his voice all the way from my cottage. He is there on his own, without me, and I have a huge hole in my heart just thinking about him there. A hole that needs filling – like the place that always needs filling with the drugs.

Later, at the doctor's surgery, I sit dutifully as blood is taken from my pock-marked arms – the scarred relics of my hospital days. I'm strapped up to a heart monitor, my blood pressure is measured and my abdomen is kneaded and prodded.

As I submit in passive surrender, I feel again that fear which still clutches tightly to me somewhere inside. The fear that I'm not ok. Fear of hospitals and nurses and tests and diagnoses.

I'm momentarily taken into a flashback, a random memory of a doctor turning up at my bedside when I'd just been admitted, apologising that she'd taken so long to bring the 75mg pethidine injection, seeing the impatience of acute pain written all over me. I remember trying to be polite while counting the milliseconds until the needle entered my vein in a blissful marriage of pain relief and oblivion. Am I to blame for this drug addiction? I ask myself, not for the first time. I had the most painful condition known to humans, according to several of the surgeons who saw me over the years. I *needed* all that blessed relief from pain.

Then I remember asking a nurse in one of the A&Es whether I could have less morphine as it was making me sick. She said my tests had come back and I had 'rip-roaring' acute pancreatitis. 'You'll need this,' she said, as the needle slid under the surface flesh and into my bloodstream. 'You are very ill.'

Then there was another time – I was rigged up to a morphine drip, one where I could click a button and the drug would be delivered straight into my vein. I was in charge of my dose. Yet I remember gritting my teeth for hours in pain, refusing to click the button because I didn't want any more drugs. I remember the nurse coming over. She told me off. Told me to start using the button because I was hurting unnecessarily.

The memories cause my palms to sweat involuntarily, I breathe deeply to bring my mind back to the room, an itch of perspiration forming on my back.

Then I realise that I'm being told I can put my clothes back on. A curtain is pulled back and it's time to go. One of the counsellors is waiting for me outside the room. It is the woman from the first meeting whose name I didn't catch. She looks up from an old copy of *Hello!* magazine as I signal it's time to go.

As we get in a cab to go back to the clinic, I thank her for coming to wait for me. She looks at me oddly, and it's then that I understand she's there to stop me running off or trying to score. I would laugh at that, except the joke feels more like it's on me. Does she know I've never bought an illegal drug in my life? That I am shamefully ignorant of the slang around drug use, the cost or even the effects of most drugs. And I wouldn't have a clue what to do or where to get it from. She mightn't believe me though. I'm starting to realise that most of what I say is taken to be a lie, an untruth. After all, I'm a drug addict, apparently.

Actually, I do remember now that I took half an ecstasy pill once on a trip to a club; a big night out, some time in the early 1990s. And I also remember smoking weed a few times at art college. It was practically the rule to do something there. Still, I've never knowingly met a dealer, though I had my suspicions about one particularly rough ex-boyfriend. But it was so long ago. And I was so laughably naive. I still am. And yet, I'm told the clinic has never had anyone on as many opiates as I am in its whole twenty-five-year history. A badge of shame, which doesn't make sense to me yet.

We get talking and this woman with beautiful big eyes, who is both my prison guard and protector, tells me her story. Her name is

Elena and she is so matter-of-fact about having been a junkie, I have to hide my shock at what she's saying. She says she was a heroin addict for two years as a young woman. She was put on a methadone programme in a clinic in Australia in an attempt to wean her off street drugs, but within weeks she was back in trouble, working as a shop assistant by day and injecting heroin by night. As she speaks, she pulls up her jumper sleeves, revealing a mass of zigzag scarring running up her arms. The jagged track marks and infected scars from the years of injecting with dirty needles have mutilated her skin. She says she has the marks over other parts of her body as well. Her drug abuse took her to dark places, none darker than the moment in hospital when she was told she risked having a leg amputated due to infected scars.

She says, 'I didn't care about the scarring or the thought of losing my leg. It had no meaning to me. All I could think about was my next hit.'

I greet her words with silence. Not knowing how to respond, I look at her lovely face. I think I can see the empty, haunted place behind her smile. The echo of her past stays with her still, as does mine, though in such different ways.

As she tells me her story, I can feel that desperate energy behind her words. I can feel it because I have it too. That thought makes me uncomfortable and I shake my head to get rid of it as Elena talks.

'I begged my parents for help, even though I didn't want to stop using. They put me in rehab and it took a while. It took several times, but I did it. I got clean,' she says with finality. 'And here I am,' she adds, a faint smile on her face.

Her skin has a grey tinge, the other visible remnant of her days spent injecting, and looking at the black kohl applied around her eyes, I think that she's beautiful in a dark way. She has this dangerous, ugly past and her scars are not just physical, she bears the emotional imprint of that time too. I am fascinated and repelled at the same time.

'And was it as bad as you thought? The withdrawals, I mean,' I ask too quickly, revealing my own fears. And I wish I hadn't asked, as she looks at me with blatant pity.

'Fentanyl is the strongest opiate on the planet. We used to buy the patches on the street – they contained enough fentanyl for three days' dosage in an ethyl alcohol liquid. Then we'd open them and drink the contents. It was the best, the purest hit,' she says, looking me hard in the eyes.

'Fentanyl is a hundred times stronger than heroin, and you are taking a lot. An unbelievable amount. It's a miracle you're not dead,' she finishes bluntly.

Then she adds, 'It's going to be hell.'

'Is there nothing I can do or take which helps the withdrawals?' Now I'm panicking. I knew it was probably going to be the hardest thing I've ever faced, but this certainty, this first-hand knowledge is fucking freaking me out.

'There's nothing, Cathryn. You just have to see it through.'

Now I can't wait to get back to the relative safety of my room and hide away from this overwhelming darkness. I want to escape from my feelings and never come back. I want to run away. I can't do this. I can't do this. I want to rock myself safe, and find somewhere else, somewhere where none of this is happening. A place where I have no concept of any of this: addiction or drugs or detox and that sweet danger that led me to here, this place, this moment, this insanity.

Later, I find out I am to see Dr Oscar, the psychiatrist. I learn this as I walk self-consciously into the dining room where five people are already eating lunch. I say hello and force some bread down as fast as I can, to get away quickly. One of the people eating is a counsellor and it's he who tells me what I'm doing this morning. It feels weird that he's eating with the residents, like we're being watched. I nod my assent and return to my room. I keep my small meal down for almost an hour until it comes up in slow judders, heaving up into the toilet bowl. I watch as the lumps of granary bread make their slow journey out of my body, fascinated for a moment by the surreal fact of my descent into all this. I still don't feel like I'm really here. The loo flush brings me back to myself. I clean my teeth. I've just finished when there's a knock on my door. The psychiatrist is ready for me. Am I ready for him though, I think, as we walk down the carpeted corridor.

'You'll never get off that amount of fentanyl,' says the psychiatrist, in his plush armchair. There's a moment's pause for dramatic effect. Then he adds, 'Especially not in four weeks which, if I am right, is as long as you and your parents are able to afford. This is very problematic, very difficult indeed.' He clasps his hands together, wringing them, as if in apology.

I don't know what to say. 'I don't have a choice,' is all I manage.

His fingers are strangely feminine, I notice in fascination, as he nods his chin against them.

'If we can get you down to the NHS maximum daily dose, then we've done our job,' he says, 'which all depends on your pain levels. I really think you should aim at reducing, then stabilising your prescriptions. You may have to accept that you'll be on this pain medication for the rest of your life.'

I don't know how to feel about this. Emotions veering between joy and worry are fighting for dominance right now. My stomach tightens, then relaxes, as the thought of staying on my beloved painkillers hits home.

I try not to smile as I reply: 'You're the expert. I'm in your hands.' And I want to laugh, as if all of this – him, his hands, me and my nerves – as if it's all terribly amusing, which, of course, it isn't.

'There's something else,' he adds with a frown.

Isn't there always, I think, and brace myself for what comes next.

'You won't be able to take the opiate substitute medication, I'm afraid. I'm very sorry for you, but you'll have to do this the old-fashioned way; the hard and dirty way.'

He means Suboxone, or Subys, as I've heard the other addicts in here call it. It's the drug I was told about at the SMS centre – the standard inpatient drug used to alleviate withdrawal symptoms from heroin, morphine, codeine and fentanyl. But I can't take it because it affects the pancreas.

Hard and dirty. No respite, no comfort. And it's further complicated by my finances limiting me to four weeks in here. Most addicts take six months to wean themselves off heroin. I have twenty-eight days.

We draw up a chart with a biro and a large piece of paper. We draw in the lines separating the twenty-eight days. Each day, I will go down by three lozenges. Even when I was trying to detox at home, it was only one a week. And that was hard. Three a day will be torture. Again, I have no choice. I write in the daily total, starting with fifty-five today, breaking each day's reduced dose down into three amounts given at 8 a.m., 1 p.m. and 10 p.m. So tomorrow is fifty-two, the next day, forty-nine, etc. I'm too daunted to fully register all this. Anyway, it won't really start hurting for a few days.

As he looks at the chart, I can see the psychiatrist thinks I won't be able to do this. I can see my failure written on his face. He says all we can do is try it and see. Who is trying here? Who is the medical guinea pig?

'We'll aim to stabilise you, sending you home on the maximum NHS dose allowed daily,' he repeats and my heart leaps again. It's the best thing I've heard in ages. I literally feel my chest thud in delight. I get to keep my fentanyl and it's officially sanctioned. My GP can't say anything to that. Thank God, thank God.

I feel so good that by the time I get back to my room, I am ready to start replying to the texts that have filled my phone since leaving home.

I'm stunned by the messages of support and love from friends and family. I have been so wrapped up in coping that I hadn't read any of them until now. With hope renewed, I reply to them all until my hands ache.

My sister has sent several a day since I got here, Adrian has also sent one each morning before he goes to work, my parents have rung twice a day and both Grace and Fran have sent messages crammed with kisses. I feel loved and not forgotten. Cameron too has been calling – he tells me news about his son, his work, his social life and how much he misses me. I can hear the loneliness in his voice; it echoes back in mine.

As I text my replies, I try to be as upbeat as possible – I don't want them all to worry (even though I know that's impossible). Especially Mum and Dad – they've been through more than enough for one lifetime with me. I want them to know as little as possible about all this and I text my sister to warn her: only happy texts, unless it gets really bad. But I don't want to think about that now. I just want to bask in all this attention and love.

The latest text from my ex moves me to yet more tears. He writes:

> C – this will probably be the hardest 4 weeks of yr life but remember this: U are the woman who walked up Macchu Picchu, u r the woman who drove thro Russia alone, who discovered nuclear bunkers in Lith [uania], who lived an amazin life. This will be ur toughest challenge yet, but it will be ur most triumphant. We r all cheerin u on. And in the midst of all that comes, never forget who u r.
> A

And with that one message, the rehab falls away. I am standing again at the top of the last section of trek before arriving at the lost Inca city in Peru, and I am shielding my eyes from the sun as I look over the ruins I have trekked five days to reach. I can see the mountain tops arch into the hazy background and the stones of ancient civilisations greet me and my strong, fit body, as the sun rises in the early morning of dawn. It is a moment of glory – and I just have to find that woman again and everything will be all right. I have to find her and walk with her through the rest of this. I have to grit my teeth and walk nobly into and through this terrible mess, accepting all of it as it comes with a fortified soul.

The feeling lasts into the night. Another sleepless night, but an ok night, not a lost night. Something has started to repair inside me and the first inkling of freedom comes like a soft breeze into my mind.

The next morning, Elaine tells me it's time for me to make the trip down to the detox centre which is somewhere in the countryside. The GP rang earlier saying the blood tests were ok, my thyroid is a little low and will need checking out at some point, but I'm good to go. Good to go. Don't want to go. Courage deserts me. It's really all happening.

My bags are lined up by the front door. Someone's already packed them. Christ, did they find the secret stash of lozenges I've still got hidden in my washbag? Panicking, I can hear my breathing speed up. No one says anything, which must mean I'm safe. They're safe. Two whole boxes of thirty lozenges for emergencies. Two lovely boxes I have been saving for when it gets really tough. Not four-hour-waiting tough, but no-more-lozenges-to-come tough. They're my safety net and my comfort. And they're safe, thank God.

The driver is running late, so I'm sent to get a massage. I complained this morning about my muscles cramping up, so Elaine has rung the local Thai massage parlour and said I'm on my way. Once inside, I'm led down two flights of stairs. It's dark and I don't like it. The massage rooms are in the basement. I feel vulnerable and disorientated as the masseuse works silently. I count the minutes until it's finished. Then I dress quickly and clamber out into the daylight.

Elena walks me back. I don't thank her this time for accompanying me. We both know why she's here. When we arrive, there's a big black shiny car parked out the front of the mews. Feeling rather ridiculous, I get into the back seat. It's cream leather.

Elaine hands me a bag with my lunchtime meds: twenty lozenges wrapped in clingfilm.

'There's no time to take them before you go; they're expecting you,' says Elaine. I feel incredibly self-conscious at being handed the drugs in front of the staff and the driver. I take the makeshift package and cringe in embarrassment. If it's possible, I hate Elaine even more.

Maybe I don't deserve privacy as I'm such a big junkie, though? But surely I'm entitled to some shreds of dignity? These questions are left unanswered by the universe as the car moves off. They stay hiding in my head, wrapping around the anger I already feel towards Elaine. I could argue the point. But I decide not to. I feel suddenly exhausted and battle-weary.

I don't think I've ever been inside anything this expensive. So this is where the fees go, I think. As the car purrs through affluent London streets, I feel utterly incongruous. I must look like I'm rich or famous, being driven in a limo. And yet nothing could be further from the truth. This is my parents' money, my parents' lifetime of hard work and scrimping and saving which is paying for this ridiculous car, this detox and everything that goes with it until my house is sold.

We arrive in the pitch black of a February afternoon. The

centre looks like a ghost town amid the flatness of bleak countryside. A tumble of outbuildings and barns with a lofty, cold-looking farmhouse in the middle, and no one in sight. Before I have a chance to wonder where everyone is, I am assigned my room – a freezing cold attic, with no bathroom or shower. Thinking of the cost – £4400 a week – I throw such a fit that I am 'upgraded' to a room in the friendlier, warmer patient block with a common room/lounge near by, an en-suite loo and enough space to breathe. I sink down on to the bed, feeling suddenly overwhelmed, realising this room is where I will spend the next month of my life. No boyfriend, no family, no friends. No drugs.

I can't decide which is worse.

CHAPTER 21

# Dawning Realisation

*14 February 2010*

It's 4 a.m. I'm in the place where the monster rises, rears and roars for more fentanyl.

Managed a couple of hours' sleep, but as the drugs from my last dose leave my system, I wake up to the sour smell of my own sweat. Yet again, I'm dripping wet, my pillow is soaked through and my duvet is cold with damp. I smell rank.

I curl up, terrified in the dark, like an animal in pain, shivering with the cold of the early hours and my damp duvet.

The good feelings went hours ago. Dissolved into nothing, leaving behind the gnawing, growing, surging cravings. The restless agitation of need, need, need, unfulfilled. Sweat pricks the cold skin on my neck. Muscles spasm all over my body. Wanting fentanyl, needing fentanyl. The urge grows minute by minute, until it's yelling at me. I'm tossing and turning in this cold bed in this cold place. The muscles in my legs start moaning, then shouting, then they roar. And the muscles in my neck and shoulders, my back and arms join in. The drug leaves and takes most of me with it. I'm left raw and hollow, mad and insane, rocking on my Egyptian cotton sheets which are soaked through, soaked through with sweat.

Four hours to go. Three hours and fifty-eight minutes to go. Three hours and fifty-five minutes before my next package of lozenges. How do I hang on? Three hours and forty minutes. Three hours and thirty-nine minutes. Three hours and thirty-six minutes. Three hours and twenty minutes, three hours and seventeen minutes, three hours. Two hours and fifty-eight minutes, two hours and fifty-one minutes, two hours and forty-seven minutes, two hours and thirty-seven minutes, two hours and twenty minutes, two hours and twelve minutes, two hours and four minutes, two hours and something, two hours and nothing, one hour and fifty-nine minutes, one hour and fifty-eight minutes ... Must stop the clock-watching, must hold on. Because there's nowhere to fall.

I huddle inside the duvet trying to get warm, a large bath towel wrapped around my body, another laid across my pillow. I'm trying to keep some kind of dignity, though it's a wasted effort. I light a scented candle and watch the flame sway gently as the light outside changes, morning comes and eventually, after a night of infinite longing, the knock on my door comes too. As I open my door to receive my morning meds, I'm praying the smell of my night sweats won't reach the rest of the clinic. I'm disgusted with myself and I'm glad no one I know is here to see this. To see me. I'm a wretched creature.

I fall upon the batch of drugs – fifteen in total – like a starving man greets a meal. I scrabble to open the first three lozenges, literally ripping the packaging apart. Each second without them is a prolonged agony of waiting. I push all three into the sides of my mouth. It only takes a couple of minutes for the first waves of numbness to creep through me. Slower now, I take three more, then hide the rest. They have to last me till 1 p.m. and it's only 8.15 a.m. When the last traces of the drug have gone, I throw the plastic applicators into the bin. Now I feel normal. The sweating has stopped. The cravings are locked away until next time. The panic is subdued and chastened.

I'm exhausted. I sit up shivering and pull a bathrobe around me. My body is slow to respond. I feel as though I am moving through thick treacle. I take a shower, feeling the hot water as if for the first time. I wash my hair and feel almost human. Almost.

The shower takes me nearly an hour. Twice I have to stumble out and vomit into the toilet. This is the part I've dreaded for months, the bit of my journey I've run from, but I have nowhere to go now.

Choking up bile and this morning's juice is my present and my future.

It is an effort to pull on clothes and walk the short way down to the kitchen which is close by my block. I have to go outside to reach it and the temperature is hovering around freezing. At least my room is warm though. As I stumble down the small path, I pray there's no one there. I don't want anyone to see me so helpless, so sick.

I am ashamed of the sickness. It's my own doing and now I have to pay for every single lozenge I sucked in wilful ignorance. It is a bit like what they said at the start of every episode of *Fame*: 'Right here is where you start paying ... in sweat.'

I miss my home. I have only been away for seven days, but it feels like weeks, years, decades. I feel I am losing everything by being here. I am selling my cottage and, in the meantime, I have had to borrow vast sums of money from my parents. I am risking my relationship, leaving my new boyfriend alone in the home we may not even have by the time I get out of here. Loss and humiliation sit like hard stones at the pit of my stomach. That, and the constant nausea make it near impossible to eat.

I get to the dining room where breakfast is laid out. There's a girl helping herself to orange juice. We look at each other warily, before saying a reserved hello. I clearly look like shit because she makes some comment about no one being allowed to look miserable in here. I don't reply, though I'd like to tell her if I can't look fucked-off in here, then where the hell can I?

We smile awkwardly at each other, then I spend most of the twenty minutes I am in there trying not to catch her eye. Despite this, she tells me the first group-therapy session is in half an hour and I'll be expected to attend.

I'm at the point of telling her where to go when I realise she's actually trying to be friendly, and she's a lot younger than she looks. It must be something about being a junkie that leaves us all looking old before our time with dark rings around our hollowed eyes.

I thank her, and this time, give her a real smile.

Later, in therapy, she sits next to me and I'm grateful that I'm not alone. It was a real battle to get to the outbuilding where the therapy is being held. Sometimes I wish my doctors and psychiatrists, my family and friends could swap bodies with me for one day, to really know how it feels to be me, and to feel the anger and frustration in each and every faltering step.

Soon, everyone lumbers in. There is a tall man in smart clothes, a shorter, more exotic-looking guy with a foreign accent – he keeps shaking his knee in involuntary shudders, like a nervous twitch. There's a woman who turns out to be Helen, the counsellor, and a man who looks barely old enough to buy illegal drugs let alone be in rehab. He's slouching like he's at college, giving off an air of nonchalant disinterest. I wonder how hard he has to work to pull off that stance.

Helen opens the session by saying, 'Hi, I'm Helen and I'm an addict.' The group all say in unison, 'Hi Helen', then she reads something from one of the laminated sheets we have all been given. It's something about who is an addict. All of us, apparently.

Then when she finishes, the group all say, 'Thanks Helen', and the next person takes their turn.

'Hi, I'm Alice and I'm an addict.' Then Alice, who is the girl from the dining room, reads from her sheet and so it goes round to me.

I feel enormously self-conscious as I say my name and I stumble over the words on the sheet. Something about an inability to take personal responsibility causing my problems.

I don't know what this means and why it relates to me, yet, and so I listen to the rest of the readings.

Helen then turns to Alice and says to her that it is her turn to be 'worked on' this session. Alice seems to retreat further into her chair, a cushion clasped in front of her as a form of protection.

This isn't her first time in rehab, it turns out. Alice refers to herself as a 'fuck-up' and then laughs, but it isn't good laughter; it is the sad kind and my heart aches a little for her.

'I'm an alcoholic. I'm nineteen years old and my life is a mess,' she says and looks down into her cushion, as if it would somehow solve her problems.

'Tell us about the mess,' Helen says and sits back.

We all look at Alice and she blushes scarlet. This is horrible, I think to myself. It's bordering on cruel, making someone expose themselves to the group. Alice speaks, though, and her voice is little. She tells us about her drinking and how she dreams about it at night. She tells us she is troubled at the moment because she has a recurrent dream that she can one day walk into a bar on a desert island and have a drink and everything will be ok. She tells us that in her mind, she knows she is planning her relapse; she has it all pictured in her head, down to the last detail. There is an audible intake of breath, as if she has said something unacceptable or troubling. I understand, though. I had dreams like those when I first went teetotal after the first bout of pancreatitis.

I understand her desires, her pain. I wish I could tell her that, but it is time to listen. Other, more private confessions are told and the counsellor challenges much of what she says.

Afterwards, Alice helps me back to the lounge where I collapse, defeated physically. We talk, and that day, Alice and I form a bond over our mutual fears and troubles. She is studying while in rehab for exams she may not be out to take. She hopes to go to uni, but is terrified of the drinking culture and where it could lead her.

I listen to her fears, but soon I feel exhausted again. I am shattered, so I make my apologies, hobble back to my room, leaning heavily on Alice's arm, and topple on to the bed where I stay for a long time.

Just as the afternoon is leaching away into evening, and just as I am starting to feel like I can go over to the common room, my door swings open (no locks).

Two men in black overcoats walk in. One of them has long hair pulled back into a pony tail. I don't like them. I am scared of them. One stands by the door like a night-club bouncer while the other, the pony tail man, announces he is going to do a bag search. They are looking for any illegal drugs. It takes a moment to realise they mean inside my bags.

Instantly, I'm angry, disgusted that my privacy and dignity are taken so lightly. But I also know I have the two extra boxes of fentanyl hidden inside my suitcase which I haven't yet got round to declaring. That doesn't make me a drug addict, though. It's just I might need them later; that, at least, I'm sure of.

Even so, I feel a lurch in my stomach as I go to unzip my case for them and reveal the green Boden bag bulging with my painkillers. One of the black overcoats takes them without a word. I can feel the atmosphere change palpably. I feel like a prisoner admitting something shameful to a guard. I can hardly breathe as they silently empty my suitcase and handbag of everything, my clothes, make-up, books, everything – even my knickers and bras. I feel totally degraded and exposed as two strangers go through my intimate things. They find some paracetamol, some ibuprofen, which my GP had also given me as pain relief, and my mirtazapine, a mood stabiliser which I have been taking throughout my four years in hospital. No guesses why.

They take that as well. At which point I panic. 'You can't take that, it's important, you're putting my mental health at risk,' I cry.

'You'll see the doctor tomorrow and they'll prescribe you your drugs,' they say as they leave, leaving me surrounded by the detritus of my bag and its contents. An island of fear and isolation in a sea of stuff.

Tears pour down my face as I pick everything up and carefully, as if to make it all better, place it back. Then I curl up on my bed fully clothed, pull the duvet over me and stay like that, trying to be ok, in the foetal position until morning. Too desperate, too confused to move. Blank mind. Blank feelings. Negative space. Until finally, finally I fall asleep, isolated and frightened.

CHAPTER 22

# Black Suits

*16 February 2010*

Two days later.

I am lying on my bed. Head spinning, feeling a kind of churning, heightened anxiety that won't settle down. It's the withdrawals, the withdrawals. This will pass. This will pass. I chant the mantra to myself and fight the tension, fight the nervous hysteria which seems to be building inside my skull.

There is a knock on the door and the clinic owner walks in. He is with Elaine. They are both wearing black suits. This seems so sinister, so threatening. Probably just my nerves, strange feelings, paranoia coming and going.

They scare me. They are scaring me.

The owner asks me how I am doing. I start to answer, but he cuts me off. There is suddenly silence and I realise this is not a social visit. Feels so sinister, so threatening. Like I'm in an Orwellian world and they are the Thought Police. They could be analysing every move I make, every word I utter.

They seem like stern parents. And I am meant to be the child. Drawing my knees up to my chest, I speak: 'What's the problem?'

It is obvious there is one.

'We want to talk about the lozenges that were in your case,' says the owner. Then there is silence as the words form loops and sounds which reverberate with strange clarity. 'We want to search your bags again,' he adds.

I know I am looking at them blankly. I am an addict, apparently, so they can do these things. They can search my bags, go through my private stuff because I'm an addict. A dirty addict. A dirty addict with no privacy.

There is a buzzing in my head and I feel sick. I draw my knees closer to me, hugging myself tight. Keeping myself together. Feeling more sick, I nod my assent and watch as Elaine empties my suitcase.

She takes out everything – my socks and boots, my knickers and bras, she undoes the side pockets, running her hands inside the material. She pulls out my books, my diary, my make-up case, my washbag. Pulling the cord, she opens the bag and takes everything out: the toothpaste and cotton buds, the moisturiser and cleanser, my mascara and eye liner, hair grips, tampons and ear plugs. To finish, Elaine shakes out a Sainsbury's bag and three apples and a packet of Hovis biscuits join the rest of the mess.

We all look at each other. There is an uncomfortable silence before he speaks again. 'There is something else.'

There is always fucking something else and it's never fucking good. That phrase sends a shiver through me, a hollow shiver, and I feel really sick now. My lunch is halfway to joining the rest of the melee.

Still clasping my knees, my arms clenched, everything clenched.

'We don't think you're showing enough withdrawal symptoms,' he says. 'We've been watching you.'

So sinister. It is a police state. I am angry now, really fucking angry. There must be better ways of handling this.

'That's shit,' I say between clenched teeth. I stare at them both defiantly. I feel anger pounding at my temples. I look at Elaine; I feel like hitting her – I feel like slapping her face.

Instead, I grab my diary and read out the first entry: '"Five a.m. I wake up this morning to the sour smell of my own sweat. Yet again, I'm dripping wet, my pillow is soaked through and my duvet cold with damp."'

'Do I need to go on?' I say. This time I'm squaring up. I'm giving them solid eye contact. This time I will win this fucking shitty argument. I read more, I start crying and I let the tears run.

'Is that humiliation enough for you? Is my suffering enough for you, yet?' I say, my voice scratchy and tearful. 'Next problem, please.'

The owner looks uncomfortable. Elaine looks back at me, like she's disengaged. I want to be cruel. I want to hurt her. Am I a monster? I fucking feel like one.

I don't know who I am any more. The nice, pretty meek and mild-mannered girl I was before would never say that. Would never even think that. They want me to behave like an addict. To look like a street addict. But I am not one. I never chose to become addicted. I survived four years of horrendous trauma in hospital, for most of which I was on an IV morphine or fentanyl drip. I left hospital an opiate addict.

I know I said I was an addict. I said it, but I'm not. Anything I said in London or in the group yesterday was only a way of fitting in, I didn't really mean it, I don't think. I can't think, there is too much aggression in the room and it's mostly mine. I won't crawl to these corporate bastards by pretending I am one of them any more.

I know who I am. They won't beat me.

*

Nine-fifteen p.m. I'm beaten. My energy is drained. My muscles are all aching and I feel so tired, ME tired, like I've been run over by an articulated lorry and left for dead in the street. I can barely lift my head off the pillow. Going out into the freezing night to the office to get my 10 p.m. meds seems an impossible hurdle.

The clinic directors said they'd work with me and my Chronic Fatigue when I originally rang the rehab from home. They said they'd make special arrangements. But despite their arrangements I still have to go out into the cold. I don't know why. Probably to make me suffer all the more. Isn't that what this place is all about?

Consumed by exhaustion, overwhelmed by homesickness, I cry fat tears into my pillow. Again. Bunch of bloody sadists, I mutter to myself.

A new patient was admitted last night. He roared up on a huge motorbike in a shiny leather jacket. Made a dramatic entrance. The clinic was a flurry of activity as people dashed out to see the commotion – they are starved of entertainment, so the arrival of this flamboyant character was a cause for some kind of celebration. I kept well away, feeling too brittle to meet this biker. Alice came to tell me that everyone had gone out to look at the bike, but I shrugged it off, murmuring that I was too flimsy in body and spirit to go see. We smiled at that – complicit in our understanding – then she went off to see this man for herself.

Anyway, at 9.50 p.m., I wrap myself in my big, furry coat and pull my Uggs over my pyjama bottoms. Doesn't matter how ill or tired or wiped out I feel, I have to get my meds. Seventeen lozenges tonight. Each day going slowly down. Every day my amounts reduce by three lozenges and each day the doses are given at the same times: 8 a.m., 1 p.m. and 10 p.m.

I make my slow, painful way to the office, situated at the end of my block in an outbuilding. Each time my meds are due, I dutifully knock, then wait for the door to be opened before I go in and collect my ever-dwindling package of drugs. Before I leave, and once I've put the fentanyl lozenges into my large coat pockets, I sign off the dose on my chart – the one I drew up a million years ago in London. I put 'CK' next to the number of lozenges, and every day, my heart sinks irredeemably lower, my body feels irretrievably older and harder and I try to make the psychological shift from plenty to nothing, step by step, reduced dose by reduced dose.

When I get back to my room, I shut the door firmly because none of the residents must know that I carry grade A synthetic smack in my pocket. I must make them believe I take my meds in the office. Then I open them in ravishing ecstasy, brushing away the thoughts that these are the last days of my using. I make sure I put aside one or two lozenges for the harder days to come. I tuck them in the right pocket of my blue coat which is hanging in the wardrobe; there is quite a nice little supply in there now. The fact that any of the patients could come looking for drugs, find them and possibly overdose on them does not occur to me. There is no price that isn't worth paying to slow down the inevitable hell of this detox. So I store them away, worrying more that I will get found out than whether I could do someone harm.

Once settled back in my bed, I can finally forget my day, forget the faces of Elaine and the owner of the clinic, forget the humiliation and despair. It is all ok because I have fifteen lozenges to take tonight, and with them comes blessed oblivion.

Evening again, and Alice has waited for me outside the office, taking the chance to light a cigarette. We're becoming good friends and we're looking out for each other – important when you're surrounded by alkies and druggies and don't know who to trust. I can barely trust myself.

We shuffle back, trailing the cigarette smoke behind us. As we reach the door, it suddenly opens and the new patient stands on the threshold, fag in hand.

'Any of you ladies got a light?' he asks in a loud voice – a voice that's used to getting its own way.

'Sorry, no, I don't smoke. I'm Cathryn, by the way,' I say and smile. His leather jacket creaks as he gives me his hand to shake.

'Mick,' he says by way of an answer, then adds, 'you don't look well, babe.'

I give him a half-hearted smile as I go inside. I can hear Alice give him her lighter and she stands outside with him. They talk, her voice barely audible, while his is sharp with a cockney slant which pins him somewhere between south and east London. He feels like trouble to me, but what do I know? I've ended up in this mess, so I cannot have a clue about what's right and wrong. All the same, my senses tell me to keep clear, keep away. There's a jagged feel to him, something too bright, too loud, too much. I don't even know him, but I can feel him and I don't like it. Alice does though, or she wouldn't be outside in the freezing cold.

In the lounge are all the other residents. Most are slumped around, either texting or talking. The TV is on in the corner, but nobody ever seems to watch it. Apparently, in the good old days there was no TV, no mobile phones and no smoking allowed at the detox centre. It was to focus everyone on their recovery, rather than avoid facing the inevitable past hurts which seem to arise out of peoples' subconscious daily. It sounds brutal to me. Feeling more relaxed now I have my lozenges, I settle down with the others.

The exotic-looking guy from therapy, Alex, is there, his knee still shaking. Every couple of minutes or so he gets up to go outside, light another in a long chain of cigarettes, then two puffs later he puts it out, walks back in and sits down. His knee starts again and it is all he can do to stay seated for that long. I don't know what is wrong with him, but he keeps repeating the same sentence, 'Today, I'm going to commit suicide; I can't live like this any more.'

At first, it is shocking to hear him tell the group that he's going to kill himself. And I see no one reacting to him, which strikes me as unbearably cruel. I cannot believe no one has rushed in to help him. He is saying it now, he is on the phone, and he says it again before reverting to his native Russian tongue. Several times a day, he has bellowing rows with someone on his phone. At these times, he marches up and down the corridor between my room and the lounge, hollering down the phone. After a while, I feel sorry for the person he is shouting at. Later, I find out it is his mother.

We are all fuck-ups. We are all at odds with family or life, we all seem to have troubled lives which defeat us daily. In the short time I have been here, I have heard so much pain from people – from Alex's continual cry of suicide and his desperate constant twitch to Alice's childhood and background, a place of neglect and unhappiness which has culminated in low self-esteem and the alcoholism which haunts her. And my own story, of course, of riches to rags, from life as a successful author and journalist travelling the high seas to a druggie, in rehab, dressed in track-suit bottoms and a hoodie with unwashed hair, no make-up and registered disabled due to the illness. And none of us really knows why we are here. We just want to know how the hell to get out.

The new guy, Mick, finishes his cigarette outside and I hear Alice giggle. The sound disturbs me and I don't know why. Mick walks back in, swinging the door open, making an entrance. I shrink back into the sofa, hoping he won't talk to me.

He sits in the chair which is central in the room, a position where he looks like he's in charge of everything and everyone in here. I don't like him. I don't trust him. He's not the 'normal' fuck-up like the other people in here. To me, it feels like there's something more, something possibly violent in his past. I meet his eyes, then flick mine away, shuddering involuntarily. I remember my door has no lock and I am secretly pleased I have the door wedge given to me by my mum before I came in as some sort of protection.

Alice sits next to him. She asks him questions about himself and I listen carefully to his replies. He is a self-made man, wealthy, feared, strong. In his own eyes, he is a god, except that he's here for his cocaine addiction. He boasts that he was spending 'a grand a day' on his habit. That he hid cocaine around the house where he lives in style with his wife and children. He hid the cocaine and his addiction was such that he gave no thought to whether the kids would find it. He got away with it, the cocaine use I mean, until one weekend recently when he hit rock bottom. He says he blew three thousand pounds on cocaine in one weekend and it was then he realised he had to stop.

He is already calling himself a recovering addict and he's been here less than twenty-four hours. At this point, I find I don't want to hear any more. I gather my things and shuffle off to my room. Mick shouts something to me about being anti-social as I leave and I ignore him. I've seen his type before and I plan to keep as far away as I can. He can't see it himself, but there is a very hurt, very small young boy inside all that shiny armour and I don't want to be around when he is finally let out.

Later, I manage to write in my diary which I still keep every day if I can. The words scrawl across the pages as I am so tired. I can barely hold the pen, but it feels important to chart all this, to see where I have come from, and to refer back to one day if I need to remember that this rehab, these people and the drugs weren't just a bad dream. They are real, very real. The words finally laid to rest,

I ease my head on to the towels kept on my pillows for the dreaded night sweats and I open a lozenge.

Mick, Alice, Alex, the residents and all the loved ones who are out there rooting for me, they all fade away as the calm of the opiate settles me into yet another long night.

CHAPTER 23

# Coke-heads, Porn Addicts, Junkies, Depressives, Anorexics and Alcoholics

*22 February 2010*

We are behaving like caged animals. There is a simmering, brooding feeling in the place today. Watching other residents prowl around the confines of the courtyard, the frustration and anger of being trapped here in posh prison is palpable. I am in the communal lounge. It is like being in an old people's home. There are seven of us dotted around the room. No one wants to be here, but where else can we go? We are addicts, dregs of society.

It feels like anything could happen in here. And very soon, something does. Alex has been circling the room in a kind of demented walk with a half-chewed cigarette in his mouth. He suddenly walks directly to the TV and turns it off.

There's immediate dissent. Mick jumps up and shouts, 'Oi, whadya do that for?' He marches over to the TV, leather squeaking, and turns it back on, this time turning it up as loud as it will go. Alice and I freeze and huddle a bit closer together. We exchange a quick glance, wondering if we can get up and leave now or whether we'll just end up in the thick of something.

The air crackles with the scent of an impending fight. As if to capitalise on his 'success' with the TV, Alex tells us to fucking get off our arses and 'do something', then shouts something in Russian, grabs the packet of cigarettes he was balancing on his shaking leg and marches out, rubbing his hands through his hair, as if trying to control whatever thoughts he was fighting in his mind.

Mick now starts to circle the room, as if deciding what to do next, making everything seem tense and jagged. The rest of us sit in expectant silence, waiting for this latest game to play out. Seconds later, the smoke from Alex's cigarette curls into the room, marking rebellion; his territory under attack, he is fighting back for the colonisation of our room through the smell of burning tobacco.

It is strictly against the rules to smoke near the common rooms. There are many rules here, and depending on how we break them, we challenge our identity and that of our colleagues in here, all fighting for air to breathe and space to feel. All living together in enforced harmony, while undergoing brutal detox and intense therapy. It is a recipe for complete disaster and chaos, yet most of the time our troubles and power struggles are played out in the mundane, ordinary acts of smoking and changing the TV channels. Alex has lit another – he's not giving up his battle to claim our space.

Just as Mick appears to reach a decision and heads for the lounge door, the outside door is wrenched open and Alex shouts, 'Forget all that, come out here and see this.'

We didn't expect that. In our confusion, the atmosphere evaporates, then we hear a woman screaming from somewhere on the country lane which runs the length of our block.

Without hesitation, we all get up en masse and head for the door. The London centre's gleaming black limo is parked up by the gate, looking as incongruous as it's possible to look against the backdrop of a farm filled with junkies. The passenger door in the back is flung wide open and we can see a woman wearing a white jumpsuit and she's waving an enormous bottle of vodka which appears empty.

'You fucking bastards, I'm not going into this cunting rehab, I'm not a fucking druggie,' she shouts.

'You, you bastards!' She's spotted us now, watching her theatre, unabashed. 'You're just a bunch of bloody do-gooders, you're all drug addicts, you must be joking if you think I'm going in there with all those losers.'

Some of the residents are openly overjoyed at this spectacle. As I've said, there isn't much to do in rehab, apart from therapy or more therapy. There's a ripple of laughter, which feels a bit mean, but the sight of this poor woman is comic in a tragic way.

The driver has got out of the car now and is talking to Alex, telling him he doesn't want to get a bottle smashed on his head.

'You should be paid danger money,' I say and he nods over at me.

'She was brought in as an emergency case and literally put straight in the car to come down here. After a mile or so, she got the vodka out of her bag and started drinking. She'd finished it before we arrived. That's some serious drinking,' the driver says.

Then, suddenly, there's a cry. Seeing we were distracted, the woman has got out the other side of the car and has legged it down the lane, screaming as she goes. The driver and two of the male patients set off after her, returning a few minutes later, red-faced, dripping in sweat, saying she managed to get across a field and is probably halfway back to London now.

We laugh, but we all know it's no joke. The woman is fucked. If she survives this drinking bout she'll go on and on and she'll eventually die.

We all know, even though we're laughing, that but for the grace of God knows what, that woman could be any one of us.

The mood softens from the release of tension and something of the tragedy of the car woman sinks into all of us, so that when we arrive at our next therapy session, Charlie the counsellor asks us why we're so subdued – normally we're all a bit feisty at the start of a session, a bit defensive until we get warmed up.

I look around the circle. There is a woman – Amanda – who arrived last night from hospital. She's a new mother but is having a nervous breakdown and has been deemed unfit to look after her child. There are dark purple rings under her eyes, where the sleepless nights and the dementia of childbirth have their grip on her. There is also Derek, who has been here for a few days. He keeps his eyes firmly on the floor and has not yet made any friends. The seats either side of him are empty (and remain so for most of his two-week stay). He tells the group today that he went to some very dark places using internet porn.

Alice shuffles her feet nervously as he talks and I can see her shrinking away from him. Later, she tells me she lives in mortal terror of him creeping into her room at night. He is the next door down from Alice and me. No locks. There are no locks on any but the bathroom doors. We are both rattled by his presence, but I tell Alice he wouldn't dare in here, of all places. But I'm not sure – and I know she isn't either.

A motley crew; each of us sick in our own way. As I look around the room I am suddenly aware of how many conspicuously wealthy people there are in this place. To my left, next to Amanda, is Raol, who is the son of an oil baron in Dubai. He is an alcoholic, but seems as relaxed as if he's sat at home. This isn't his first time in rehab. There don't seem to be many that come in just once, and this doesn't bode well. It is something I have to ignore because I know I can only do this once. There will be no second chance for me; this is the only chance I have, the only time I'll ever be able to pay the extortionate fees. So it has to work. And it is the fear of failing that spurs me onwards through this process. I have no safety net. It is as simple and as effective as that. In some ways, I feel sorry for the magnificently wealthy clients because they have no boundaries in their lives. They can fly off at a moment's notice which sounds like heaven, but to an addict it is the gateway to hell – you escape the shit and land in another pile in another country with the same problems. And with money to burn, they live lives of excess compounded by privilege. Honestly, I wouldn't swap my little life for theirs, not for the world.

Jason, the nineteen-year-old coke dealer from London, who is paying for his rehab out of the ill-gotten gains from selling coke and crack to London's wealthy elite, is slumped on his chair, his practised air of calm looking less convincing in the face of Derek's continuing confessions. Derek is still speaking when Jason breaks the cardinal rule of silence when someone is talking. He mutters something to himself and wrenches back his chair. He gets up and says he's leaving, he can't listen to this and that Derek is a pervert.

Charlie asks Jason to sit down, says that we are all sick people and we all deserve to be listened to. I admire her resilience, her calm in the face of our outrage and our fear. We are all the same – whether it's painkillers, gambling, cocaine or sex, we are all using things to fix how we feel, to avoid facing ourselves and our problems, medicating ourselves against the pains of life, both real and imagined.

There are differences though. Even among junkies, there are hierarchies – things that we decide make us unique in our addictions. There is a subtle but clear set of rules. The first thing we do after saying hello to each newcomer is establish each person's drug of choice. The d-o-c is believed to determine personality types, the friendships made within the rehab and even the chances of recovery. The alkies and the heroin addicts stick together and are known as the sensitive types. The chances of recovery are perceived to be higher for the druggies than for the alkies. It may be just a matter of alcohol being far easier to procure than H, but whatever the reason, many alkies bounce in and out of rehab, or so the perception is anyway. The cocaine addicts tend to be more like the alpha personality – high achievers, driven to succeed. Some accuse them of being egotistical, but we are all hiding shattered self-images, so maybe it's just that they hide theirs better. The coke-heads put themselves first for therapy and, at times, think they are in charge of the group. The smack-heads generally keep their distance – unless the coke-head has multiple addictions, in which case there seems to be more common ground.

The sex addicts are treated with ill-disguised unease, sometimes even by the staff. Elena told me back in the London clinic that sex and love addiction is the hardest form of addiction to recover from. It's easier to log on to internet porn than it is to access drugs or even alcohol. The hierarchies are, of course, a script made up by mad people in the grip of addiction. They are meaningless, yet somehow we all conform to the stereotypes, as if we are trying to understand each other in the simplest way. The suicidal depressives are pitied, then ignored inasmuch as anyone can ignore someone who is living with them 24/7.

I sometimes think that being here is like being a participant in one of those tests they do on TV – like the experiment where a group of ordinary people is divided into guards and prisoners with the accompanying power struggle and left to fight it out. It is a curious alchemy at work in here, just like that on TV, and despite having counsellors around during the day, we are pretty much left to fend for ourselves at night with maybe one member of staff on till 10 p.m., then just a security guard till 8 a.m. It is a long time for a group of crazy, withdrawing junkies to play out the battles witnessed by day. And sometimes it gets scary in here.

Amanda is speaking now, and her voice brings me back to the room. She is pleading with the counsellor to send her home to her baby. Her face is a mask of misery and she is crying and shaking, her head in her hands.

The counsellor is impassive. 'Tell me about the thoughts you have,' is all she says.

Amanda looks up and starts to plead more, begging now. In a minute she'll be on her knees, I think.

'You are addicted to the thoughts in your head,' says the counsellor.

What does that mean? It is sometimes like the counsellors speak another language in here.

Amanda repeats her requests to leave, she wants to see her baby. Her eyes are dark with tears, but there is something else, like there is something blank within her. This pain is confusing. I don't know who is right or wrong any more. My heart bleeds for her, but I know she's one of us. She's definitely tarred by the same brush as the rest of us.

And how do I know this? Because she came to my room last night. Her gentle knock pulled me out of bed and I went to the door, opening it a fraction of an inch, wary as always in here.

'Have you got any mirtazapine?' she asked, no formalities, no small talk.

'What do you mean?' I asked, genuinely shocked by her front.

'I need that drug. If you give me that drug, I'll get some sleep, then I can go home to my baby.' It sounded plausible enough, but I felt unqualified to deal with this, and was also concerned that a patient had come asking for drugs from me.

'I'm sorry, I can't help,' I said, even though I had my night's tablet in my bedside table drawer – it was dispensed at lunchtime, but I take it in the evening.

'Let me come in, Cathryn, you can help me,' she said, this time more insistent, but I felt uncomfortable and I backed off, telling her to go to bed. I said I was sorry and tried to shut my door. Amanda's hand was holding the handle.

'But you're the chemist in here, everyone knows you're not a real drug addict and that you just took prescription drugs. You must have some to spare.'

Reeling in shock, I slammed the door shut harder than I wanted to. I heard her footsteps shush down the carpeted hall and I realised my heart was pumping with anger and something else, something I couldn't define. There was so much wrong with what she was saying, I could not begin to untangle her reasoning. I waited till her footsteps disappeared, then I got dressed again and headed out into the night to find a counsellor. I was worried about her state of mind, but also about my security. People obviously think I've got a supply of drugs in my room. Does that mean I am unsafe in here? I make the decision there and then to stop stashing extra lozenges in my coat.

I am a prescription drugs junkie. I now know this must be true. I didn't want to admit it for the first week in here, but finally the label has got to me and found a home. It makes life easier in here to say it and mean it. It gives me a chance of recovery. How can I keep denying sixty a day? And as a junkie, I relate to all of these people in here in ways so profound and confusing that in a strange sense, I feel I am finally at home, in a tribe of my own.

It isn't a happy thought, however good it feels to relate to people, because we are all the shunned masses, part of the bands of outcasts of a society that worships self-control and despises addiction as a moral failing. We have mostly realised we were probably born this way, born without the normalising brain functions which tell people to stop after one drink, one cake, one drug, one gamble or one fuck, and it is a source of resentment and frustration that the compulsion which overcomes us with any mood-altering substance – be it food, sex or drugs – is perceived as a failure of will when, in fact, it is mental illness in its cruellest, most rampant and destructive form.

Still, the label I will have to live with for the rest of my life sits uneasily on me. My preconceptions about myself are undergoing complete reinvestigation – and, frankly, I don't like what I'm finding. As my acceptance starts to break down my barriers, I find I am softer, more forgiving when I'm dealing with the others in here. I see Alice talking to Mick, sitting too close on the settee, laughing too loudly at his jokes, and even though I wince inside for her, I know she is just lonely and this man is paying her some attention. We all need that, by God that is true.

I have been missing my family and Cameron, and so I am really happy to discover that Mum and Dad are coming this weekend. Cameron will come next weekend, which is something that freaks me out a bit, as I know I will be coming closer to the last ravages of the withdrawal then and I cannot say what state I'll be in. I am still shy around him. I still want him to fancy me, and the thought of him seeing me like this, so small and frail and destroyed, makes me want to cancel him with some excuse. I can't though. I have to risk seeing them all.

I miss my life now, which must be a good thing. All I cared about before was making sure I had enough of the drugs to keep me going, but that is changing. I know exactly how many I will have every day and so I am becoming free to remember the other stuff. You know, the life stuff – like friendships and love and even a faint whisper of a future.

It all seems a long way off still, though. And so I bunker down, getting through each day the best way I can. I don't complain, what would be the point? I just want this done. I grit my teeth, which are already tight in my jaw, as my body takes on a cramped gait all over and I surrender to the onslaught of the fentanyl reduction.

CHAPTER 24

# Trouble Brewing

*4 March 2010*

Four weeks into my detox, we sit down to start yet another afternoon therapy session. We have had a full-on day and we are all pretty twitchy and unsettled.

This should have been my final week at the clinic but the effects of the withdrawal are leaving me too ill to go home yet. I have been cutting down my lozenges daily, as per my bloody chart, and I feel like I am being dragged into Hades slowly, with each excruciating new symptom ripping apart the shreds of me which still remain. My neck muscles are now so tight I cannot turn my head at all, there is a feeling the counsellors call 'snakes in muscles', which is a continual sinewy, crushing feeling moving inside my muscles; my legs, thighs, arms, even my fingers, hands, neck, head and jaw are stretched as tight as a drum, which is being hit repeatedly.

Getting to the sessions is a torment – sitting in them utterly unbearable. Many times, I have to lie on the floor, twitching and moaning just outside the circle, as the therapy continues with no absence of leave, no escape possible. It is sheer agony. I cannot find any words to bring it home, which could possibly shape those sensations into any form, into something recognisable. My body feels like it is dying – and it is taking my sanity with it.

Ebbing away into panics which stay, day and night, formless fears which ride my brain like a charging horse, quivering neuroses, sounds which aren't real, words which make no sense. I am drowning in this withdrawal, drowning and flailing, washed into a dark vortex where I spin and curdle inside. Will there be anything left of me?

I tell the counsellors I am mad now. I am mad. I will always now be mad. How can I come back from this? They look at me with such compassion, and they tell me – I can't remember who it was, was it lovely Charlie? No, I hate Charlie at the moment because she's the one that makes me go to the office for my dwindling meds; maybe it was Helen? Now I love Helen because she tells me she went through detox from prescription tranquillisers and she knows the physical and mental agonies endured. She is kind, she tells me to lie on the floor, with a hot-water bottle. She soothes the seemingly unsoothable parts of me. No, it was the clinic owner, I'm sure it was. Have I drifted off again? That happens a lot these days. Someone told me I am not mad – I am going through a kind of madness, but it is the drugs, it is not me. It is the drugs.

For every lozenge I ever sucked in my stupid little mouth, I am taken to hell. For each and every one. Walking through the shadow of the valley of death, I think they call it. And I still have a week to go until I hit the big, fat zero. Because that is what I've decided to do now – even though the counsellors were aiming to stabilise me on a small daily amount of fentanyl, I'm going for the magic number zero. That place beyond imagining. This is all so hard, so brutal that I never want to have to have to go through it all again. I want to go for it, to hit the zero – come off the drugs properly and for good. I have hopes for the future now. I want to learn how to live in pain and see if I can do it. The longer I spend here in rehab, the more I realise that I want to be free of my prescriptions. Just the thought of going to the doctor, then the chemist to collect a script, leaves me feeling sick and tired. I want this done, finished. Even though I'm told it takes three days of the climactic withdrawal pains for the last of the drug to physically leave my system. So even at the end, there will still be somewhere new to experience, a dragging out of this nightmare.

Today, I am propped up in a chair, shifting every second or two as my muscles spasm and twist. I am hot at the moment, I know this will change within minutes, maybe seconds and I will be cold again, cold enough to shiver and shake, my teeth rattling, my jaw trembling. Then it goes again, and I am back in an internal sauna.

Oh God, I am moaning. I keep forgetting that I am moaning and I have to keep trying to stop.

Our counsellor Peter announces we will work on the coke addict Mick and asks him to pick out someone to play his 'sister' as role play for dynamic therapy. I don't know how I know, but in that instant, I realise he is going to choose me. Oh God, please don't let him say my name.

He says my name.

I look at him, recognising his choice, but also trying to play ball. Though I mistrust this guy and don't like too much interaction with him, I agree, hoping this will be some phoney half-arsed therapy shit which we can all laugh about later, as we often do after more lighthearted sessions.

Mick turns to face me, moving his chair directly in front of mine. Already I feel hemmed in. I am forced to make eye contact, something I don't really like doing with him. His eyes are penetrating, fierce even, but that might just be me feeling ultra-sensitive. I feel like I have had my outer layer of skin removed and I have nothing to hide behind. The air is piercing cold, the draughts even worse, as they are unexpected. I can smell everyone, and worst of all I fancy I can smell myself. I can smell the kind of scent an injured animal gives off, rank with that bitter tang of fear.

Peter starts Mick off, asks him to pretend I am his sister and to tell me why he feels such hurt from his childhood. Self-consciously, Mick begins – and it soon becomes clear there are years of hurts, layers of them – it's like peeling an onion – and they start to flap open and hang there for all to see. I am uncomfortable for him and his exposure, but he carries on. I am starting to feel the pain and the hatred, all understandable, as he describes his childhood. My heart breaks for him, but I am also afraid. He is staring at me so intently, I think for a moment he really feels like I'm his sister and he looks like he wants to throttle me.

Peter finally stops him, and the room draws a collective breath. The counsellor turns to me and says, 'Now it's your turn to respond to his pain as his sister; tell him why you did what you did, why you hurt him.'

I am bewildered for a second. How can I possibly know? I cannot find any words for a moment, but then I realise I have to speak, for Mick's sake, if not mine.

'I'm so sorry,' I begin, hesitantly. 'I didn't realise I had hurt you so badly. I had my life, my friends, my hopes and dreams and my needs and I lost you as I tried to live them. I am so, so sorry,' and with that I trail off, looking to Peter for support. I cannot work him out. I instinctively like him as a counsellor because the work he does with people is challenging and interesting, but now I am part of one of his experiments I am not sure I like it. I know I have somehow been dragged into Mick's drama – probably as a representation of part of his past. Maybe that is why he is so 'off' with me, always digging at me slightly. I obviously remind him of his sister, and I sympathise, but where does that leave me? I shift uneasily in my seat, my muscles are screaming blue murder at me and my mind feels brittle today. I can't cope with this.

Mick starts to cry and we all sit and watch him. We know it is good to cry, especially when the men break down, as some of them won't have expressed any sadness except through anger, for most of their lives. But I am sore at being the 'cause' of it.

He starts talking again, through his tears, and soon his raw grief turns back to anger and he has nowhere to direct his anger but at me, and I have no escape from the release of this pent-up wrath as he is directly opposite and now shouting, crying and raging at me, at his sister. His pain is evident, his hurts are decades old and I feel for him, even as I receive his anger. I tell him I am sorry again, but it isn't anywhere near enough.

Normally, when a session ends, there is a release of laughter or talking as we say the Serenity Prayer, but this time, there is silence. We are all rattled and there is little chat.

When I get to dinner later in the evening, Mick won't look me in the eye and I start to feel something more than unsettled, something closer to fear.

There is no Narcotics Anonymous meeting tonight, so the group is shut in for the evening. The counsellor on duty is not around and the brooding feeling intensifies. I make my excuses and leave the common room and head back to my room, sighing with relief as I shut the door. I sink back on to my bed and cry more tears into my sodden pillows. I am too shaky to take on this man's anger and I feel raw and vulnerable. My mind is also playing tricks on me and I keep thinking I can see spiders crawling along the walls of my room. Now and again, I have to get up, touch the wall to make sure they aren't real. The fridge in the corner of my room is making a strange sound and I keep thinking there is an orchestra playing out of the plug socket. I am confused, alone and sinking in a mental mire, and this time, it isn't of my own creation.

About an hour after I get into bed the music playing in the lounge is turned up to full volume. The centre has a decent stereo and it is throbbing through the rooms in a violent, dark bass beat which is as unnerving as it is disturbing.

The music builds up and up to a crescendo it never quite reaches and I start to feel scared. But after twenty minutes of this brutalising sound, the fear vanishes and is replaced by anger. I throw on a sweatshirt over my pyjamas and go down the hall, which is pitch black. They have turned the lights off, the music is fierce and pounding, I feel sick with it. I reach the door, I open it and inside is black with furious noise. I shout for them to stop.

'Fuck off, bitch,' is the reply from somewhere and I know it is him. I know he has mixed me up into the molten swirl of his hurt and hatred for his sister, and who can blame him after the session today? And, of course, we are left in this shit until tomorrow morning. But I won't be left because I am frightened. I slam the door and head down to the office, half-afraid he will leap after me, try to hurt me. I get there and even though it is only a quarter to ten, there is no one there. Peter has left, so I do the only thing I can think of and ring the clinic owner.

He picks up the phone immediately. I tell him that Peter has gone and there is trouble at the rehab. He calls Peter and sends him back to the centre and when he arrives I try not to look aggrieved. I tell him what is going on and head for my room. I don't want anything more to do with this fucking place. I don't feel safe tonight. I won't feel safe until the counsellors are back at eight o'clock tomorrow morning.

It is the longest night I spend in treatment. All night, my ears are trained towards the door, wondering if he will try to come in. Nothing happens though, except that by six the next morning, when the centre starts to wake, I am broken into pieces.

At breakfast, I take the food back to my room and eat alone. I just want to go home – and the thought brings fresh tears. I am sure the guy is suffering too, and I don't blame him. We are all fucked-up people and trying these therapies on us, then leaving us together in our own mess seems negligent at times.

I cannot go home, though. I have to see this through.

CHAPTER 25

# Coming Clean

*Saturday 6 March 2010*

I can hear the sound of a car turning into the lane outside my window and I know it's my parents. They are visiting me today and I have looked forward to it all week. I have taken special care to dress myself in something a bit more flattering than my usual joggers and hoodie, even putting on a small amount of make-up because I don't want them to see me in the state I am in.

It has been a difficult week. My daily lozenge total is down to five for the whole day – it should've been four, but I begged the counsellors for an extra one as I am falling too fast to that zero. Mum and Dad are also here for another reason – I am in such pain and delirium from the withdrawal that the clinic is worried about me and wants me to stay at least another week, so I can do the final detox at a slower rate. I am sick at having to ask them for more money, but I am also so wretched now that I am within a whisper of not caring if I live or die.

I can honestly say that this last week has been the worst of my life. I cannot move, I cannot speak, I cannot sleep or eat. I can only lie in an ocean of terror and pain as the effects of years of drug abuse tear at my body. I panic all the time that I won't be able to get to the loo, as I have diarrhoea and vomiting pretty much constantly. I have even dragged myself and a blanket on to the floor next to my tiny toilet cubicle, so I can at least be assured I stand some chance of getting to the loo in time. How I think I can hide all this from my parents is a mystery, but I know I have to try, for my own peace of mind at least.

I have one thing that brings me comfort. It is a shell posted to me by Cameron from the beach outside the flat which we are hoping to buy. I have heard that I have a buyer for the cottage and it is time for a new start, a chance to leave all this behind. It cannot come soon enough. I have no feelings now towards that place where I sat in lonely reverie, taking all those lozenges and convincing myself it was all ok. I feel nothing, except maybe an urge to be rid of it, to let go and wash clean my life. A new beginning is what I want now – I just have to get through this. I clutch the grey shell – fragile, yet tough enough to survive posting and the grip of my cold, sweaty fist. The shell is a promise of something – a spiritual connection to my new home maybe, or just a reminder that we are all atoms, all together part of this entire creation.

There is a knock at the door and I manage to say, 'Come in' from where I lie on my bed. I may be dressed in a skirt and several layers of T-shirts and tops, but I cannot get up to open the door. Mum comes in first and then Dad. We say tearful hellos and hug each other, the three of us. Mum brings a stack of cards from friends and family wishing me well, and a hand-drawn picture by my nephew, Freddie. More tears follow before we get down to business. They can't stay long – they have to get back to 'put the chickens away'. It is a long drive to the clinic and visiting is only allowed from lunchtime, so we haven't much time. It is great to see them, even though I know they will be frantic with worry, but there is absolutely nothing I can do about that.

'You're so skinny,' Mum says, and she's right. I haven't eaten a meal for at least two weeks as all food makes me so nauseous I simply can't force it down, so I am surviving on sweets that Cameron has sent me. I can't get myself to the dining room anyway now, I am way past being able to walk. I am in the shit, on every level, back in my sickbed, ambling through insanity, trying to be cheerful.

They have an appointment to speak to Helen and the clinic owner, so they excuse themselves and go down to the office. I know they'll all be talking money. I am embarrassed, but the feeling is deluged under this swamp-like fatigue and sickness and muscle cramps, so even this doesn't touch me like it used to.

'Whatever will be, will be,' I mutter to myself and wait for them to return, all the while clutching my shell.

Dad is the first to arrive back. He looks agitated. Mum follows and she has that look on her face, the one that says, 'Don't upset your father.' I saw it a million times as a young girl.

Dad paces a little around the room and then flusters over his words. The upshot is he has seen my chart, seen how much fentanyl I was taking when I was admitted and he is shocked to the core.

'How could you do this? How could you have been on all those drugs? You lied to everyone,' he says, his voice harsh with disappointment.

I nod my head. What can I say? It is all true.

'We knew you needed the drugs, but we never thought for a minute you were taking this many. I don't understand how you got in so deep, Cathryn. After all, I've never taken a drug in my life – how did I get a daughter who does?'

I never expected my problems to be a reflection on him, but it seems they are. I am. This, I had not expected. I nod again.

'Does Cameron know how many you were taking?'

'No, Dad, and I want to be the one who tells him,' I say slowly.

I can see where this is going. Mum looks stern behind Dad and I don't know if it's me or him that's pissing her off.

'Cameron has a right to know, Cathryn.'

'Don't you dare tell him, Dad. It's my truth, my problem and I'll tell Cameron when I'm good and ready,' I say. If I had the energy, I'd shout.

'If you don't tell him soon, then I will. He has a right to know.' Dad has this face that sort of sets when he decides to be stubborn. His face is like this now.

'Yes, Cameron has a right to know, but I have a right to decide when and how to tell him,' I say, but I already know that Dad wants to do it. I can see it on his face. It is dead set.

'Dad, I love you. I'm so happy to see you, but will you please let me tell Cameron myself?' I say, hoping this will end our discussion which is fast becoming a row. At this point, Mum steps in.

'Albie, we need to talk about the money. Can we just get this sorted out as we're going to have to head back soon?' She's brilliant at defusing him.

Dad nods and we move on. I see Dad is hurt over finding out his daughter is a proper drug addict. It's hardly what every parent hopes for.

I forget that it must be awful for my family – harbouring a druggie in their midst – where once there was a blonde-haired daughter posing for her degree or MA photos with the certificate as proof of her intelligence and promise. What a distance between that image and this woman, in detox: broke and with a history of heroin addiction – because you can dress up fentanyl as a prescription drug as much as you like, but underneath it's no different to smack. It's all the same. I am a heroin addict.

It was hard enough for me to accept – it must be impossible for my dad. All those years of being proud of me and boasting to his friends, all crumbled now into this madness. Things will never be the same again, I can see that now and it saddens me. How I have let them down. I feel a lump in my throat as I listen to the upshot of their chat in the office.

I am to stay another two weeks, give or take a couple of days. I am on five lozenges today, and this will go down by one a day starting next Saturday. Ground Zero will be Thursday, 18 March and I will have to leave two days later. I will be leaving at the climax of all this, at the point where the withdrawal pains peak. I am frightened, but it's all the money I have and I have to go with it. I have to surrender and trust I will get through.

I kiss Mum goodbye and hold her tight. I tell Dad I love him and I hold him for longer. I want to convey how sorry I am to have brought all this down on their heads, to be spending their hard-earned money on rehab. I am heartbroken – and I guess they are too, but we will get through. I know that now.

However angry or disappointed they are in me, they are still here, still supporting me and I owe them my life. Of that I am convinced. Without rehab I would be dead. I was told I had three months left to live when I got here. Mum and Dad may have bought me my recovery, but the hard work is up to me. That I know too.

I wave from my window and cry like a little girl when they leave. I love them so much and yet I bring them so much pain. When will it stop?

Another week goes by and the atmosphere in the clinic has calmed down. Mick and I have called a truce and are on speaking terms.

Cameron is due to visit and I have been thinking only of that, counting the hours until I see him. I have been away from home for over a month now, and I am desperate for his company. I have missed him so much. I am also desperate for something else, which has nothing to do with therapy or reduction charts or group sessions. He feels the same. But it is another of the absolute no-nos here: couples do not spend time together in single rooms. I am expected to be abstinent on all levels for the duration of my stay. We know this, and yet when he pokes his head through the door, when he comes to my bedside and kisses me, I know that we will break the cardinal rule of the rehab – and risk being kicked out.

It's a stupid thing to do, but the risk spurs us on. We calculate we have half an hour at most before someone comes looking for us for the afternoon therapy session. Quickly, Cameron shoves the wedge under the door and gets out of his clothes. I am amazed that he still finds me attractive as he gently, carefully pulls off my joggers. I am drenched in sweat and trembling, but he appears not to notice and kisses me so tenderly that I don't care that we may get found out and shamed. I don't care if anyone hears us. I just want my man to make love to me. I want to feel like a woman again and not a hideous mess of a human being.

He has to be slow and careful. I am so bloody ill, feel so sick and woozy that it is not one of our finest lovemaking sessions, but it is something, and when it is over, Cameron collapses, laughing, on to the bed. I ask him to dress me and he helps me into a fresh pair of leggings and a soft cotton dress. I ask him to get me a scarf, a cardigan and two pairs of socks as well, as by now I am freezing cold.

He laughs at me. He is naked, bronzed and says the room is boiling – a picture of health. What the hell does he see in me, I wonder for the millionth time. Almost the minute that we have got my clothes on, there is a knock on the door. Cameron dives under the duvet, still as naked as the day he was born. I slowly open the door and creep outside, wobbling a little at the exertion. Helen is standing in front of me. She takes one look at my flushed face and raises both her eyebrows.

'I hope you are not doing what I think you are,' she says sternly. I move into the corridor, pulling the door shut behind me and look back at her with wide, astonished eyes.

'Of course not, I was just giving him a massage,' I tell her.

Helen looks at me. I imagine she knows full well that I have just told her a bare-faced lie, but she chooses to believe me.

'We're starting the therapy, be over in two minutes,' she says, and I realise I have just deceived the woman who has done the most for me during my stay, whom I love because she challenges me and everyone else in here to speak truthfully at all times. I love her fierce honesty – and I have just thrown it back in her face to save my own shallow skin.

'Well, you are dressed, at least,' she adds and a crooked smile escapes the side of her mouth. 'We are waiting for you in the therapy room; we are having a lecture today.'

'Ok,' I say as brightly as I can manage and shuffle back into my room. I make a face at Cameron and he laughs.

'Thank fuck she didn't come ten minutes earlier.' He is thrilled with himself.

'It's not funny, Cameron. We could have got me into major trouble.' I now feel guilty and I rub my hands though my hair for want of something else to do. I throw my naked man his T-shirt and say, 'Come on sexy, get dressed.'

Then I realise I haven't told him. I've 'forgotten' to tell him how many doses I was really taking when I came in. In therapy this week, I finally admitted to the group how many lozenges I was taking. There was silence after my confession before one of the more experienced heroin users whistled a long, low note in disbelief which was greeted by the group with nervous laughter. I felt the hot flush of shame brand my face as I stared back at the circle of faces. Once I'd done it though – and lived through the reaction, which turned into a kind of respect as my image as the uptight middle-class girl who just took too many was shattered – I was relieved. They all know what I am, and who I am now. But Cameron doesn't, and I know the time has come to tell him. I have lied to him for too long under the guise of protecting him from the truth, when all along, I've been protecting myself. But I know in my heart I can't bear to lie to him any more. If I do, then there is simply no future for us. It has to be real. I have to tell him.

'There is something I have to tell you, and I'd really rather tell you now, so that if you want to leave you can,' I gush.

He looks at me strangely, surprised by my sudden change of mood.

I try to speak, but the words fail me; my tongue is thick and dry and my heart jumps as everything I have composed for this awful, dreaded moment dissolves into nothing.

'Spit it out then,' Cameron says, still puzzled.

'Oh God, I'm so sorry, I'm just so sorry, Cameron. I lied to you.'

He stares at me, as if I am insane.

'I mean it, honey. I wasn't taking twenty lozenges a day as I told you. Well, I was, but that was a long time ago now.' The words start to fall from me and sink into the waiting silence of this too-pink room. They come in fits and spurts now, leaking out, then pouring in torrents as I tell him everything.

'When I came in here, I was on sixty lozenges a day. That's the truth. I was on twenty till about six months ago, then it just went up and up and ran out of my control. I don't know how it happened, I really don't know. First it was twenty, then twenty-five, then thirty, then forty, then forty-five, and then, by the time I got here, it was sixty . . . ' My voice trails off and I find I can't look him in the face. I know he's going to leave. I can feel the horror, the disbelief and the anger rise in him.

'You lied to me,' is all he says. His voice sounds all wounded and sore. 'I can't believe you lied to me. How can I trust you again?'

The question moves into my silence this time and I cannot reply. I don't know how to reassure him. I don't know if I can be trusted again and that, finally, is the real truth.

'I'm so sorry. I was really ill with addiction,' I say feebly, and it sounds hollow and meaningless, so I sit and wait while Cameron digests this unpalatable reality. His girlfriend really is a junkie – not the pretend one he thought, not the misunderstood one he imagined, but a real one. A lying, shameful, real one. And this floors him. He leans back against my pillows and shuts his eyes.

There is a very long silence. Then Cameron speaks.

'I don't know what to think about you or us yet. I need some time, but I can see what you're going through to get rid of this drug from your system and I still love you.

'In a stupid way, I love you more for doing it – and I know being honest was really hard.'

I gulp down my reply; my own tears have started. 'Ok,' is all I can say, and I manage a smile.

He smiles back and, eventually, very slowly, very carefully, he kisses me before getting up to leave.

I watch him disappear down the corridor. My mind is frozen with fear that he will leave me. My heart aches already at the loss of him and I just want to curl up and wait until he decides.

CHAPTER 26

# Two Paracetamol

*The Final Week*

I am vaguely aware that my jumper is being pulled off me carefully, then my T-shirt, and the air feels cold and razor sharp against the goosebumps which cover my skin. Helen's voice comes from somewhere above me, urging me to try and get up as I have to remove my underwear. I think this is real, but my mind is strange and unfocused, veering from hallucination to a blurred reality, none of which makes much sense. The light is harsh and the sound of the running water in the bath I seem to be slumped against is deafening. Confusion and delirium make me weep and moan. Then Helen's voice comes again – I look up and there she is.

She helps me to my feet. I was on the floor and now I'm half-standing, shivering as I comply. Once everything is off, I realise I'm having a bath. The water brings me back into myself again. It feels scalding as I dip one foot into it.

'It's not hot, it's warm,' she says, kindly.

It is a struggle getting in and over the bath sides. Helen helps me, but her grip hurts and I wince, even as she helps me to keep my balance until I can sit, then lie in the water. 'Come on, this will make you feel better,' she says. Her voice is as warm and dreamy as the water I'm now sinking the rest of my body into.

The first thing I notice are the bubbles, they are extraordinary. How come I have never noticed them before? The light is refracted inside the air and soap and shines a million different colours where the oil of the bubble bath separates.

They twinkle and glow at me and I am held suspended in wonder. My chin sinks under the water and, for the first time, I feel some relief for the muscles in my back, shoulders, lower back and legs, my arms and even my jaw, which has been clenched tightly for days and days. I'm still gazing at the bubbles when Helen takes hold of my hand which is on the edge of the tub and I hear her lovely voice. I don't catch everything, but I do remember how gentle and calm her voice is, quiet even.

'You've rewritten the rules, Cathryn,' is what I eventually hear after my thoughts about how soothing her voice is have finally trailed off. 'When we get heroin addicts in here, rolling about on the floor saying they took heroin twice or three times a day, I will tell them about you.

'I will tell them how much you were taking, and how you saw it through without the fuss, without the drama. We are so proud of you, darling,' she adds and looks at me. She's normally so direct, so forceful, which is why I love having her as my counsellor – there is nowhere to hide with Helen. But this time, it's her gentleness that provokes my tears. This time, I am crying with delirious love for her and for the rehab and for everyone who takes this journey.

There is a reason why so many heroin addicts die of their affliction. And the reason is this: the withdrawal process. It is so desperate, so frightening and all-consuming that it is simply very often the only 'logical' choice of an addict to keep using, to keep clinging to the chains of their addiction, rather than go through this. I understand that even as I do it, go through it, and I don't judge or blame. We have to be ready somewhere very deep inside to take this path. And once through it, there is no escape, no place to hide, no shadow to linger within because we will be abstinent. No drinks at the office party, no glass of wine to take the edge off the day, no cannabis or cocaine to be sociable at a dinner party, no painkillers to cope with hurt, physical or emotional. All of it goes.

This is a clearing-out time and it hurts like hell. I would roar in horrified rage and disbelief at how fucking bad this process is, but I don't have the strength. Instead, I shake and quiver, like a tiny dying bird. I have lost so much weight. I must have lost a stone and a half in the time I have been in rehab. It has fallen off me because the nausea and anxiety make it impossible for me to swallow anything. I have a permanent hard lump in my throat which makes even speaking difficult. I have diarrhoea, cramps, tremors, hallucinations, uncontrollable weeping and desperate fear. I have insomnia and haven't slept at all most of the time I've been here which is leaving me madder still.

But as Helen washes me with intricate care, I feel I am a million miles away, in another galaxy. This is not my body which she is gently making clean. This is not me undergoing this treatment. I am here and yet a very long way away. The room is cold, but the water is warm. There are sounds of people talking outside and the drifting smoke from lit cigarettes.

'I'm going to be sick,' I say suddenly, and clamber for the sides of the bath.

'Ok darling, hang in there. I've finished washing you, let me get a towel,' Helen replies and hurries out of the room, down the corridor to the towel cupboard.

'I'm going to be sick,' I say to myself. 'I can't bear this any more. I can't bear it.'

Helen comes back, I stumble out of the bath, she wraps me, trembling, inside a large towel and I lurch towards the loo. I make it in time for a steady stream of steaming vomit to launch into the toilet bowl. It is the third time today. Helen says she has to go back to the office. I tell her thank you and that I'll be fine. I puke again then sink on to the floor. The door is not locked so, in theory, anyone could walk in, but I know there is a group-therapy session on at the moment – and anyway, I don't really care.

After what seems like hours, I rise up and slowly, agonisingly slowly, I get dressed, back in the same joggers, T-shirt and jumper. I hadn't washed for days before this bath. I have been too ill, and I'm aware that my clothes probably smell, but I cannot put a wash on – the idea of it is too momentous, I literally haven't the strength to pick up my clothes and carry them to the washing machine. Most of the time now, I have to crawl along the floor if I need to move anywhere. And I do this now, crawling on all fours, like a baby, back to my room. I'm now freezing cold. Everything has tightened up again and I feel, if it is possible, worse.

Back in bed, I stare at my wall. I stare and shake, occasionally crawling back to the loo, but otherwise marooned in this bed, pinned down by the pain which is screaming at me from every part of my body and mind. The Xanax I was given at lunchtime is wearing off and peculiar thoughts keep swimming through my frazzled mind. There are tiny ants walking up the wall in front of me. Whole leagues of them walking up my wall. Where have they come from? Did the spiders tell them about my room? In the bit of my mind which still clings to reality I know they aren't real, but their imagined presence frightens me, makes me worried I am really mad, despite what Charlie and Helen say.

The visions are with me all the time now. So is the orchestra, which keeps playing and playing the same tune, puzzled, I look round the room to see where the sound is coming from. Eventually, I isolate it to the far side of my bedroom, by the window. It is the sound of the fridge humming – but it is like an orchestra is playing down the electric wiring from it. I have heard it before, but not as loud or as insistent as it is now. I must go and tell someone. I think I am going mad properly now.

It takes me twenty minutes to crawl to the door at the end of the corridor. I then have to rest, lying like a dying tramp at the end of the building. Then I have to haul myself up and negotiate the uneven pathway to the office, which is less than fifty metres away. This journey takes me a shockingly long time, but I am spurred on because of the noises in my head and the ants on my walls. Once inside the office, I collapse on to a chair. Charlie is there. I love Charlie, too.

It was Charlie who told me I was using the drugs to escape my painful memories of all the pancreatitis and the trauma of hospital. It sounds so obvious now, but it was a revelation to me. My GP had really been focusing on my relationship breakdown and the emotional causes behind me taking more and more of the drug, and while that felt authentic, it never seemed to hit the nub of my problem with fentanyl. And I was – still am – in a state of permanent terror that the pancreatitis may return. I still have nightmares about hospital and it is two years since my last admission. Those nights in A&E haunt me, and will probably do so forever, with their brutality and pain. No wonder I took a bit more, then a bit more, until it all spiralled out of control. No wonder I tried to run from those damaging memories into the arms of mother opiate.

Charlie looks up at me and sees I am in a state.

'Are you busy?' I say. I must look pitiful, but she treats me like any of her colleagues. There is no pity from Charlie, and I love her for that as well.

'Yes, I can see you. What is it you want to talk about?' she says calmly, looking me straight in the eyes. So many people have not been able to do that since my 'problem' with painkillers came to light.

'I am going mad. I really am demented this time,' I say, wringing my hands a little with anxiety. 'There are ants crawling up my walls now and the orchestra is back, playing in my fridge, and it's much louder this time, much louder in my head,' I say, hearing my utter lunacy.

Charlie does not even smile. She says: 'You are not going mad. You are going through a difficult journey and you are nearly at the end of it. All of this is perfectly normal. The Xanax can sometimes give people hallucinations, but I think that as you are taking so little of it, it is probably the withdrawals.'

'But I feel mad,' I say. I'm really desperate now and I don't know whether to believe her.

'You will feel mad. You are taking a brave path and it is hard. This is part of it.' Charlie's face is so sincere, so direct and trustworthy that I sink into acceptance of her words.

'Thanks,' I whisper and get up, ready to do battle with the door, ready to brave the slicing cold air outside and go back to bed. Charlie sees how weak I am, but she does not open the door. She sits, calm and still, while I hobble over and wrench the door open. Part of me hates her then for not helping me when I am so weak and pathetic, but the bigger part of me knows it is tough love. I have to do it myself. I have to do this journey myself. It is the big lesson of being here. Tough love. Take responsibility. Feel the pain of it and don't be a victim. Stand up and get better. Have self-respect. Still, it's hard going and the childish, battered part of me wants to be mollycoddled a little, just a little.

Outside, the March sun is already setting in a deep, golden glow which highlights the bitter cold. Coming off heroin is like the outer layer of skin being stripped off. My body, which has been desensitised by the drugs for so long, is now naked and vulnerable, its self-regulation functions having been annihilated by the opiates. As a consequence, I am now either always freezing cold or burning hot. Tonight, I am cold to my bones, down to the marrow and beyond.

I have barely rung anyone since arriving here. It is like I don't want anyone to know how miserable this is and how close to breaking point I feel. They ring every day though, and I either ignore the calls or I lie, telling them it's ok, not as bad as I thought it would be. I know they're not convinced, but it is better than dragging them through this as well.

I've received a message from my parents. Apparently there are problems over money again and I need to talk to the owner and sort it all out. I don't really care about the money right now, but I go to the office and ask for the owner anyway. He's not around. But Helen is. And it is Helen who puts me straight.

'We're really worried about you leaving here at the acute stage of the withdrawal process and we want you to stay on for another week after you hit zero lozenges,' she says without blinking. 'Can you borrow more money?' Her tone is direct, the message clear as the ice which traces the outline of the farm with delicate white fingers.

'One more week. Christ, what am I going to do?' I say, panicky now, breathing faster, my mind racing. 'I haven't got any more money and I cannot ask for any more off my parents. I'm stuck, Helen.'

We both turn to look at my chart which is pinned in a rather haphazard fashion to the noticeboard. Several weeks of my life are on it, reduced to days and their corresponding lozenge tally. I started on fifty-five lozenges and I am now fast approaching zero. I know for a fact that heroin addicts usually take six months to detox. I have had five fucking weeks – and now it is crunch time.

'I won't borrow any more money. My parents have done enough. I mean, Jesus, what happens to people who don't have parents with money? How the fuck do they go into detox?' I guess I already know the answer to that. They don't. They die. Or they lose their homes, their money, their jobs, their partners until they hit the bottom, far off the social register, until they are picked up by the law or A&E and put into NHS detox alongside all the other poor sods who have walked the same treacherous path.

I am one of the lucky ones – but even my luck has run its course. I have to stick with it, get off this shit before I leave or who knows what will happen. I do know that I can never, ever go through this again. Once in a lifetime is more than enough. 'Let's keep going. Let's crack this thing,' I say in a hard voice. It is time.

Helen's face is grim as she looks at me. She knows as well as I do what we have to do.

'It's three today and the last one is on Wednesday. Thursday will be my first morning without any lozenges and I am leaving here on Saturday,' I say, defiantly, knowing the worst is to come, yet feeling that new sensation, that glimmer of the heady, fresh scent of freedom.

We lock eyes, as if we are going into battle.

'Once the last dose is taken, it then takes three days for the opiate to leave your body,' Helen reminds me. 'You will undergo terrible suffering in those days, but you must hold on to this: this is your chance for freedom. Don't ever stop, don't fail in your courage.

'You have to do this. It is just remarkable that you have done it from so much, actually the highest level of opiates we've ever had here in our entire twenty-five-year history. You've come down from sixty a day to three – that is an amazing achievement. But this is the final stretch, and it will be the hardest.'

I cannot fathom what could be harder. I take the last two lozenges of the day and Helen helps me back to my room.

'Do you know what, Helen? I'm going to write a book about this. I'm going to write and tell people they can do this, that there is help out there and, most importantly, that however bad it gets withdrawing, it is never worse than a day spent hiding, cheating and using drugs. Nowhere near.' And with that, I fall on to the duvet and start to cry the tears which don't stop for a long time.

I'm going to have to go cold turkey now and I'd better get my head down and do it because there is no safety net; not here, not in hospital, not anywhere. Without my parents and their care for me while I was ill, and without their money which I am shamefacedly borrowing from them now, I would be dead either of pancreatitis or addiction.

And I'm lucky. What about those people who don't have parents like mine – parents with spare cash, parents who love me so much they would do anything to support me? The anger helps me, makes me feel less of a victim.

By the next morning my rage and desolation have been engulfed by a burning abdominal pain which makes me beg to be taken to hospital. I haven't slept or eaten for weeks now, I can barely swallow liquids and the pain holds me so tightly I am driven half mad by it. It is a delirium of sorts.

One of the counsellors drives me to the GP. There is a queue of people, and I am writhing in agony in the waiting room. We see the doctor. He says we have to go straight to the hospital. I start to whimper with fear, as he suspects it might be pancreatitis. Is my old enemy back to sear the memory of all that hurt back into my body and brain?

We drive to the A&E department of the main hospital in the area. The trip takes almost an hour. By the time we get to the front desk, a worried-looking nurse ushers us into the acute admissions unit. Grateful to be somewhere safe, I curl up on the trolley clutching a pillow and the counsellor's hand. He doesn't seem to mind, but I know I am digging my nails into him as the waves of pain break inside me. Then the worst comes. I have to tell the nurse I am a rehab patient and I must not be given opiate medication unless my condition is life-threatening. I tell the nurse with dark hair and kind eyes that I am a drug addict and I am in withdrawal from fentanyl. At this, she carefully strokes my arm and tells me how brave I am. She says she can only give me these – and with that opens her palm to reveal two small white tablets. Two paracetamol. In a moment, I am transported back to a hospital bed all those years ago, and I am screaming at a nurse with dark hair and scared-looking eyes. I am screaming at her because she has just tried to give me two paracetamol in the face of pancreatitis. Only this time, I take them and say thank you in a quiet voice, all the while saying a silent apology to the unknown nurse who bore the brunt of my distress all those years ago.

Within the hour, the blood tests come back. It is not acute pancreatitis. The doctor comes round with the nice nurse. He looks at my notes and says that it takes three weeks for the body's endorphins to recover from their long opiate holiday. In the meantime, the body becomes the playground for excruciating pain, as there are no natural painkillers, nothing to counteract the chronic pancreatic pain I live with all the time. He tells us that I am withdrawing too heavily, too fast, and I should go back to wearing the lowest fentanyl skin patch (25mcg) while I come off the final lozenges.

As we leave, the nurse holds my hand briefly and says, 'Good luck.' The touch of her soft hand stays on my skin for the length of the drive back, her kindness etched deep within me.

CHAPTER 27

# The Last Post

*17 March 2010*

The time has come. I feel so emotional about collecting the last lozenge from the office. I am half-carried, half-pulled by Alice outside into the bitter night, down the steps, across the grass to the office. The light is on, like they are waiting for someone. I knock and we go inside. There is a feeling of expectancy. Like something is happening. Takes me a moment to realise the something is me.

'We didn't think you'd do it. We all said, she'll never do it.' The voices are kind, incredulous maybe, but kind.

I'm trying not to throw up the three bites of bread I managed to get down earlier and don't realise at first they mean me. Looking up, I see everyone is watching me.

Everyone is looking at me. There's Jeff, one of the counsellors, Charlie, a couple of the residents, including Alex, and, of course, me. Inmates and jailers alike; all alike.

Looking down, I realise I am wearing pyjama bottoms, a pair of Ugg boots, three T-shirts, a hoodie with 'Champion' emblazoned on the front, a ski jacket and a pair of glasses. Alice is holding me upright and I must feel like a tonne weight on her with all these extra clothes on.

My hair is in unwashed, matted confusion around my face. I'm not wearing a bra – I don't have the strength to reach behind me to do it up – and I look like the worst bum on the street. But I don't care. I can barely stand. I'm feeble. Ill. Scared. Hunted.

It has finally come to this. The sum total of my life. My hopes and fears and dreams and efforts, my work and play and trying so hard all the time. It has come to the last lozenge in my hand. I want it so badly, but if I take it, it will be gone. For ever.

Briefly, I toy with the idea of keeping it, as a treasure, but I know I'll take it when the monster rears again.

It is 6 p.m. It is the last one.

Jeff asks everyone to be upstanding, then he puts his hands to his mouth in a trumpet shape and starts 'playing' Last Post. Slightly comical at first, but then something in the room settles into a momentous feeling, just like when the real instrument plays the opening chords. I am emotional and blessed, wretched and relieved all at the same time. Yet more tears make salty wave lines down my face. I hardly notice them. There have been so many.

I will take this, the last lozenge, then I will be plunged into the madness of remorse and longing. I can feel it at the edge of me, like blinking and missing it. It is waiting. The sting of it is waiting. And I am going to feel so bad. The worst is here. It is fucking here – and, at long last, I am ready.

The Last Post finishes. Everyone claps. I try to look like a champion, but I know I am really a dirty junkie.

'We never thought you'd come this far,' someone says.

This far where? I want to say. But nothing comes out. I just stare back, staring in dumb terror at the zero written on to my drug-reduction chart which is still pinned to the office noticeboard.

'Let's get you back,' says Alice. Her eyes are filled with tears. 'You're amazing.'

I wonder why she's saying this. I don't feel amazing. I look like shit. I am shit. I'm an addict getting my last fix. What's amazing about that? How did I end up here? How? Thoughts don't fit together any more. I hover between their world and the derangement of mine.

Did someone say something? Perhaps I'm hallucinating.

We shuffle back to my room. I know I'm walking, sort of. And I know it's cold. The wind seems to slice my skin raw and I pull my jacket closer around my emaciated body. Haven't eaten for weeks now. Still shitting every hour or so. Throwing up at regular intervals too. There's nothing left of me and I don't care.

My world has been reduced to a white lozenge on a plastic stick which is pure fentanyl; 200 micrograms of the finest medicinal smack. Built to fit the opiate receptors of the brain to perfection; heaven to take, hell to wean off. And now it is my turn.

Fentanyl was my best friend, my worst enemy, my lover and destroyer, my numb friend and blind enemy. It was my gentle joy and my worst self and it is leaving me. I hold the last lozenge I will ever take in my hand. It is a hand which trembles and curls tightly round the white plastic stick which holds the solid white medicine. It is a medicine which has held me, spellbound, for two years, yet it promises very little tonight. It is not nearly enough to register in my sickened body, but it is all I have.

I feel like a savage hole has been ripped through my soul and my heart. There will be no more lozenges, no more pain relief. No more comfort and no hiding place.

There will be nothing to protect me from the harsh winter outside of me and the colder one inside. There will be nothing to dull the too-harsh lights of the real world. Nothing to console, nothing, nothing, everything. Emptiness punches me in my stomach. I'm curled up and crying, writhing into loss. How can I live without it?

And this is going to hurt. I note that with a kind of twisted pleasure. As if the hurt justifies the loss. I think I am now so used to pain of whatever description that things only take on meaning for me if they contain it, hold it, have it. Sick. I know I am sick. I am told I'm spiritually and emotionally sick every day, here in this clinic. I have barely been listening, in truth. My thoughts have been watching, waiting for this moment.

And here I am. Alone in my room. The light turned down low. The heating turned up. Everything made ready for this last meeting with mother opiate.

Ophelia is finally getting out of the stream. I am seconds from taking this white stuff into my mouth. I have a moment's indecision: which is the best way to make this last? Should I have half now and the rest later, when I'm desperate for it? Or should I gorge on this last beauty, suck it dry, take whatever sensual pleasure I can from this last seductive escape?

In the end, I break open the sealed package, carefully, so I don't lose any of the chalky tablet, and I lie back, get comfortable on my pillows and I take it all. I sink the sweet-tasting lozenge against the inside of my mouth, careful not to make too much saliva, in case it dissolves too quickly. I lie down in unhurried anticipation and wait to receive whatever it has left to give me. It's like a gentle caress. A kiss which hardly touches the lips, leaving an imprint on the heart, rather than the mouth. It's goodbye. It's a sweet goodbye to peace and serenity. Leaving me to the ravages of chaos and insanity.

The moment is still sacred though, however brief and unsatisfying. It's God, it's nature, it's everything. And it is gone. Five minutes later and I'm sucking the plastic stick and the fentanyl is gone. I can still taste the sweet last traces of it on my tongue. It's over. There's only an empty wrapper left as proof of the years of longing and loving, taking and using, all the cravings, anxiety and paranoia. I decide to keep it as a talisman. To remind me if I ever need it, this is all it amounts to – and it isn't much. Not much at all. And you know what? There is a tiny piece of me which wasn't shredded by the drug, which talks to me quietly now, saying I am relieved. I am relieved it is over. And I'm ready to face what I have become. And I am ready to feel it go, however hard, however painful. I am ready.

I manage to sleep for three hours because the night counsellor took pity on me and wrote me up for two zopiclone, which are strong sleeping tablets. In the entire time I have been here I can count the hours I have slept each night on one hand – despite a daily sleeping pill, plus the dopey effects of the mirtazapine. I have the body of a dead sparrow, but the constitution of a rhino.

Waking at 3 a.m., I feel moved to write in my diary, to record the last stage of this experience which has seen me break out of the cocoon of my own making and hesitantly spread my wings in faltering flight. It is probably a bit premature, I'm hardly out of the woods yet, but I want to celebrate. Three hours' sleep is nothing short of a miracle.

I write that this has been the best and worst experience of my life. The sound of my pen scratching the surface of the paper calms me, prepares me for what I feel I must set down, in case I ever forget.

I add details to everything I've already written about all the people I've met in here. Every last one who has loved me, challenged me, frustrated and annoyed me. I pay homage to them all, and thank them for being part of my journey. I set down every last kindness, big and small and somewhere in between, recording the person, the time and the context, and I thank each and every one of them too.

Then I write the real stuff, the dirty stuff. The secrets and lies, the battles and surrenders of each of the people in here and I know, as I remember them all, that I have witnessed sacred ground in here. I have explored, joined and separated from each and every person's path; by going into rehab, I've prevented the loneliness of an addict's life – and death.

I write about the group, how we as a collective charted the internal maps which we brought to this place, this strange and special place. And I feel a sense of magic and reawakening as I record it all, I really do. The dynamics and the troubles have ebbed and flowed every moment in here, but we've done it all together, as a group, as a fellowship.

I note down the sight and sound of the tides of repressed emotions which have flooded to the surface of these damaged souls, my damaged soul. And it may be the hour, the lack of sleep or my brittle mind, but I feel honoured and humbled to have shared their journeys too, to have seen and felt others tear themselves out of their cocoons and dare to tread.

And now, with my departure in sight, I see that I must go out and live my own life, at last. This is where my pen stalls. It waits for my courage to catch up and then we start again, writing into the darkness all the astonishment and terror of living free and sober. I write that I have to take responsibility for my life – and that means for my feelings, my needs, my decisions and my actions. I am daunted and free, wild and scared, like a bird in the seconds before taking the plunge and leaving the nest. I write that I am astonished as well. Amazed by the thrill and excitement in that first step, the joy that feels so small and so new, but will widen and grow as I do. As I dip towards the ground and then trust that I will, eventually, fly.

Still, it is 3.30 a.m., so I might be overdoing it on the emotional front. My tears have run freely while I've been committing all this to paper – and now I can't stop them, even if I want to.

I also have a strange, tinny buzzing in my head, or my ears, I can't decide which. I hesitate before continuing, I am so used to my insanity now that I just try to concentrate on how to take this diary, this pen and everyone else with me.

Eventually, I close my diary, and reverently place it by my suitcase, ready for Cameron to pack away when he arrives on Saturday – a literary umbilical cord which will unravel into who knows what after I leave here.

It is then I realise I really will go mad, if I stay in bed, sitting in my thoughts like a baby in a dirty nappy. So I get up, pull on my Champion jumper and shuffle down to the common room. One of the night watchmen is in there; not my favourite – Gerald, with his tales from his country home – but another man who is friendly and seems unsurprised to see me wander in.

He makes me a cup of tea and I take it gratefully, watching the spirals of steam rise into the rafters. I force myself to stop thinking and instead concentrate on staring at the TV screen. There's a violent film playing, I don't know which one, and I find it strangely soothing. It quietens the noises in my head and the tugging feeling at my heart where all the emotions for tomorrow are stored.

I know I'm scared to leave. Even though I've hated this place at times, and hated some of the residents and counsellors more, I know that leaving will be like being spat out of a claustrophobic yet warm womb. Out into the daylight, to have my arse slapped before I let out my first indignant yell of my new, reborn life. I feel too fragile to face it, but the money has run out and, in my gut, I know it's time to go.

As the night wears on, other residents appear from the silky indigo night sky outside, like ghosts from the main haunted house, to smoke, drink coffee, then disappear.

Silk turns to velvet, indigo to pale blue, and I sit until I can sit no longer. Feeling safe from the onslaught of my thoughts which have been put to rest temporarily by company and bad TV, I return to my room to greet the day – my first without a lozenge.

The next two days pass in a complete blur. My memories of them are very hazy – non-existent, if I'm honest – and the nights that follow are sleepless, but somehow, time passes, taking me along with it.

D-day, and as the cold light of dawn finally breaks across the sky, I crawl, shivering, into the shower. The water droplets are like miniature crystals, they feel sharp and unwelcome, beautiful but hard, beating into my skin which has been made so sensitive by the detox.

Gradually, the crystals become water again and I let the warmth seep into my skin and bones, bending my head into my hands as I sit on the shower floor and embrace the water, melting away the fear and strangeness of the night before. I almost wish I could stay this way, feeling everything in a sensual, heightened way. The cold air outside is like a knife, the warm water inside is like summer rain, each droplet felt as it hits and nudges the pores of my skin.

I realise I'm starting to meander into my mind again. I turn off the shower and, slowly, I quiver my way to my bed to lie down wrapped in towels, waiting for them to dry me as my last energy is spent.

An hour later and I'm finally dressed. This time, I make an effort by applying mascara which almost blinds me as my hand is shaking so much, drawing on my eyebrows which I haven't dared do for weeks because I couldn't hold the pencil steady enough to not make them wonky. I look at myself in the mirror and laugh. I look like a transvestite. I'm so unused to seeing myself looking anywhere near feminine after weeks spent in a dishevelled disarray of unwashed hair, no make-up and sweatpants that the sight of me looking like a woman again, albeit a wrecked woman, is so unfamiliar that I can't take her – me – seriously.

Feeling incongruous, I make my way down to the common room to wait for the rest of the inmates to wake up. Alice is already there. She announces she got up early so we could spend as much time as possible together before it is time for me to leave. Before she's finished talking, I wrap my arms around her and hold her until we are both crying and promising to write and email and see each other regularly. We sit huddled together until one of the men decides to make coffee and we drink it, slowly, on the worn sofa in the lounge watching MTV until breakfast is ready.

I still can't force much food down me. But I've lost too much weight to care now and I nibble at half a slice of toast with Marmite until it's time for our morning meditation.

At precisely 9.25 a.m. everyone troops out to the lounge, which is unusual because most people skive off this part of the day, preferring to get an extra fifteen minutes in bed before the first of the group sessions. All the counsellors are in there too, which is even more weird as they mostly let us do the meditation ourselves (another reason why most people don't attend).

The room is filled, all the chairs are taken. Ben, a counsellor, starts to speak.

'Today we thought we'd do something special,' he says, smiling. I realise he's looking at me. 'One of us is leaving and we'd like to honour her stay with a small ceremony we sometimes perform with the longer-term patients,' he adds, still smiling.

I breathe deeply, unsure of what's to come, but everyone else is smiling, so it must all be ok.

Ben hands me the meditation book and asks me to read today's piece of wisdom. My voice is so tiny and fledgling and I stumble over the words, a little in awe. After I've finished self-consciously reading the passage there's a short silence.

Ben then produces a large coin from his pocket and says, 'Every person in this room is going to take this coin and tell us something about you. About how you've affected them or helped them or anything they want to say about your journey with us in here.'

I am stupefied, floored by this gesture. Gulping in my speechlessness, I nod. It's all I can do to respond. Then Ben takes the coin out of its cellophane wrapper and starts.

'When I first saw your case notes I thought, Oh my god, this woman is going to be a total nightmare.'

I laugh at this, along with everyone else, and fidget in my seat, clutching the edges of my skirt for protection, for anchoring. Everything hurts, but I try to separate from the continual physical endurance test and stay focused on this room and these people.

'And you were a nightmare, at first,' he says with a laugh. 'But then you did it. And we watched in amazement as you came off all those drugs. We watched your pain in disbelief, we witnessed your battles with yourself and other people and we couldn't believe that this woman who came to us in such denial and anguish could take this on – and beat those drugs.

'You have such courage, an indomitable spirit, and you are an inspiration to us all.'

I stare back at Ben, and I feel like an adult, like a grown-up, like I've finally stood up and been counted. I have a lump in my throat, but I force out the words: 'Thank you.' I cannot think of another moment in my life – except, of course, hearing of the birth of my nephew – that was so heightened and so special.

Neil takes the coin from Ben. He holds it up like a beacon and tells me I have a sense of 'magnificence' about me. I am stunned, and think, Is he joking? But he looks serious enough. He passes the coin on, but keeps his eyes in contact with mine, sure and steady, telling me without words somehow that he is speaking his truth and so I believe him. I let those words in to glow as a manifestation of something beautiful. Something I hope to carry with me for the rest of my life. I nod, feeling complete wonderment, and I hope he knows that is a thank you too.

Alice then takes the coin, which I see now has part of its edge missing, to remind me, perhaps, that we are all imperfect, that to be human is to be imperfect (as if I need reminding). She is crying, and I realise by now I am too. She says simply that we've become best friends, and I can't help but agree. I get up and hug her tightly. I tell her I feel the same about her.

It is several minutes before I realise the coin is still being passed round. The rest of the words are a blur, some more heartfelt than others, I suppose, but the feeling in the room is good, connected and supportive. In the weeks I've been here, I haven't seen another such ceremony and I know I've been blessed with this accolade, this honour. It makes it all the harder to leave.

At the end, we join in our circle, holding hands. Then, instead, we have a spontaneous group hug. I feel included. That's the warm, fuzzy, loving feeling. It has taken me the last half an hour to work it out. I feel properly included. It is a new feeling. A shiny, bright new feeling. And one which I shall store in my new emotional toolbox until a day when I may need it.

As the group breaks up, Cameron walks past the window. He is still struggling to come to terms with his new picture of me. His focused energy as he heads straight for my room tells me he would rather this was all a dream, a figment, an illusion which disappears, leaving no trace. But he is here, he has stayed with me and he is not leaving, and I find him packing up the last bits when I arrive in my room after the meditation.

Cameron loads the car as I say my final goodbyes, then the patients trudge off to their next therapy session, my triumphs forgotten, the circle already moving onwards, and I walk slowly out of the rehab, leaning heavily on Cameron's arm. Once in the car, he says simply, 'Let's go.' And we do.

We go. It is not a pleasant ride home. I am sick several times as I finally give in to the force of the last part of my detox, and I am shivering so much now I have to be wrapped in the picnic blanket. Picking off bits of stray grass and leaves, Cameron bundles me into his arms and carries me up to the front door. The front door I have dreamed about, crooned over, worshipped from afar. The key turns, the door opens and I see an empty house. The furniture is in storage ready for moving and the weeks of being almost empty and a bachelor pad have rendered the insides of the cottage musty and untidy. Cameron carries me up to bed and lays me down on the duvet.

I'm back. I'm home. Only it isn't my home any more. It has finally been sold and we have days left until the move is complete. I'm not sure I care as much as I thought I would. I am too busy being amazed that this blond Viking boyfriend of mine is still here, with me, tonight. The rest? The rest is just extra.

I'm finally home, I realise. But it isn't the cottage that tells me that. It is being with him.

CHAPTER 28

# Shaky Start

*March 2010*

It has been three days, four hours and five minutes since I left rehab. I feel like a duckling breaking my way out of the egg shell and launching into the crisp glare of daylight. Everything hurts, my back, my shoulders, my arms, my teeth from grinding them in my scant sleep, my eyes, my head, my legs, calves, ankles, feet. Everything. My muscles are all screaming out for fentanyl. Opiates are stored in muscle tissue which is why they object so loudly when it's taken away.

Withdrawals. It's all withdrawals. And now I'm going to be reducing my dose of Xanax every week as well. Xanax is the tranquilliser I was prescribed during detox for some relief from the severe muscle cramps, agitation and anxiety. The only problem is that it's highly addictive and it scares me. Really scares me.

I'm already down by nearly half my daily dose, which, of course, I am doing too quickly. And so I'm getting the flashing lights and hallucinations I know so well. I must get off them though. I have to get off them. I never, ever want to end up in rehab again.

I want to describe the last three days – how the climax of the weeks of reducing fentanyl played out – but I cannot. They passed in a mania of torment, physically, emotionally and mentally. In some ways, the climax, for me, was that last lozenge in rehab – because that was the end of the road. I just had to live through that last bit. I now have to detox off the small patch they gave me at A&E, but it is such a tiny amount that already I can see it will be as a mere drop in this, my life's ocean.

So I'm reducing the Xanax and the patch in unison now. I have drawn up a chart, just like the one for my lozenge reduction. And I'm doing it religiously. Experience has taught me I cannot be trusted with my medication, not by myself, not by anyone.

Mum drops me off at my doctor, Dr M. I sit in front of him in that same yellow room, the same place I discovered I was a heroin addict a mere three months ago. It feels like three decades. I can't find words to express where I've been during that time.

I look a state. I'm dressed in baggy black jogging bottoms to soak up the DTs, a purple cotton top and a black fleece. My hair is scraped back into a bun and I'm shaking. We look at each other in watchful silence. He nods, but says nothing.

I'm the first to speak.

'My name is Cathryn and I am an addict,' I say, as boldly as the nausea, cramps and paranoia of the Xanax and fentanyl withdrawals will allow.

There's silence for a short moment which stretches out like a desert in my confusing, confused mind. Looking down into my lap, I can see my hands shaking. Shaking.

Then he claps. He stands up and he claps. And the sound is like a peal of ancient church bells. It's a sound of rejoicing, of triumph, of release and renewal.

He is clapping, for me, for him, for our grand achievement.

I stand up and I clap with him. And together we stand and face each other, clapping and clapping until my hands hurt.

'You're free,' he says, eventually.

Simple, but so exquisitely true. The sound of these words is like fresh mango juice and sparkling seawater and the Flower Duet – it's every good thing there is in this world. I'm free.

'Thank you,' I reply as an encore. 'I bet you didn't think I could do it. I expect I've taken you to the brink of suspension for malpractice,' I grin as we sit down again. Doctor and patient now. Dealer and junkie no more.

'Yep,' he says. 'But you had to get there yourself.'

'Bloody risky business,' I say sharply. 'I nearly lost my life.'

'But you didn't,' he says.

And he's right, I didn't. In fact, I gained a life. A tiny, shiny new shaft of sunlight which is my very own life. The miracle of it seems utterly extraordinary. Incredible and magnificent.

I show him my chart. I show him the packet of Xanax I was given on leaving rehab with the letter written by Helen telling him how many tablets there should be inside. Just to make sure. Just in case this junkie falls at the first hurdle.

Well, I haven't fallen. They're all in there. All the tiny white Xanax pills I am growing to hate. We make an appointment for a week's time. He measures out the number of tablets I will need, according to my chart, between now and then and he gives them to me, solemnly, as if the expectations of many lie heavy on my thin shoulders.

I get up and open the door with some difficulty. He doesn't get up to help. He stays there. Sitting. Watching. Making me do it myself. And so I do it. The next door is worse; I can barely push it open. Christ, I'm so frail. Will I ever be fit and strong again?

Getting the short few metres from the car to my temporary home proves trickier still. I have to keep stopping as my legs shake, my sweats start and waves of nausea plough over me; the combined effects of illness and withdrawal. It's ok though, and I get home.

I fall on the sofa and I lie there for a long time. And I think about everyone whose stories I shared, whose grief I witnessed and whose pain I felt in rehab. I think about them all, and from a deep place inside me, I miss them. I miss my brethren: the ones who know.

The light fades from the day. Cameron arrives home. His face lights up as he comes in and sees me there. At home. Admittedly, looking awful, but at home properly now, and not just here in spirit.

Later, when he's cooked dinner and washed up and he's settled on the sofa next to me, he kisses me lightly on the forehead and I feel safe. I feel like I've come home to the man I love. Maybe this time I can make a go of this relationship and these feelings.

By 10 p.m. I was normally in bed, taking my last lozenges of the day. In our old life, our dead life. So he's surprised that I'm still here sitting with him, quietly. I don't want to go upstairs to our bed alone. I want to stay beside him, breathing in the feelings of being here and not there, with him and not alone. I want to watch him as he taps on the computer keys. I want to touch his hair and his neck and tell him over and over that I'm back, I'm home.

But it's moving day tomorrow, so we have to go to bed soon. The day I thought I was dreading for so long has arrived. I wept many hot tears in the clinic in mourning for this home – the home I described as my sanctuary and my safe place. I thought my world had ended when I realised I had to sell it.

Sentiment and nostalgia for this place followed me all the way up to London, into rehab and then down to the detox centre. I held it close, holding on to something which I felt symbolised something of my past. Its creaking beams and gentle draughts formed a quiet, reclusive place where I put all my fear and pain and was comforted.

But now, looking at the shell of my old life, I realise it was all a lie. None of it was ever true. Now I see this cottage simply as the place where I took all those drugs, the place where I first decided to take 'an extra lozenge' because it couldn't hurt, could it? This is the place where I was cheated on and abandoned. This is where I lied to my doctor, my family, my Cameron. And now, on the brink of leaving it, I feel like a snake shedding its old, worn skin. I shuffle through each of the tiny rooms, run my hands along the 250-year-old beams, touch the whitewashed walls and wooden floors. And I feel nothing for it, and nothing for the lost girl who lived here. I'm glad she's gone. I'm glad that the person who needed this house has gone, leaving me in her place.

And it's good, so fantastically, marvellously, magically good that the tears come, thick and fast. And this time, they're tears of joy and happiness and new beginnings.

As the new day dawns, I'm not feeling so good. I've been sick twice overnight and haven't slept at all, as I fought panic attacks through the early hours. I feel really shaky.

Cameron leaps into action, packing the last boxes and stuffing clothes into bin liners. Suddenly, it feels like it's all happening so fast. I feel cut loose again, alone and anchorless in a fast current. I try to eat, but throw it all up minutes later. I should be used to the inside of a toilet bowl now, but I'm not. Each violent tremor forcing food out of my sore stomach feels like an insult, a setback.

I hear Cameron's footsteps behind me up the stairs. Jesus, he exclaims, maybe you should go to your parents' today. I'll do the move, you just look after yourself.

I'd had dreams of us getting into the car and driving off into the sunset and a shiny, happy future together. So I am unprepared for the reality of today, the dispelling of the fantasy world I am still prone to living in. But reluctantly, I agree.

I call Mum and ask her to pick me up. As I hear her voice at the end of the phone, I vow silently to myself: This is the last time I will ever ask for your help. From now on, *I* will look after *you*.

Instead of the soulful, tearful farewell to this crumbling 'sanctuary' that I had imagined, I leave the house in a bundle of pyjama bottoms and furry jumpers. I surrender it to its new owner without a murmur, without any grace. I leave, shut the door behind me, almost absently, and I'm gone. I stumble into Mum's car with only my chart, the remaining Xanax and a book.

As the day wears on, Cameron rings to say everything's in. Dad has put together our bed, we have a sofa in place and all the boxes are wherever anyone could find space. There's some mix-up with the keys to do with the old cottage and Cameron has to drive all the way back to drop them off and pick me up. We do, eventually, get to drive down together, but not into the sunset, as it has long since set.

We have teabags and no milk indoors and everything feels strange and unfamiliar. After opening up the grand shutters to try and see our new view of the sea which is almost on our doorstep, I realise we overlook a dark car park. Somehow, my idea of this place did not include the car park opposite which sits between us and the frothy swell of our seafront.

With disillusionment hovering at our shoulders, we turn away, shut the shutters and decide to head to bed early. An utterly unremarkable day. Maybe it was better this way. Maybe all the tearful, soulful stuff gets too much after a while and a short, sharp dose of reality is preferable.

Several weeks later and things are slowly starting to improve. Cameron has packed away most of our belongings. I have begun to make short, trembling walks outside to the seafront – a journey of five metres. And life is looking altogether cleaner and fresher.

Then, one day, Cameron tells me, 'We need to talk.'

At once, the toast I am munching on becomes like a dry bone stuck in my throat.

'Meet me on our beach at 8 p.m. There is something I have to say,' he tells me, then kisses me on the cheek before leaving for work. Something in his tone tells me this is important and I spend the day bracing myself for the news, absolutely convinced he has had enough of all this and is finally walking out.

These first few weeks out of rehab have been hard on us both. In spite of my silent vow, I have spent a lot of time back at my parents' as the strain of caring for me has worn both Cameron and myself out.

The woman who barely walked out of rehab seems so different from the one who was dragged in. I have strange moods, fits of temper followed by long periods of weeping. My sponsor – the lady (an ex-drug addict herself) who has kindly agreed to watch over me during this vulnerable time – tells me it is all normal. That coming off drugs is like opening a valve and everything comes tumbling out: fear, loss, moments of ecstasy and bliss, followed by tears and tantrums. It all comes out – and I fear this has all been too hard on Cameron. I am angry with him as well for not coming to the counselling sessions at rehab because he would know what is going on and what to expect. But he didn't want to face them, and so I now feel alone and misunderstood in all this and helpless in the face of both our ignorance.

Time moves so slowly, but 7.50 p.m. comes, eventually, and I pull on a jacket and scarf, plus big winter boots, even though it is May and the green shoots of spring have been in evidence for weeks now. I make it down to the beach, though walking on the pebbles proves difficult and tiring. I simply don't have the muscle strength in my legs nor the lungs for exercise. I sit on a bench almost directly outside our flat and wait in tense silence, watching the waves wash into the shore and drag out again and seeing the silver path of the moon's reflection on the mercurial darkness of the sea.

Moments later, Cameron arrives. He seems a little agitated. I must keep smiling, I tell myself. He's done so much for me, I mustn't be rude or angry when he leaves, though I can feel myself shake at the thought.

Cameron says nothing. Instead, he reaches inside his rucksack and brings out a little blue box.

'You know you said you wanted to get hitched one day?' he says, still looking so solemn and serious.

'Yes,' I reply, cocking my head to one side, waiting, watching him.

'Well, do you fancy it?' he says. The words catch the back of his throat which he clears, sheepishly.

'Fancy what?' I say stupidly, all logic and reason having flown out of my mind.

This isn't the talk I thought we were going to be having.

'Do you fancy marrying me?' His words are clear now, as clear as the diamonds which twinkle and tease the moonlight as he takes my hand and places the ring in my palm.

'I thought you'd like this,' he says and he is now smiling.

I think I squeal, or say something stupid or exclaim in delight. I can't really remember, but I am sure I say yes because the ring, a blue Tanzanite stone in a heart shape surrounded by proper diamonds, is on my finger.

Later, I am still stunned. I call my friends, family, anyone who'll pick up the phone to tell them. It all feels so surreal. Life has literally turned on its head and everything that was bad has gone, leaving everything shiny and new in its place.

We set the date. We decide to get married on our beach. We book our ceremony. We even start to make lists of who to invite – and every now and again we look at each other and laugh at the crazy wonderment of our life together. Yet every day, I still clutch the imperfect coin I was given at the end of the rehab as if it is a talisman to guide me through these early weeks and months. It *is* a talisman, and it guides me with the residue of the love and acceptance shown to me, helping to calm the fears, the worries, the anxious beginnings of trying to get it right this time, trying not to hurt people, trying to be different, yet stay the same.

It is a confusing time. I don't really remember who I am or what I like. It is like being reborn, which sounds very glamorous and triumphant, but feels vulnerable and strange. It is as if an old skin, one worn for a very long time has been ripped away from me, like a duvet off a warm bed, and I am exposed, naked, trembling with the newness of being alive.

Feeling delicate, I sit on my bench opposite the seafront on the days I feel well enough to go outside. I sit and watch the waves and start to find it in me to trust life and the world again. It is a fragile awakening. I know that anything could strike it dead. And so I sit, listen to the summer winds and the seasonal undercurrents and watch the light glint off the surface – and it is all I can do.

Slowly, cautiously, the grief starts to flow as the events of the past few years catches up with me. I see the frightened shouting woman in hospital in my mind's eye and I see the frightened shouting woman in rehab and I see her now, here, on this beach, except she is shouting a bit less these days. Only a bit though.

I have to come to terms with the loss of my prospects as a mother and that really hurts. It is not like the old, buried pain though; it is a new pain in the name of sadness which is true and beautiful in its own way. I grieve for my ex and for the betrayal and also for his love and care for me. I listen to my heart strings play out the last notes of our tune together and I cry for him, for me and for all those expectations, all those nights in A&E and for all those promises which were never kept. I remember the debility of all those years, which is still ongoing. There is, after all, no magic wand to make me better. And I wonder how I didn't go completely out of my mind. I live in pain from the chronic pancreatitis and it wears away my moods and my energy as surely as the sea wears down the rocks into smooth pebbles. Maybe I will become something as beautiful from all this. It is a hope, at least.

As I sit with all this, the plans for the wedding roll slowly onwards. The venue is fixed, chosen because it is yards from our flat and so I can be taken home if unwell. The dress is finally bought. I know I will shock everyone when I turn up wearing a traditional white dress, as they will all expect me to be quirky or outrageous. It is vintage though, and I will have a beehive and flowers in my hair, so it won't be too far out of the ordinary for me. The guest list is drawn up and the invitations all sent. It will be as low-key as we can make it. We have asked our guests to dress casually. Our biggest fear is that I won't be well enough to go through with it – but with that we are, again, in the hands of the gods.

The last thing, the most important thing, is Harry, the eight-year-old boy who holds Cameron's heart in his keeping. Cameron sits him down one sunny Saturday and carefully explains that he is going to marry me, which means that I will now be his step-mother. Harry cocks his head to one side like a baby bird and considers this for a moment.

'We will buy you a linen suit like your dad's and you'll be the ring bearer which is the most important role on the wedding day,' I say hurriedly, hoping he won't need to be swayed.

I know Cameron is on tenterhooks waiting for Harry's answer. It means everything to him. One word from Harry and the whole wedding would be off, postponed at the very least.

Harry – gorgeous, innocent, trusting Harry – knows nothing of this. He considers for a moment longer, then delivers his verdict.

'Cool,' is all he says. And it is more than enough.

CHAPTER 29

# Shocking Discovery

*June 2010*

Time stands still. I am in the bedroom of our new flat, peering into a box which I have been feebly trying to unpack, as I half-listen to *Woman's Hour* on the radio, half-hum a tune in my head as I potter the morning away. Except all that has stopped. The seconds and minutes have frozen and something is beating a harsh note inside my skull at the sight of what I have just discovered.

I sink back on to the bed, sitting and staring at the box I've been unpacking, not knowing what the hell to do. I've just lifted out a white pillowcase I had carefully packed six months ago in the week leading up to rehab, but as I reached in, instead of white broderie anglaise, I have found a white box. A white box with thirty fentanyl lozenges inside it. A white box worth hundreds of pounds to a dealer on the street, and it is sitting inside my pillowcase.

I have to stop and think. I don't know how it got there, do I? I put it there, didn't I? I did. I know I did. I keep looking, making sure this isn't the result of a fevered spell, a nightmarish fantasy, but no, it is real. The box was hidden away, by me, for me, to find on a day just like today. I screw my eyes up and put my head in my hands as the room shifts slightly. It was me. I know it was me. I think I can remember, but I am not sure. I don't want to be sure. I vaguely see myself in my old cottage bedroom and I have the box on the bed and I am packing things, but do I remember packing *those* things? Hiding away those terrible things? Preparing for my own relapse, my own tragedy, even as I was selling my beloved home and borrowing thousands from my hard-working parents? Even against that heavy emotional backdrop, I was hiding drugs to take after finishing rehab.

If it has not hit me already, then it does now. And by the 'it', I mean the full extent of my sickness. The ferocious grip of the addiction to this most powerful of enemies, this satanic demon inside me which prepared for my own undoing. I suddenly scream, cry out into the warm silence of the flat. The radio sounds tinny and far away. I realise what I have done and I cry again. A sound like 'No' leaves my lips and I start to rock backwards and forwards on the bed, in this room, all alone with my fentanyl. Then the thought leaks in, creeps in, slowly winds round my mind that I am here, and no one would know, and there they are, and what do I do? What the fucking hell do I do? The question startles me into action.

'Fuck, fucking hell, fucking shitting hell!' The fear escapes in obscenities which sound hollow and small in this very lonely, scary place.

'What do I do? I don't know what to do,' I say out aloud to the air and the walls and the ceiling and the doors, the bed and the furniture. 'What do I do? Help me please, help me.'

And with the new sounds comes a tiny moment of clarity: ring Mum and Dad. I can't be trusted. I cannot be trusted with this box of heaven and hell; it is temptation and terrible, terrible fear all contained in one rectangular cardboard box, the label on which reads 'Actiq Fentanyl Lozenges 200mcg' on the side.

I find the phone, and dial too quickly. I botch it and have to put the receiver down and try again. All the time talking myself through it, so that I don't forget myself, go back to the box, open it and rip out a lozenge. I have to keep the monologue going to avoid the pull of the box and its contents. I dial and it rings.

On the ninth ring, Mum answers the phone.

'... 024,' she says calmly, like it is an ordinary day.

I interrupt her flow because I know that I have to tell her straight away and become accountable or I am lost. I am truly lost.

'Mum, please listen. Look, I've been unpacking a box from the move and I found something, I found a box of lozenges. They're unopened and I don't know what to do with them. I'm scared I'm going to take one. Please come, please come now and help me get rid of them. I don't know what to do ...' I burst into sobs at that point.

I hear my mother reel in shock before saying, wearily, 'Don't do anything. Just leave the box alone and we'll be on our way down there.'

I don't even wait for Mum to ring off. I put the phone down and head to the kitchen. I'm convinced now that if I am sat in the same room as this box, I might open it. I am so bloody terrified I will succumb to the horror of it all again for that brief moment of heady, unadulterated bliss that I have to get them out of the flat. I need to get them out, but how and where?

I see a pile of Tesco bags under the sink in the kitchen and I take out four. With unsteady hands I take the box, holding it at arm's length, as if it were contaminated. I drop it into one of the bags, then tie a knot. Then that goes into the next bag and so on until I am looking at a fat plastic shopping bag filled with other plastic shopping bags and one extremely dangerous box of class A medical opiates. Satisfied, though I know I am acting like a mad-woman and that Tesco bags are no guarantee against craving a drug stronger than heroin, I pull open the front door and expel the mess of bags on to the landing. In my crazy, stupid mind, addled by withdrawal symptoms, it makes sense to try and hide them from me, even though I know where they are and even in my weakened state, four carrier bags won't exactly keep me at bay, if it comes to it. I have to think that it won't. I have to concentrate on something else, wait for Mum and Dad to arrive and bring some common sense into the delirium that is my life.

I wait like an obedient child, grateful that help is on the way. I sit on my bed, watching the ebb and flow of the sea outside my window for an age until eventually, I see their car turn into the car park opposite the flat. I watch the two harassed and hunted-looking people who must be fucking sick of looking after me as they get a parking ticket and walk up to my buzzer. I let them in and they appear in my doorway. I point to the plastic bags sitting in a rather pathetic heap, looking as un-frightening as it is possible to look, and Mum picks them up as she comes in.

'Don't bring it in!' I say, my voice verging on hysteria.

'Stop it, Cathryn. Now what are we going to do with it?' Mum asks. Her voice is harsh and she is looking at me strangely.

'I promise you I haven't taken any. It was such a shock, I was so addicted to them I almost scuppered everything, I was planning to relapse before I even went to rehab, I just can't believe how sick I was, Mum.' My words fumble about, making little sense as they escape. My mouth feels clumsy and slow, even as I gabble to her.

'We can't just throw them away, in case another addict finds them – there is enough in there to kill someone with an overdose,' I tell them, hoping they will listen to the frantic woman–child in front of them.

'We'd better take them to the chemist, then,' says Dad logically, and so they walk down to the nearest pharmacy, returning ten minutes later. Then we sit together, sipping hot tea until they finally say they have to go. I can barely look them in the face.

Something odd happened today, which we are all uncomfortable with. Maybe it is the realisation that the addiction did not end when I took the last drug and still gnaws away at me, tearing at my mind and heart, even though I have been clean for three months. Whatever it is, I am tired and feeling low.

When they leave I lean my back against the cold smoothness of the wall in my bedroom and sink slowly to the floor. I stay like that for a while, not daring to move, feeling like an empty shell.

Gradually, I find the strength to get up. I cannot keep living in the past. I did resist those drugs. I did the right thing, and now I must move forward as there is still much to do. I am getting married in a month's time. I have the menu to finalise, the drinks to organise, the wedding car to book. These are all good things and I must do them, shrug this off and get on with starting to live the life I have been given a second chance at living.

Even so, the ache of the discovery is sore like an open wound. Will there ever be a day I can be free of this demon inside me? It is a question I have no answer to now, and one I may never have an answer to. In the meantime, I must pull myself back together and begin again. This time, with the knowledge of myself a little keener, a little sharper inside.

CHAPTER 30

# Perfect Day

*31 July 2010*

I swing the shutters open to revel in this, the most splendid day of my life – and find that July has turned into November. Thick fog greets me. I cannot even make out the seafront which is only metres from my window. Rain, pouring down the glass windows in milky abandon, is every now and then swept off by gusts of wind. Blinking back my reaction, I grimly remind myself it is only 6 a.m. and I seem to have woken in the middle of a squally storm.

Climbing back into bed I sneak a glance at my dress which is hanging from one of the large shutters. The beading which covers the entirety of the fabric winks at me in the dismal daylight and I snuggle down, grinning in childlike delight and worrying about the weather in equal measure.

It is a couple of hours before the boys wake up – I insisted Cameron slept in Harry's room last night as I wanted us to have some semblance of tradition about our life and our wedding day. We didn't have the money to go to a hotel, and we don't have the money for tonight either, so we will spend the first day of our married life back in our bed, in our flat and that is exactly how we both want it.

Harry wakes up first. I can hear him creep into the lounge and look for the TV remote control. I get up then and greet him cheerily, give him some milk and put his favourite Saturday-morning programme on for him. I put the kettle on and make a cup of tea for Cameron – he won't thank me for waking him, but I need him and our boy to be up and out by 10 a.m. because that's when the make-up and hair lady is coming. I didn't want any fuss this morning, there has been enough of that to last me a lifetime over the past few years, and so only Francesca is coming over. Grace is in Cuba working on a guidebook, and although we are both devastated she couldn't make it back, we know it was just too wildly impractical. My sister will be here a bit later as well, but I've told everyone else that I'll see them at the venue on the beachfront.

Thinking of the outdoor beach ceremony makes me panic again about the weather. Must not think about that now, I tell myself. And I have a funny feeling it will all be ok – everything else in my life has sorted out, so why would this be any different? Sometimes, it is possible to get a sense of how something will be – and today I know that the rain and fog will disappear as quickly as they arrived. Don't ask me how I know – I just do.

Cameron grills some sausages for him and his son and runs me a bath. As they eat, and watch telly, like any normal weekend, I sink into a hot bubble bath and watch the refracted light from the oily bath cream make rainbows in my bubbles. Why did I need to go to rehab to notice how beautiful everything is? All the little details – the feel of the hot water melting my bones, the twinkling bubbles, the smell of good sausages grilling – all of it suspends me in a kind of sensual reverie. I missed all this stuff before. I missed life itself. The thought chokes me a little – I am old to be experiencing such a rebirth, thirty-nine in a month's time, and I am only now seeing how much of my long life I simply was not able to enjoy or experience. But I must not dwell today of all days – regret is such a useless emotion, such a waste of precious time. I have been given a chance to live – how many times was I expected to die? First from the acute pancreatitis and then from the drug addiction? So many times – and yet I didn't. I don't know why I was spared, but I was. And now, just like Sleeping Beauty, I am rising from a century-long sleep and can start to enjoy being alive and being human. And I have a gorgeous prince to kiss me out of my slumber, my old ravaged, drug-induced reverie. I am finally awake and keen to smell, taste, see, feel the world and everything in it.

At 10 a.m., Cameron is still getting himself and Harry together. The hairdresser arrives and sets up in the lounge. The weather is no different. The sky is still bleak and the fog has cleared only enough to reveal grey waves tipped with white, foamy streaks. It doesn't look good. She is cheery though and so am I. We finally get Cameron and Harry packed off. They are going to his mum's where I suspect she will iron their matching linen suits.

I am wrapped in my favourite kimono – one I bought in a market in Tokyo on one of the travel trips that made up my life before all this drama. I keep my travel heirlooms close to me to remind me I am not just the sum of these parts – illness, addiction; rebirth.

As the hairdresser lays out her stuff and sips her coffee I muse about another trip, this time in Cambodia where I was working and travelling for a month. I remember another market – this one slung under drapes of plastic sheeting and parts of plastic bags and old hessian, frayed and ripped, but enough to cover the largest market in Phnom Penh. I remember walking through this market, filled with old car parts and cheap wooden carvings of Buddhas from China, then turning down by a small stall laden with bags of bitter-smelling spices and finding, eventually, a magical stall – a tiny, cupboard-like hovel stacked to its plastic ceiling with kimonos of all shapes and sizes.

As a self-confessed fabric-fetishist, I can still feel the sense of being spellbound by the glories held within this ragged space; the rich textiles folded carefully and stacked one on top of the other. There must have been thousands of them. A woman sat in the middle of the stall, surrounded by the teetering treasures, most of her teeth missing and talking to me in gummy clicks, while weaving delicate smoke tendrils from a pipe into the confined air.

It was like stepping into a fairytale: the witch's cottage filled with beautiful booty for those who dared to enter. She was selling each kimono for just three US dollars. Three measly dollars. If I could go back to any of my trips, any of the places where I wandered and mused and walked, it would be here to this place – to buy all those treasures and carry them home to revel in sumptuous fabric heaven. I wish I had bought them all. I didn't though. I bought two – a plush red silk kimono with a blushing pink silk lining in an erotic contrast, and a purple one with a turquoise blue lining.

I still have the kimonos. They are folded away carefully in boxes, yet to be unpacked, nestled alongside my Moroccan and Turkish rugs, my Burmese monks' prayer mats and incense, my Laos Buddha with the arching cobra forming an umbrella to protect the sitting metal figure, my Burmese textiles, a suitcase filled with decorative longhis, my Russian shawls and matrioshkas, my Baltic samovar for brewing black tea, my ceramics from Sardinia, my blankets from Peru, my Spanish throw, my candles from Thailand ... the list goes on. All those beautiful things to remind me of who I was and what I did and what I loved.

I loved the adventure and excitement of travel. I loved not knowing where I would stay that night, or who I would meet while finding a good meal or where I would be the next day. I felt connected to and part of the world in a way I have struggled to feel since those days. I know that, and while I appreciated the times abroad, I am trying to be grateful now that I can live at a slower pace, with plenty of time to see the details, feel the magic of living, rather than the constant need to move on and on, to more and more wondrous or beautiful places.

It is hard though when there is pain – lots of pain, and the strange depressions which sit on me and taunt me along with the tiredness, so complete that I feel sometimes I have already died. I know my challenge now is to find that wonder right here in this place, putting down roots at last. This is a new town for me, a new place to live and I admit I fight the claustrophobia of being in one place already, despite only having lived here for less than four months. But I am happy to fight it, to sink my feet into the ground here and see if I can't build a solid life at last.

The hairdresser interrupts my mind's wanderings by asking if we can start as we are a little behind schedule. Fran has arrived and is toasting bagels in the kitchen. There is no champagne because I have learned that I must stay away from all drugs, and that includes alcohol, if I am to live wisely and recover well.

I don't miss it, today of all days. A few people have remarked how awful it is that I can't get drunk on my wedding day. I just smile and say nothing, thinking that it is a small price to pay for my health and wellbeing.

As I sit in surrender, my hair is dried and sprayed, then moulded into something that is somewhere between a chignon and a beehive – just as I wanted it – with artificial flowers pinned into one side. I wrap my kimono tighter around me and suddenly feel very small and very tired. It will be a struggle to sit and stand for the whole afternoon. We booked our ceremony for 4 p.m., the last slot of the day, to give me enough time to rest beforehand and to keep the wedding as short as possible. Neither of us knows how great the toll from the day's activities will be on me, but we suspect it won't pass without decimating my body for days and weeks to come.

Still, I am going to stand upright and walk the short walk to my new husband to say my vows. We have my wheelchair as back-up, but I have been doing small walks every few days for the past couple of months, and while I am physically very weak still with ME and the effects of years of illness, as well as the withdrawals which still plague my beleaguered body, I am determined I won't be wheeled into my own wedding. I have said all along that I will stand for my vows, just like any normal bride.

Because I want so much to be normal now – to live a normal, settled life with a mortgage and bills and Harry's football subs and the weekly supermarket shopping to be paid for. I have never done any of these things, never had a life that could be described as 'ordinary' and now feels like just the right time to start fitting in and getting on.

But suddenly, I feel overwhelmed and tearful. There are beloved friends and family arriving, but it all feels too much, too big, and I wonder what the hell I was thinking of. I find I am crying and Fran goes to get me a tissue. She smiles at me and tells me it's just pre-wedding nerves. I nod, knowing this to be partly true. But I am also terrified of how little strength and energy I have, and conscious I may not make it through the afternoon, and so the nerves don't go. When my eyes have dried enough, my make-up is applied, but I know we're now behind schedule.

My bouquet has been delivered, bought for me by Mum, with flowers for the wedding breakfast bought by Fran. The white vintage 1949 Chevrolet is due in twenty minutes – and there is still the small matter of getting my dress on. Fran holds me up while Laura, my sister, pulls it over my head. The panic makes everything so surreal and, finally, funny.

Dad arrives, the car arrives, and still the wind is blowing strong against the grey sea. There's a light drizzle now and I am starting to think my instincts may all have been wrong.

'Let's have a glass of bubbly water before we go,' says Laura.

Dad cracks open the San Pellegrino and we pretend to be filling our glasses with champagne with a slightly ironic chorus of 'Oohs' and more laughter.

'Cheers,' we all say and clink our glasses together.

'Time to go,' says Dad, when the chauffeur comes up to the flat to tell us we are late, nudging us gently into departure.

Now it all feels surreal. I gather up the length of my dress and turn to face the door. My short veil is pinned in place, my bouquet of white and cream roses is in my right hand, while the other smoothes down the dress. Dad grips me tightly as we descend to the waiting car.

At that moment, the clouds part, revealing the splendour of afternoon sunshine. The wind has dropped a little, the sea is still churning against the shore, but is blue with light dancing off the water like millions of tiny glances on a bed of diamonds. We stand, transfixed for a moment, in absolute delight at the sudden, dramatic change in the weather.

'A good sign,' says Dad.

We all nod, then Fran helps me and the dress into the red velvet interior of the car, and we are in. We are ready to go. With my white dress, my vintage-red lipstick and my hair dyed the colour of a post box set against the delicate white veil and my white and cream bouquet, I feel like a princess, not an ex-druggie for once, but a bona-fide queen of the day.

It only takes a couple of minutes to get to the venue. As the car pulls up, the shout goes up and the windows which line the seafront are filled with smiling faces cramming to see us arrive. It takes a moment to ready myself to be able to step out of the car, and by this time the doors to the venue have opened and several people have gathered outside to help me in and say hello. All my fears dissolve away. This is already the best day of my life and I haven't got to the ceremony yet. I'm so glad everyone is here. I am surrounded by the people I love and my heart swells like the sea, which is washing against the shoreline more calmly now. The sun is arching brightly overhead, though there is still a breeze, which feels good, like it is wiping away the dead wood from before, rendering me clean and renewed.

I lose count of the kisses and hugs, the smiles and good wishes which greet us as we walk slowly into the back of the venue, out of sight of the groom who is waiting on the beach side, on the crescent-shaped terrace where we will wed.

Dad, Fran and I wait for the longest ten minutes of my life until the registrar comes down to confirm I am not being coerced into the marriage! Fran and I hold hands. I am trembling with exhaustion already, I'm not sure I can last much beyond the ceremony, but that is ok, that is enough.

We wait and Dad tells jokes and we are finally ready to go to the balcony where everyone is now waiting. There is chatter as I stand to one side, and I suddenly feel I cannot breathe. So much has happened in the past few years and it has all ended here, with this wedding. I am hyperventilating a little and the venue owner tells me to calm down and breathe slowly.

The first chords of the Flower Duet sound above the waves, and it is time to step out.

I don't recall much of the next few minutes. I see faces I know and love, and they are all smiling at me. The wind is quite blustery and I have to hold my veil on as I walk up to my husband-to-be. He takes an age to look at me, but when he does, I see his eyes and know myself to be loved by this tall man of mine who has brought light to my world of darkness.

Harry takes his part as ring bearer seriously, as he solemnly holds the rings in his proffered hand and we say the vows. I had been dreading saying them, but it turns out to be the most special and emotional time of the day. Giving myself to someone, and him giving himself to me, is so much more than I ever dreamed. We both say our words with meaning, looking deep into each other's eyes, smiling and holding hands so tightly I remember they hurt when he finally lets go for the kiss. And the kiss? Well, it is the best kiss to seal a new marriage that has ever been witnessed. No polite peck on the lips for us. Instead, Cameron sweeps me into his big arms and I hold my head and my heart up to him in total surrender as he kisses me, holding me tight into him while the guests clap and cheer. As we turn round to the crowd, they laugh even harder. Cameron is now wearing my red lipstick as he has kissed it off me, and when he realises he puckers up back at them, laughing as he does it.

Afterwards, there is a sweet interlude when our guests are busy talking and drinking, and we – Harry, Cameron and I – have a glorious moment of quiet and reflection. We sit together by the seafront, taking in the view, watching the tide as it goes further out, exposing the rocks and pools of the shallows. The wind has now dropped completely and the water is lapping gently against the pebbled shoreline.

We are a family now. We are married and life will never be the same again, thank God.

After the last of the guests has finished eating Cameron rises up to signal the start of the speeches. He keeps hold of my hand as he grabs the microphone. I think he is handing over to my dad, but instead he has a speech of his own. As he talks, I find that the happy tears I have wanted to cry all afternoon finally come spilling out. He turns to me and tells me how he respects me for everything I went through. Everyone here knows I was in rehab, everyone knows the illness and long years of degradation and debility. He tells me I am the most courageous woman he has ever met and he is proud to be my husband. My eyes are fixed on his, and his voice finally breaks as he sheds tears of his own.

I am amazed and humbled by this man who has changed everything for me, who supported me through my torments, who did not judge me or abuse me. Who believed in me – and does so still. His speech cements something deep within me, and I know that no matter what trials lie ahead, his words will be the flame that guides us through into our future.

There is hushed silence as he finishes, then riotous applause. I can see my whole family crying and I am joining them too. In my mind and my heart, I thank whatever it was that pulled me through.

Whatever benign energy in this blessed universe got me here, now, to this day, I am more grateful to it than I can express. I feel enclosed in a safe space with my husband, a protected island, and it is as if we are in our own world, separate together.

Over a year later, my stepson Harry is staying for his usual weekend with us, and I decide I feel well enough to take him on a nature trek in nearby woods, where he can run free while I sit, soaking up the late autumn sunshine.

We walk slowly. I am still in pain and still hampered by physical constraints, but it is a beautiful day and I choose to ignore it all. Harry skips around me as we look for the rest of the nature party, and I watch, sitting on a felled tree trunk in the glow of the sunshine, as he hunts for insects with the other children.

Heading back to the car an hour later, I feel his hand slip into mine. I make no move to acknowledge this, as I am terrified he will pull away as he usually does, like a small frightened animal. At last though, he is relaxing with me; at last, he trusts me enough to hold my hand and is content to be with me, chattering away in his usual fashion.

The day is suffused by orange light and something deeper, quieter. The gulf inside me which yearns for my own child, which will remain forever empty, softens and shrinks. It will never go away. I will always only ever be Harry's step-mummy – I have no wish to try to be anything more – but it is something, it is something very good which I feel right now. It is a blessing I could never have foreseen. We talk and walk, slowly and carefully along the short woodland track, and his hand stays firmly in mine and I feel, at last, I have reasons plenty to live, reasons to love – and the terrible theatre of my grisly past fades into nothing, sinks away, out of sight, like the day's setting sun.

EPILOGUE

# New Beginning

I pray every morning on waking. I feel awkward as I do it. It is a squirmy, embarrassed feeling. But pray I must or the delicate cords that carry me into sanity might tangle and break. It's the same feeling as putting on a life-jacket – a bit of a nuisance, but it makes the difference between floating and drowning.

I pray to whatever it was that got me through the darkness. Whatever it was that pulled me through it all: pain, hospital, loss, loneliness, terror, addiction and withdrawal. I pray because I'm terrified of the pain which hums an insistent note through each of my days. I am always afraid of the possibility it may crescendo into an acute attack. I can still feel the imprint, the echo of that horror inside me. By the time my last operation took place I had lost most of my life to it. I hoped the op would kill me. There was a fairly good chance it would, as it was difficult and dangerous surgery. I felt my spirit had been ripped from me over the years in dirty, dingy, uncaring, soulless hospital wards. I couldn't move, couldn't walk, couldn't live. Pain pulled me deep into my grave and something, I don't know what, pulled me out again.

Kicking and screaming.

I don't know what each day will bring. My specialist tells me each day is a gift, and they cannot tell me my prognosis. The pancreas is a delicate, highly-strung organ and you mess with it at your peril. So I have to live in the moment. Or I will go crazy with fear. My father recently told me that in 2007 he was told by a surgeon that I would live a maximum of seven years because that's what pancreatitis does to people. It destroys them. I wish he hadn't told me that as the thought of it sends a cold spear into my heart. I must go on thinking it will all be ok.

Because in lots of ways it is already. I have overcome so much, and I have the proof of it right here, right now. I am a married woman, I live on the seafront in glorious disbelief at my good luck and I have friends, family and a naughty, gorgeous, beloved stepson to keep it real for me. I am blessed. I am grateful.

But even so, every morning, I wake up frightened by the terror that an uncertain future brings. And every morning, I have to fight for perspective along with the panicky breaths I take. I don't know if I'll be ok today, let alone tomorrow. Hospital feels like it is a hair's-breadth away, and I still have to live, knowing that. So that is why I have to shut my eyes again and ask for help. I feel silly saying it. I've never been a prayer. But I do know that I was saved for something, for some good reason.

Maybe just to tell my story. Maybe just to be a good stepmummy or wife. I've learned that the most important stuff doesn't have to be dramatic. There was a time when I aspired to accomplish epic things. I'm pretty sure I won't be conquering the world or finding the cure for cancer now; instead, I'm yearning for a quieter, domestic miracle. Keeping my own house, being a loving wife, being a better sister and daughter. These are epic enough for me to grasp.

So many people have told me I must have a guardian angel. Throughout my time in hospital, undergoing the sometimes brutal and tortuous treatments, I received angels and fairies from friends and loved ones. Little carved treasures, dolls made into magical totems, all symbols of hope, calling to help me when they could not.

Did they work? I don't know, but here I stand today, broken but not beaten, emerging into a life, an ordinary person's life. So maybe they did, maybe they did. Miracles don't surprise me any more. They happen every day – if we remember to look for them.

Even the simple fact of waking up in my own bed every morning. Such a small thing, we all take for granted, yet I cannot because I have been to the other side of life, to the edge, even over it, gripping the precipice with my fingers, hanging on, no matter what. It is a mystery how the human spirit is spun of such fragile material and yet can withstand such enormous destructive forces. It's like that saying that a room in darkness only needs one small candle flame to have light. In my own small way, I feel I am becoming that flame. Bobbing and weaving into life, laughing with the joy of existing.

And with this comes such a blessing. As my friends start to notice their physical decline, a few wrinkles, grey hairs, weight that won't shift as they reach forty, I realise I have all of those worries and yet I am simultaneously free of them. Each day is a gift, literally a gift. I don't give a shit about my wrinkles or my white hairs – I wear them with pride. I earned each and every one of them.

Cathryn Kemp, March 2012

# About the Author

Cathryn Kemp is a journalist and travel writer. She was a journalist for the *People*, *News of the World*, the *Sunday Mirror* and the *Mirror* for seven years before falling ill literally overnight in 2004. She has written several Lonely Planet books, including *Romania and Moldov; Estonia, Latvia and Lithuania; Eastern Europe* and *Europe on a Shoestring.*

# Useful Resources

## Addiction – definition

If I had to choose one word which, for me, summed up the entire gamut of my insanity and compulsive behaviours while in active addiction, I would have no hesitation. I know the word. It is the word 'prison'. Being stuck in the chaos of addiction to a substance is like being trapped inside a prison which squeezes and constricts tighter and tighter like a hungry python until there is nothing left of the person inside.

While I was having to take the enormous amount of painkillers my body and mind were craving, there was always a part of me – a very small part – which could see how deeply I was trapped. I simply had no focus other than the continual fear of running out of my supplies of fentanyl, of not being able to convince my GP to give me another prescription, of calculating how many lozenges I had left, how many I would need, how many I had binged on the night before and how long I would have to wait until I could drag my broken body up to the pharmacy for the next lot. For the circle of shame and pain and terrible fear to start turning again; each time ending up back in the same place. There's a classic saying in Alcoholics Anonymous 'Don't tell an alcoholic (or addict) to go to hell, they've already been there.' That, for me, is the definition of addiction, which is why any terrible day in recovery is still a thousand times better than a day using drugs.

## Do you have a problem with addiction?

My denial of my deep-rooted problems with painkillers was the single most harmful aspect of the disease of addiction as it manifested in me. I fought my doctor head-on for months as he became convinced I was dependent on fentanyl. I simply refused to believe that I could be an addict. After all, wasn't I formerly successful as a journalist and businesswoman? Hadn't I had the best education my parents could provide? Didn't I have qualifications aplenty, lots of friends, my own home? And yet, when the truth came crashing in on me I found I could fight no longer. It was at that point of complete surrender, knowing I'd lost the battle of my life, that recovery finally could happen. It is an irony of this disease that isn't until we stop fighting and give in to the people who are trying to help us that things can finally change for the better, or so it was for me.

Self-delusion is the cornerstone of addiction. Despite our lives being chaos, our relationships failing, our finances a mess, our inability to stop taking whatever substance has a grip on us, we still believe we can sort it out. We can't. We need help, and admitting that is the first, most important step on the path to recovery.

The below questionnaire from the Narcotics Anonymous literature, may help you decide if you have a problem:

## Am I an addict?

Only you can answer this question.

This may not be an easy thing to do. All through our usage, we told ourselves, 'I can handle it.' Even if this was true in the beginning, it is not so now. The drugs handled us. We lived to use and used to live. Very simply, an addict is a person whose life is controlled by drugs.

Perhaps you admit you have a problem with drugs, but you don't consider yourself an addict. All of us have preconceived ideas about what an addict is. There is nothing shameful about being an addict once you begin to take positive action. If you can identify with our problems, you may be able to identify with our solution. The following questions were written by recovering addicts in Narcotics Anonymous. If you have doubts about whether or not you're an addict, take a few moments to read the questions below and answer them as honestly as you can.

1. Do you ever use alone? Yes ☐ No ☐
2. Have you ever substituted one drug for another, thinking that one particular drug was the problem? Yes ☐ No ☐
3. Have you ever manipulated or lied to a doctor to obtain prescription drugs? Yes ☐ No ☐
4. Have you ever stolen drugs or stolen to obtain drugs? Yes ☐ No ☐
5. Do you regularly use a drug when you wake up or when you go to bed? Yes ☐ No ☐
6. Have you ever taken one drug to overcome the effects of another? Yes ☐ No ☐
7. Do you avoid people or places that do not approve of you using drugs? Yes ☐ No ☐
8. Have you ever used a drug without knowing what it was or what it would do to you? Yes ☐ No ☐
9. Has your job or school performance ever suffered from the effects of your drug use? Yes ☐ No ☐

10. Have you ever been arrested as a result of using drugs? Yes ☐ No ☐
11. Have you ever lied about what or how much you use? Yes ☐ No ☐
12. Do you put the purchase of drugs ahead of your financial responsibilities? Yes ☐ No ☐
13. Have you ever tried to stop or control your using? Yes ☐ No ☐
14. Have you ever been in a jail, hospital, or drug rehabilitation centre because of your using? Yes ☐ No ☐
15. Does using interfere with your sleeping or eating? Yes ☐ No ☐
16. Does the thought of running out of drugs terrify you? Yes ☐ No ☐
17. Do you feel it is impossible for you to live without drugs? Yes ☐ No ☐
18. Do you ever question your own sanity? Yes ☐ No ☐
19. Is your drug use making life at home unhappy? Yes ☐ No ☐
20. Have you ever thought you couldn't fit in or have a good time without drugs? Yes ☐ No ☐
21. Have you ever felt defensive, guilty, or ashamed about your using? Yes ☐ No ☐
22. Do you think a lot about drugs? Yes ☐ No ☐
23. Have you had irrational or indefinable fears? Yes ☐ No ☐
24. Has using affected your sexual relationships? Yes ☐ No ☐
25. Have you ever taken drugs you didn't prefer? Yes ☐ No ☐
26. Have you ever used drugs because of emotional pain or stress? Yes ☐ No ☐
27. Have you ever overdosed on any drugs? Yes ☐ No ☐
28. Do you continue to use despite negative consequences? Yes ☐ No ☐
29. Do you think you might have a drug problem? Yes ☐ No ☐

If you are an addict, you must first admit that you have a problem with drugs before any progress can be made toward recovery. These questions, when honestly approached, may help to show you how using drugs has made your life unmanageable. Addiction is a disease which, without recovery, ends in jails, institutions and death.


## Where do I turn for help?

The first point of call is your GP or your local Substance Misuse Service (SMS). Your doctor may refer you to your local SMS which may encourage you to attend an NHS rehab facility. Another option is to do a self-referral by walking into the local SMS where you will be assessed by drug workers and a doctor with inpatient treatment as an option. All of this is funded by the NHS. You can also walk into any A&E at any time and say you need help in the form of hospital detox.

Private rehab clinics are expensive but provide 24-hour collection services for emergency cases. There are lots of private clinics out there, as any quick look on Google shows, and I recommend searching online to find the clinic which would be most suitable for your needs. When contacting a treatment centre I would advise asking several questions to determine if the centre is right for you:

- What treatment plan/method do they follow?
- Do they cater for people with your addiction (prescription drugs, gambling, sex, alcohol, sugar, cocaine etc)?
- Are there adequate medical facilities nearby?
- How long would your detox be expected to take?
- How much does inpatient treatment cost per week?

## Resources for addicts seeking recovery

### Anonymous fellowships

Anonymous fellowships are free to join and open to anybody seeking help for an addiction without fear of legal or social repercussions. They provide worldwide support and help for addicts using the twelve-step approach to addiction.

**Narcotics Anonymous**
*UK*
Website: www.ukna.org
Helpline: 0845 373 3366
Email: helpline@ukna.org
*Australia*
Website: http://na.org.au
Tel: 1300 652 820 (for recorded information about NA meeting times and locations)
Email: info@na.org.au
*New Zealand*
Website: www.nzna.org
Tel: 0800 628 632
Email: nzrsc@nzna.org
*Worldwide*
Website: www.na.org
Tel: (818) 773 9999
Email: fsmail@na.org

**Alcoholics Anonymous**
*UK*
Website: www.alcoholics-anonymous.org.uk
Helpline: 0845 769 7555
Email: help@alcoholics-anonymous.org.uk
*Australia*
Website: www.aa.org.au
Helpline: 1300 22 22 22
Email: national.office@aa.org.au
*New Zealand*
Website: www.aa.org.nz
Helpline: 0800 229 6757
Email: nzgso@xtra.co.nz
*Worldwide*
Website: www.aa.org
Tel: 212 870 3400
Email: international@aa.org

## Other anonymous fellowships

**Cocaine Anonymous**
*UK*
Website: www.cauk.org.uk
Tel: 0800 612 0225
Email: helpline@cauk.org.uk
*Australia*
Website: www.caaustralia.org
Helpline: 0 432 040 023
*Worldwide*
Website: www.ca.org
Tel: 310 559 5833
Email: cawso@ca.org

**Sex and Love Addiction Anonymous**
*UK*
Website: www.slaauk.org
Tel: 07951 815 087
Email: contact@slaauk.org
*Australia*
Website: www.slaa.org.au
Tel: 0410 650 355 (Sydney)
(03) 9513 2084 (Melbourne)
0452 074 974 (Byron Bay)

Email: secretary.sydney@slaa.org.au (Sydney)
secretary.melbourne@slaa.org.ua (Melbourne)
*New Zealand*
Website: www.aucklandslaa.org.nz (Auckland)
www.slaawellington.org.nz (Wellington)
Tel: 09 377 1800 (Auckland)
Email: slaainauckland@hotmail.com (Auckland)
*Worldwide*
Website: www.slaafws.org

**Gamblers Anonymous**
*UK*
Website: www.gamblersanonymous.org.uk
Tel: 020 7384 3040
Email: young.private@gamblersanonymous.org.uk
*Australia*
Website: www.gansw.org.au
Helpline: (02) 9628 5065
Email: info@gansw.org.au
*Worldwide*
Website: www.gamblersanonymous.org
Tel: (626) 960 3500
Email: isomain@gamblersanonymous.org

**Debtors Anonymous**
*UK*
Website: www.debtorsanonymous.org.uk
Tel: 020 7117 7533
Email: infor1@debtorsanonymous.org.uk
*Worldwide*
Website: www.debtorsanonymous.org
Tel: 800 421 2383 (US only) or 781 453 2743
Email: office@debtorsanonymous.org

## Other organisations

*UK*
**Talk To Frank**
Email and telephone support for young people, parents and carers concerned about drugs. Calls are free from landlines and won't show up on the telephone bill.
Website: www.talktofrank.com

Helpline: 0800 77 66 00
Email: frank@talktofrank.com

**Release**
A national helpline offering advice in relation to drugs and the law.
Website: www.release.org.uk
Helpline: 0845 4500 215
Email: ask@release.org.uk

**Council for Involuntary Tranquilliser Addiction**
A national helpline, support and information for people who have become addicted to prescription tranquillisers.
Website: www.citawithdrawal.org.uk
Helpline: 0151 932 0102
Email: cita@citap.org.uk

**Addaction**
Information and advice to help individuals and communities manage the effects of drug and alcohol misuse.
Website: www.addaction.org.uk
Tel: 0207 251 5860
Email: info@addaction.org.uk

**DrinkLine**
Free, national service providing counselling, support, advice and information.
Tel: 0800 917 8282

**Smoke Free**
NHS website providing advice on how to quit smoking.
Website: http://smokefree.nhs.uk/
Helpline: 0800 022 4 332

**Quit**
Information and an online email service to help smokers quit. Includes advice for young people, pregnant women and health professionals.
Website: www.quit.org.uk
Helpline: 0800 002 200
Email: stopsmoking@quit.org.uk

**GamCare**
Provides information and counselling services to gamblers and their families.
Website: www.gamcare.org.uk

Helpline: 0845 600 0133
Email: info@gamcare.org.uk

**MIND**
Provides support for anyone with a mental health problem.
Website: www.mind.org.uk
Tel: 0300 123 3393
Email: info@mind.org.uk

**SANE**
Provides emotional support, practical help and information to anybody affected by mental illness.
Website: www.sane.org.uk
Tel: 020 7375 1002
Email: info@sane.org.uk

**Samaritans**
A confidential emotional support service for anyone in the UK and Ireland.
Website: www.samaritans.org
Tel: 08457 90 90 90
Email: jo@samaritans.org

*Australia*
**Counselling Online**
A free service where you can communicate with a professional counsellor about an alcohol or drug related concern.
Website: www.counsellingonline.org.au
Tel: 1800 888 236
Email: CounsellingOnline@turningpoint.org.au

**Australian Centre for Addiction Research**
A correspondence treatment program for people who wish to cut down their drinking on their own.
Website: www.acar.net.au
Tel: (61) 411 286 109
Email: acar@acar.net.au

**Cannabis Information and Helpline**
A confidential information and support line for cannabis users.
Website: http://ncpic.org.au
Helpline: 1800 30 40 50

**DrugInfo**
A service provided by the Australian Drug Foundation offering information about alcohol and other drugs.
Website: www.druginfo.adf.org.au
Tel: 1300 85 85 84

**Quitnow**
An online resource for people who want to quit smoking.
Website: www.quitnow.gov.au
Helpline: 13 7848
Email: quitnow@health.gov.au

*New Zealand*
**Alcohol Drug Association New Zealand**
A national organisation that aims to minimise the harm associated with alcohol, other drugs and gambling.
Website: www.adanz.org.nz
Helpline: 0800 787 797
Email: ada@adanz.org.nz

**Addictions Treatment Directory**
A regionalised database of the publicly funded addiction treatment and advice services available in New Zealand.
Website: www.addictionshelp.org.nz

**Gambling Helpline**
A twenty-four hour Freephone support service for people with gambling problems.
Website: www.gamblingproblem.co.nz
Helpline: 0800 654 655
Email: info@gamblinghelpline.co.nz

## Resources for families of addicts

Watching a loved-one fall into the hell of addiction, and living with their compulsive, addictive behaviours is, to say the least, not easy. Many of us watch while our partners, husbands, wives, fathers, mothers, sons, daughters or friends behave in the full volatile spectrum of active addiction with mood swings, depression, anger, cheating, lying, manipulation, mania or just plain insanity. The list of 'bad' behaviours is endless. It is in fact a list of sick behaviours. And while the addict seeks help, so must family members embark on their own 'recovery' in groups such as:

**AL-ANON Family Groups**
Support for families and friends of alcoholics.
*UK and Eire*
Website: www.al-anonuk.org.uk
Helpline: 0207 7403 0888
Email: enquiries@al-anon.org.uk
*Australia*
Website: www.al-anon.org/australia
Tel: 1300 252 666
*New Zealand*
Website: www.al-anon.org.nz
Tel: 0508 425 266
Email: nz-al-anon-gso@xtra.co.nz
*Worldwide*
Website: www.al-anon.alateen.org
Tel: (757) 563 1600
Email: wso@al-anon.org

*UK*
**Families Anonymous**
A self-help group based on the twelve-step programme for families of drug abusers.
Website: www.famanon.org.uk
Helpline: 0845 1200 660
Email: office@famanon.org.uk

**National Association for Children of Alcoholics**
Support for children growing up in families where one or both parents are alcoholics or have a similar addictive problem.
Website: www.nacoa.org.uk
Helpline: 0800 358 3456
Email: helpline@nacoa.org.uk

**Parents Against Drug Abuse (PADA)**
Support for the parents and families of drug users.
Helpline: 08457 023 867
Email: admin@pada.org.uk

**ADFAM National**
Support for families affected by drugs and alcohol. Also runs direct support services at London prisons for families of prisoners with drug problems.
Website: www.adfam.org.uk

Tel: 01970 626 470
Email: admin@adfam.org.uk

*Australia*
**Family Drug Support**
Information, advice and support for family members where there is an alcohol or other drug problem.
Website: http://fds.org.au
Helpline: 1300 368 186
Email: admin@fds.ngo.org.au

## Can I recover?

Recovery is a one-day-at-a-time process. I can only know that today I am clean. Today I don't have to pick up a drug or a drink to make myself feel better. I work a programme, I have a beloved sponsor, I am one of the lucky ones. I hope and pray I stay that way. Recovery is possible. I know people with twenty and thirty years of sobriety. At the time of writing I have just over two years clean time. That's all I can say.

I hope my story touches someone's journey somewhere, I hope by writing this you know you are not alone. I hope my words inspire others, who like me, have experienced feeling they have nowhere left to go, who are ready to embark upon a path of recovery. I know that writing this book has taken me back through some of the darkest days and nights of my life. I know that at times, reliving the pain pushed me a little closer to the teetering edge of the cliff we all know so well, and one extra bleak footstep might have sent me hurtling over its edge. I didn't though, because of the love and support of my husband, recovery friends, sponsor and programme. Today, I am clean and sober, and right now, that is enough for me.